just enough

# just enough

lessons in living green from
traditional japan

azby brown

kodansha international
tokyo • new york • london

Distributed in the United States by Kodansha America LLC, and in the United Kingdom and continental Europe by Kodansha Europe Ltd.

Published by Kodansha International Ltd., 17-14 Otowa 1-chome, Bunkyo-ku, Tokyo 112-8652

First edition, 2009
18 17 16 15 14 13 12 11 10 9    10 9 8 7 6 5 4 3 2 1

Library of Congress Cataloging-in-Publication Data

Brown, Azby, 1956-
  Just enough : lessons in living green from traditional Japan / Azby Brown. -- 1st ed.
    p. cm.
  Includes bibliographical references and index.
  ISBN 978-4-7700-3074-0
  1. Environmentalism--Japan--History. 2. Sustainable development--Japan--History. 3. Japan--Social life and customs--1600-1868. I. Title.
  GE199.J3B76 2009
  333.720952--dc22
                      2009015550

*www.kodansha-intl.com*

# contents

foreword
# just enough

This is a book of stories.

They are not fables. They are depictions of vanished ways of life told from the point of view of a contemporary observer, based on extensive research and presented as narrative. The stories tell how people lived in Japan some two hundred years ago during the late Edo period (1603–1868), a period when traditional technology and culture were at the peak of development and realization, just before the country opened itself to the West and joined the ranks of the industrialized nations. They tell of a people who overcame many of the identical problems that confront us today—issues of energy, water, materials, food, and population—and who forged from these formidable challenges a society that was conservation-minded, waste-free, well-housed and well-fed, and economically robust, and that has bequeathed to us admirable and enduring standards of design and beauty.

I hope that from these stories readers will gain insight into what it is like to live in a sustainable society, not so much in terms of specific technical approaches, but in how larger concerns can guide daily decisions and how social and environmental contexts shape our courses of action. These stories are intended to illustrate the environmentally related problems that the people in both rural and urban areas faced, the conceptual frameworks in which they viewed these problems, and how they went about finding solutions. More than anything else, this book is about a mentality that pervaded Japanese society then and that can serve as a beacon for our own efforts to achieve sustainability now.

This book was prompted in equal part by large questions and promising answers. The large questions concern our environmental crisis—global warming being the most threatening, of course. But realizing that the mechanisms that propel global warming are enmeshed with those of deforestation, the degradation of the watershed, the looming possibility of global famine, and the impending exhaustion of limited material and energy resources, the most pressing question became, "How are these problems connected?"

As for answers, the point at which a sense of hopelessness gave way to glimmers of hope for me, personally, came when I attended the Sun Valley Sustainability Conference a few autumns ago, and realized that the quiet and continued efforts of individuals and organizations around the world had begun to coalesce, and that their combined body of knowledge and experience was reaching the sort of critical mass necessary for igniting widespread change. A shared language was developing as practitioners of diverse specialties found their own work extending into new areas. Urban planners wanted to know what farmers knew about soil, architects wanted to know what hydrologists knew about purifying rain runoff, foresters wanted to know what waste specialists knew about naturally treated sewage, and everybody wanted to find out how to power everything from the sun. In every field, people were bringing answers to the table and walking away with a sense of partnership. Among the specialists in any area of green, sustainable, or environmentally sensitive design, no one underestimated the enormity of the tasks ahead. But everyone agreed that the necessary change is doable.

Still people shrug and ask, "Is it worth the effort? Won't the sustainable life be annoying at best?" The problem is that none of us has ever lived in a sustainable society, so it's hard to imagine what it will be like. Will we have cars? Will we have air-conditioning? Will my neighbors report me for not composting my table scraps? What if I want mangoes in December? Answers to questions like these depend upon how well the best recommendations for environmental remediation are implemented, and how quickly.

In the most optimistic scenarios, our power infrastructure is rapidly overhauled to eliminate the use of most fossil fuels, and we are able to use electric-

Is sustainable life worth the effort? The problem is that none of us has ever lived in a sustainable society, so it's hard to imagine what it will be like.

ity much as we do today. Plug-in hybrid autos become the norm. Reuse and recycling, along with improved product design, allow us to approach the goal of zero-waste while still buying and selling huge quantities of products. Deforestation is halted and reversed by massive replanting, and sustainable forestry insures a continued supply of wood for building and other uses. Freshwater is available but is conserved, and people enjoy what they're eating. In short, in this scenario it is possible to make the transition into a new way of providing for our needs so that our future life closely resembles our present one.

However, we have nearly lost the race against time. As government and industry dither, as individuals delay making crucial changes in how they travel, eat, and use household energy, as inertia and denial continue to overcome proactive decision making, our margin for avoiding unpleasantness has largely evaporated. We should all be prepared for social disruption, for shortages, for being forced to accept unpalatable changes and lack of choice in areas where, even today, we can choose how and when to change. Sustainable society will come, because the alternative is no society at all. The bleak prospect of the collapse of our civilization may seem fantastic to many, but in fact most environmental specialists are forced to concede that their less-optimistic scenarios point to exactly that.

Japanese society once faced the prospect of collapse due to environmental degradation, and the fact that it did not is what makes it such an instructive example. Japan entered the Edo period in 1603 facing extreme difficulties in obtaining building timber, suffering erosion and watershed damage due to having clear-cut so many of its mountains for lumber, and virtually unable to expand agricultural production to the degree necessary to feed a growing population. The needs of the urban population, particularly those of the capital city of Edo, but also those of Osaka, Nagoya, and numerous other growing cities, conflicted with those of the rural areas, and the life of farmers was made all the more difficult by their legal obligation to surrender one-third or more of their harvest to support the warrior classes.

In terms of environment and natural resources, Japan was both challenged and blessed. The archipelago is extremely mountainous, and arable land is limited to a handful of broad coastal plains and many narrow mountain valleys, amounting to only about one-fourth of the nation's land area. At the start of the Edo period, nearly all of the potentially arable land had already been opened to cultivation and was feeding, just barely, a population of about twelve million. Agricultural land in many areas was showing signs of exhaustion and degradation, and output was declining. But the country benefits from a temperate climate

*Japanese society almost collapsed due to environmental degradation. The fact that it did not is what makes it such an instructive example.*

and warm ocean currents, and it is blessed with abundant rainfall and a long growing season. Freshwater from snowmelt is generous and fast-flowing, and the extensive watersheds drain into innumerable fertile river valleys and wetlands. The virgin forest that originally covered the mountains of the archipelago was extensive and diverse in both broadleaf and coniferous species, and it provided an extremely rich habitat in which all manner of flora and fauna flourished. Nature itself had endowed Japan well for human habitation, but by the early 1600s the land was suffering from overexploitation by the large population.

All the more remarkable, then, that two hundred years later the same land was supporting thirty million people—two and a half times the population— with little sign of environmental degradation. Deforestation had been halted and reversed, farmland improved and made more productive, and conservation implemented in all sectors of society, both urban and rural. Overall living standards had increased, and the people were better fed, housed, and clothed, and they were healthier. By any objective standard, it was a remarkable feat, arguably unequalled anywhere else, before or since.

This success can be credited partly to technological advances and partly to government direction. Agricultural breeding played a part, as did improved hydrology. Design was crucial, as was the timely collection and distribution of information. But more than anything else, this success was due to a pervasive mentality that propelled all of the other mechanisms of improvement. This mentality drew on an understanding of the functioning and inherent limits of natural systems. It encouraged humility, considered waste taboo, suggested cooperative solutions, and found meaning and satisfaction in a beautiful life in which the individual took just enough from the world and not more. The stories in this book describe many of the more remarkable technical aspects of life during this period, as well as relevant social, political, and economic factors, but their real purpose is to convey this mentality of "just enough" as it guided the daily life of millions throughout the society.

How do we know how the people of Edo Japan lived and what they thought? For one, we have surviving material culture in the form of houses, clothing, and the implements of daily life. Archaeology has literally dug up the old infrastructure and clarified its design and workings. We have been left with a wealth of writings, both printed sources and the handwritten records of individuals and families. The number, variety, and quality of pictorial sources that have come down to us—mainly woodblock prints, but also drawings and paintings—are astounding. All of these sources have undergone decades of collection, curation, commentary, and analysis both in Japan and overseas, with the result that

> The mentality of the time found meaning and satisfaction in a life in which the individual took just enough from the world, and no more.

a rich body of knowledge exists within reach of anyone who seeks it.

There has never been a better time to study Edo-period Japan, and the discoveries and observations of many specialists are finding such a ready audience at home that the country can be said to be experiencing an "Edo Boom." Museums of Edo life and culture in Tokyo and elsewhere are packed most days, and the era's approach to various problems is presented frequently in the mass media. The appeal of Edo is quite broad in Japan, but in the hands of successive generations of specialists—in architecture, agriculture, industry, and economy, as well as in environmental history, to name a few areas—information and understanding is reaching a great depth as well. We know a lot about the price of fertilizer in certain regions, and the literacy rates of farmers. We know quite a bit about the lumber industry, how wood was cut and transported, the uses to which it was put and the prices it brought. We can reconstruct networks of paper recycling and estimate the extent of the used-clothing market. And we can describe how energy was used and not used.

Many sources were drawn on in writing this book: observation and examination of what exists, written sources in both Japanese and English, pictorial sources, museums, archives, and consultation with experts. The result could easily have been a volume or two of academic research, which in itself could have been quite gratifying. But as I immersed myself in the project I soon realized that, although superb commentary by specialists in many fields existed, each illuminating a small corner of the subject, as did books for popular readership, most in the form of illustrated anecdotes about food, homes, and clothing, there was very little that described how everything fit together—urban and rural, food and waste, making and recycling, nature and the manmade—and how we might learn from it today. This "fitting together" became the overall theme of this book. Being something of a generalist myself, I felt prepared to take a stab at it, but how well I have succeeded in making the interrelationships and interconnectedness clear is something readers must decide.

Though confronted with a wealth of material from which to draw, I also gradually became aware of gaps in the existing body of knowledge of Edo life. For instance, hundreds of farmhouses from the period have survived throughout the country, and probably an equal number of urban townhouses originally built for commoners; quite a few of the best examples have been thoroughly researched, dismantled and rebuilt, and carefully preserved both in situ and in the country's several excellent open-air architecture museums. But very few samurai houses survive anywhere, and none to speak of in what was formerly Edo, today's Tokyo.

*We can reconstruct networks of paper recycling and estimate the extent of the used-clothing market. We can describe how energy was used and not used.*

There are a few extant examples, however, in places like Kanazawa, as well as quite a few pictorial sources and a handful of written accounts describing the daily life of samurai. In constructing my depiction I have availed myself of as much research material as I could find on the subject. Very little of anything from the Edo period survives in Tokyo, victim to successive fires, earthquakes, bombing, and sadly, disinterest, but we have excellent detailed maps of the old city, many pictures, and lots of written commentary.

More significant perhaps is that, although actual buildings from the period and entire neighborhoods have vanished without a trace, anyone who knows how to read the townscape can still find blocks in which the scale and pattern of use that once characterized Edo, with its two-story shopfronts and back alleys, can be discerned. Many farming villages have survived with only superficial changes, however, and occupy their valleys much as they did two hundred years ago. But yet, all in all, whether one speaks of buildings or natural environments or ways of thinking and of behavior, very little of Edo survives anywhere in Japan. The change since industrialization began in the mid-nineteenth century has been too great.

Though Japan today must be credited with admirable efforts in reducing its pollution, improving the efficiency with which it uses energy, and maintaining its forest cover through regenerative forestry, and though it has high rates of public transportation use, strong standards for recycling, and excellent designs for small, resource- and energy-efficient homes, no serious observer would ever suggest that it is a model for sustainability. Though efforts are being made and things are improving little by little in many areas, there is now far too much that is done wrongly, or left undone. Though in comparison with China, Japan comes out looking pretty good, the country continues to destroy its environment in innumerable ways. What Edo Japan did well and beautifully, modern Japan either undervalues or fails to understand entirely. This is why instead of being able to illustrate valuable principles by showing how things are done now, this book tells stories about how they were once done.

Is it accurate to describe the Japan of that period as "sustainable"? Though some might say any comparison between then and now is inherently misleading, given the radically different contexts, I say emphatically: "Yes. By most of our most accepted current definitions, theirs was a sustainable society."

According to the report of the UN's Bruntlandt Commission of 1987, which might be credited with first popularizing the term, sustainable development is "development that meets the needs of the present without compromising the ability of future generations to meet their own needs." While admittedly vague,

*Insted of illustrating valuable principles by showing how things are done now, this book tells stories about how they were once done.*

this describes what Edo accomplished quite succinctly. More specifically, the widely acclaimed Hanover Principles for sustainable design, drafted by William McDonough and Michael Braungart in preparation for the Hanover Expo of 2000, can be summarized as follows:

- Insist on human rights and sustainability
- Recognize the interaction of design with the environment
- Consider the social and spiritual aspects of buildings and designed objects
- Be responsible for the effect of design decisions
- Insure that objects have long-term value
- Eliminate waste and consider the entire life cycle of designed objects
- Make use of "natural energy flows," such as solar power and its derivatives
- Be humble, and use nature as a model for design
- Share knowledge, strive for continuous improvement, and encourage open communication among stakeholders

As this book illustrates, Edo-period Japan met all of these objectives, taking into account the different conception of human rights that prevailed. It achieved sustainable and renewable forestry, sustainable agriculture, sustainable architecture, sustainable city planning, sustainable transportation, and sustainable use of energy and materials. At this time, Japan lacked a global perspective, but it operated locally with no negative environmental effects beyond its borders. It sustained its high population of thirty million and kept it very stable for two hundred years.

*Edo-period Japan achieved sustainable forestry, agriculture, architecture, city planning, transportation, and use of energy and materials.*

Its technical solutions bore all of the characteristics now most sought in new designs, including low-impact materials, quality and durability, renewability, design for reuse and recycling, energy efficiency, and reducing consumption by providing group services wherever possible, as in public baths and the prepared food market. Its designs and techniques depended upon natural biological processes and solar energy wherever possible, and they closely mimicked natural processes elsewhere.

E. F. Schumaker, author of the groundbreaking *Small is Beautiful* of 1973, would undoubtedly have held traditional Japan up as a example of a "Buddhist economy" that values well-being over consumption. As he put it, instead of assuming that someone who consumes more is necessarily better off than one who consumes less, "since consumption is merely a means to human well-being, the aim should be to obtain the maximum of well-being with the minimum of consumption." Again, this accurately describes the mindset of the people of that era.

From time to time others have recognized the importance of what Japan accomplished in doing so much with few resources and with traditional means, particularly in agriculture. As far back as 1911, in *Farmers of Forty Centuries, or Permanent Agriculture in China, Korea, and Japan*, American agronomist E. F. King wrote glowingly about Japanese multicropping and interplanting, use of night soil for fertilizer, rice paddy hydraulics, and the general efficiency of farm production, which was still being carried out largely along traditional lines. The author stressed that in Japan, as well as in China and Korea, traditional methods had allowed the same farm plots to remain productive for centuries, whereas American farms were wearing out after only a few generations of use.

King's book is now considered an early bible of organic farming, and it greatly influenced the thinking behind the permaculture movement formulated in the late 1970s by Australians Bill Molison and David Holmgren, which takes many of its primary principles from traditional Japanese agricultural and gardening practice. Many other aspects of traditional Japanese culture have been singled out for praise and have influenced design in the West. Its wooden architecture has long been held up as a standard of environmentally sensitive use of materials and space, and the compact and economical design of household goods such as boxes, trays, cabinets, and other furnishings has been a strong influence on the things we use today. From the garden to the dinner table, Japanese ways of doing things have been hailed and emulated, but rarely does anyone look at the overall conditions and systemic responses that made these achievements possible, even necessary, in the first place. We should recognize that almost everything we have learned to value from traditional Japan emerged during the Edo period in response to scarcity.

That the carefully nurtured sustainable systems that had been so painstakingly put together during the Edo period broke apart so completely later under the impact of industrialization should strike us all as tragic, for it represented the sudden evaporation of generations of know-how of the sort we desperately need now. The Edo solutions were inherently local ones, arrived at with almost no input from beyond Japan other than what the ocean and atmosphere brought directly. After the country opened its doors to trade and industrialization in the 1860s, the self-sufficiency imperative gave way to an import-export economy tied to the production and surpluses of the world at large, which soon affected every aspect of life.

Though the conservation ethic persisted well into the twentieth century, perhaps even until the beginning of the postwar period, and though the nation still strives to maintain its self-sufficiency in rice, for over a century it has basically shared the production and consumption patterns of the developed West,

The solutions were inherently local ones, arrived at with almost no input from beyond Japan other than what the ocean and the atmosphere brought directly.

and to revert to Edo ways on a significant scale now would be impossible.

But just as in retrospect it is possible to outline scenarios in which Japan might have developed globally competitive industries while maintaining its overall sustainability one hundred years ago, it is possible for us to profit, perhaps vastly, from the experience of Edo even at this late date. The challenge that faces us now is to redesign our production and our consumption so that they share the virtues of their Edo-period counterparts, to link our sophisticated technical systems to the kind of mentality that those prescient forebears displayed.

We will need to learn again what it means to use "just enough," and to allow our choices to be guided by a deeper appreciation of the limits of the world we have been bequeathed as well as a determination to leave future generations with better possibilities than what we have given ourselves.

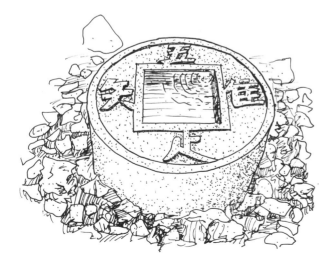

"Ware tada taru wo shiru"

The Japanese characters that appear on the jacket are taken from the inscription on this 17th c. stone basin at Ryoanji Temple in Kyoto. It is an important Zen saying that can be translated as, "I know what 'just enough' is."

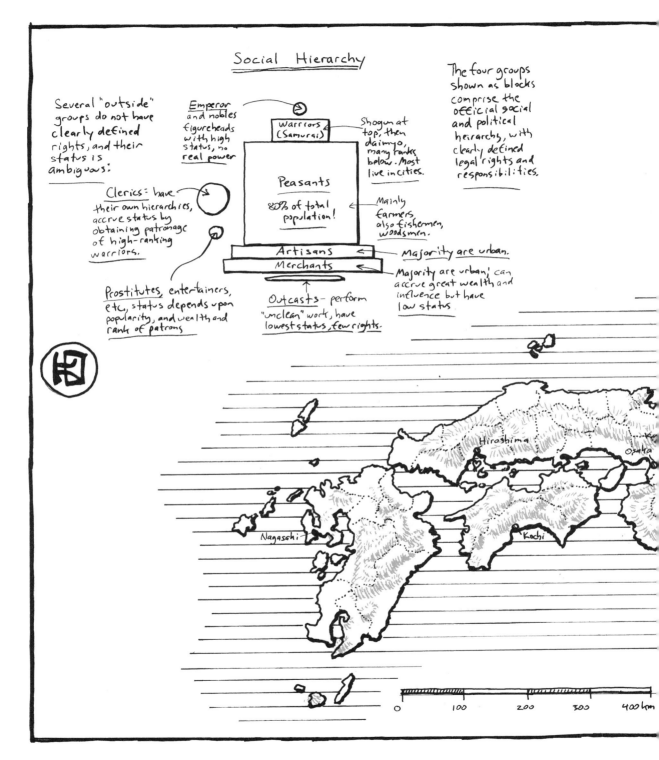

## Social Hierarchy

Several "outside" groups do not have clearly defined rights, and their status is ambiguous:

Clerics - have their own hierarchies, accrue status by obtaining patronage of high-ranking warriors.

Prostitutes, entertainers, etc, status depends upon popularity, and wealth and rank of patrons

Emperor and nobles figureheads with high status, no real power

Warriors (Samurai)

Shogun at top, then daimyo, many ranks below. Most live in cities.

Peasants

80% of total population!

Mainly farmers, also fishermen, woodsmen.

Artisans

Merchants

Outcasts - perform "unclean" work, have lowest status, few rights.

Majority are urban.

Majority are urban; can accrue great wealth and influence but have low status.

The four groups shown as blocks comprise the official social and political hierarchy, with clearly defined legal rights and responsibilities.

Hiroshima

Osaka

Nagasaki

Kochi

0      100      200      300      400 km

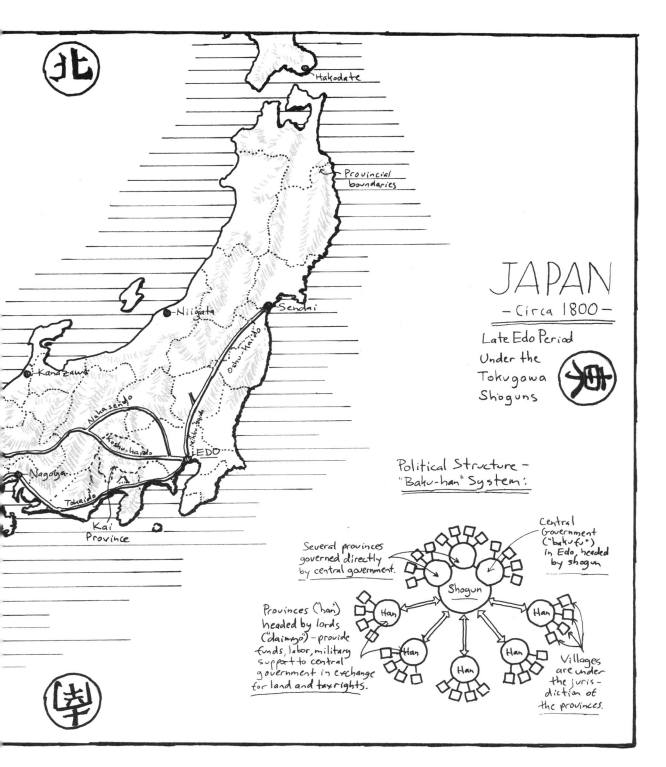

北

Hakodate

Provincial boundaries

Niigata

Sendai

Kanazawa

Nakasendo

Koshu-kaido

Oshu-kaido

Nikko-kaido

EDO

Nagoya

Tokaido

Kai Province

JAPAN
— Circa 1800 —

Late Edo Period
Under the
Tokugawa
Shōguns

江戸

Political Structure —
"Baku-han" System:

Several provinces
governed directly
by central government.

Central
Government
("bakufu")
in Edo, headed
by shogun

Shogun

Han    Han

Han    Han    Han

Provinces ("han")
headed by lords
("daimyō") — provide
funds, labor, military
support to central
government in exchange
for land and tax rights.

Villages
are under
the juris-
diction of
the provinces.

学

# field and forest
## the farmer from kai province

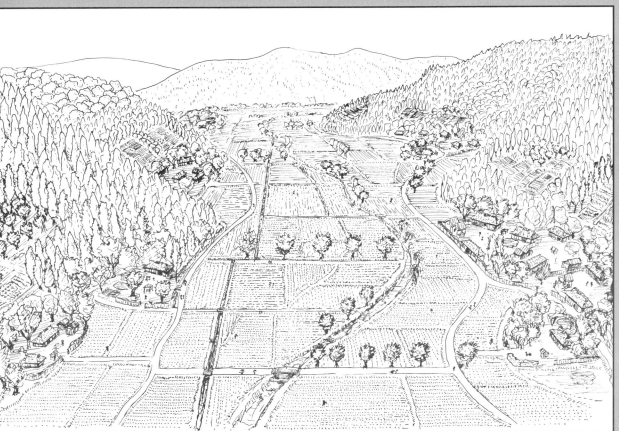

The year is 1798, Kansei 9 by the Japanese calendar—the eleventh year of the reign of Shogun Tokugawa Ienari. It is high summer, and the hillsides of the Kai province of central Japan are at their most verdant, alive with the flowering climbers and shoots that flourish during these brief months, only to seed and die as fall approaches. The ground cover is speckled with tiny parti-colored blossoms, and the air shrieks with the deafening call of cicadas.

We have walked for several days from Edo, mostly along the Koshu-kaido, one of the five great roads that link the capital with the rest of the country. Our journey has taken us nearly due west, the first day through the flat, monotonous belt of farmland that surrounds the city, followed by two days of steep mountain passes, narrow river gorges, breathtaking views, and gravity-defying bridges.

Acorns from the "Shii" tree

Though the main road was wide enough for a military detachment, we met no carriages or draft wagons along the way, and only an occasional mounted rider—although idle palanquin bearers milling about at every stopping point badgered us for business. Even those have not been seen since we took a narrow side road heading north, deeper into the mountains. Though this road is narrow and dusty, the walk has not been overly strenuous, and we are rarely more than a half-day walk from a farmhouse or settlement where we could obtain a night's lodging on an informal basis.

"Shiitake" mushrooms

After one last winding, uphill trudge, we crest the hill and sigh with relief to see our destination, the village of Aoyagi*, spread in welcome across the valley below. Wispy tendrils of hearth smoke drift skyward from its thatched rooftops, and the gentle breeze brings the comforting smells of domestic life. From our present vantage point one might be forgiven for assuming that the village below endures an isolated and independent existence.

Chestnuts - "kuri"

The forest seems to have hiked its skirts to make room for the village. Conifers like cryptomeria predominate but are healthily interspersed with copses of chestnut, zelkova, oak, and other towering deciduous hardwood trees, as well as large stands of bamboo. The understory teems with variety: shrubs and seedlings, ferns and vines, moss and fungi.

* a fictional composite based on the regions villages.

Along the journey, we have passed entire hillsides covered in white birch, all growing naturally, as well as lanes and fields bordered with ornamental cherry trees intentionally planted by human residents. And from time to time we have encountered vast plantations of Japanese cypress and cryptomeria growing in straight lines, prominently posted with notices reading, "Do not enter under strict penalty, by the authority of the Shogunal Forest Warden." The forests themselves have begun to be cultivated.

Though we are still a half hour or more away from the village proper, the nearby hillsides are alive with human activity this morning. Household teams of villagers, mainly women and children bearing woven bamboo baskets and wooden carrying frames fitted with large sacks of woven rush straw, work their way methodically through the undergrowth, gathering essentials. As the seasons change, so do the objects of their gathering, particularly in the case of food that resists cultivation but can be found growing wild in significant amounts.

Late spring brings bamboo shoots, which must actually be dug rather than gathered, as well as many kinds of "mountain greens" like mustard flower and various ferns. Autumn is a particularly rich time, since the ground is liberally littered with chestnuts, walnuts, acorns, and other edible nuts and seeds, and many of the most desirable mushrooms can be found in abundance, as well as burdock root and other tubers. Even the winter months present several desirable foodstuffs, like shepherd's purse, chickweed, and the other herbs that go into *nanakusa*, a special dish eaten on January 7.

But it is summer now, and the food-gathering teams are hunting for water chestnuts, mugwort, butterbur, and other edible greens. Although the villagers don't realize it, their stone-age forebears foraged for the same items on the same slopes; these hills are capable of supporting small populations through foraging alone, and in times of famine they still provide significant sustenance.

On other days during the warm months of the growing season, the villagers gather fallen leaves and other organic matter to use as "green" fertilizer and mulch. That part destined for fertilizer is mixed with human waste in the compost pit—where the naturally occurring high temperatures caused by bacterial decomposition kill most pathogens—and is then applied to the fields at specified intervals.

Rural communities like this one depend upon gathered fallen wood for all of their fuel needs, and fuel consumption is strictly limited to that which can be satisfied by the amount of wood found lying on the ground—limbs and branches, mostly, with special permission required to take possession of fallen logs. Enforced by both custom and government policy, this practice has far-

Summer Gathering

"Fuki"

"Kuwai"
water
chestnuts

"Kuwa
no mi"
mulberries

reaching implications. In essence, with very few exceptions, fuel needs have been satisfied for centuries by a fully renewable resource, that is, trees. But by eliminating tree-cutting for fuel, a potentially major source of environmental pressure from the rural population has been eliminated, and more lumber is made available for building and for producing charcoal fuel for the cities.

Though foraging and forest maintenance are essential activities for the community, it is obvious on our walk through the village that its central purpose is farming. In Aoyagi, one hundred families tend both irrigated rice plots—the average family holding being one *cho*, (about one hectare—1000 sq. m.)—and "dry" fields, averaging rarely more than one-fourth that size, and often quite a lot less. A typical homestead is about 150 square meters. So the largest environmental impact by far is from the rice fields. The area considered adequate for gathering forest fertilizer is five to ten times that devoted to crops.

Several factors influence the size and siting of the farm plots, the most significant being the slope of the land. Because flat bottomland is scarce throughout the country and the construction of rice paddies requires flat land, almost every acre of it has been cleared for this use. Terracing is a common method of converting sloped acreage into paddies, and though such fields require more effort to maintain and to irrigate, in many cases terracing has already been taken to extremes, particularly in the more remote and rugged regions.

The relationship between irrigated fields and those for non-irrigated crops is defined by local geography. With all of the flat land devoted to rice, other crops, such as vegetables, dry grains (wheat, millet, and barley), yams, and cash crops such as cotton and hemp, are usually planted on the lower slopes of the surrounding mountains. Even steeper slopes can support orchards and crops such as tea, with the result that agriculture is practiced in a stratified manner that conforms to the local environment. Except in the widest of valleys or the rare expanses of coastal lowland, the farmhouses themselves are likely to be nestled in clusters against the nooks and hollows of the hillsides, often somewhat distant from the family's fields.

"Shungiku" can be found in winter

Spring gathering:

"tsukushi"

"takenoko"

"yomogi"

Obtaining fuel without damaging the health of the forest

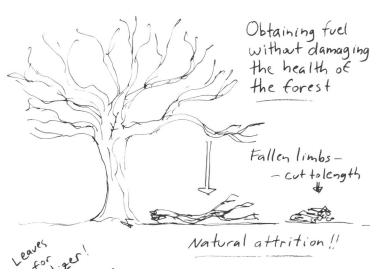

Fallen limbs —
— cut to length

Natural attrition !!

Everything needs to be hauled out on backframes — this imposes a natural limit !!

Leaves for fertilizer!

Trees toppled by wind or rot are usually okay to use.

Farmers use gathered wood for fuel almost exclusively. Since they comprise about 90% of the total population, overall fuel use does not add significantly to deforestation.

The Japanese "kamado" cookstove does a good job with twigs, sticks, and just about anything else that burns, enhancing fuel economy.

## CHARCOAL

Oaks and other hardwoods are grown in clusters called "coppices"....

They regrow quickly!

Charcoal-making is a common winter occupation for farm families. It is usually sold on the market for use in cities. The kilns are built in the mountains.

Charcoal hauled out

## approaching the village

As we approach the village, we are passing through a very green but very human-influenced landscape. Certainly the largest environmental effect has been on the valley floor, where the previously existing ecosystem has been selectively dismantled and replaced with paddy agriculture. Trees have been cut down and the ground subdivided into shallow pockets. These paddies provide a ripe environment for other species that benefit from the changes humans have brought: frogs and fish flourish, feeding on insects whose numbers have increased with the new food source that rice represents. The frogs and fish in turn attract ducks, egrets, and other predators, and so on up the food chain.

What have declined are many weeds, bushes, grasses, and other botanical species, as well as boars, foxes, rodents, snakes, and other animals that seek dry ground during the summer. The result could be considered damage from the purely natural point of view. But by designing the agricultural process in a manner that makes the fullest possible use of naturally existing features, by seeking to maintain the fertility and productivity of the forests, and by the

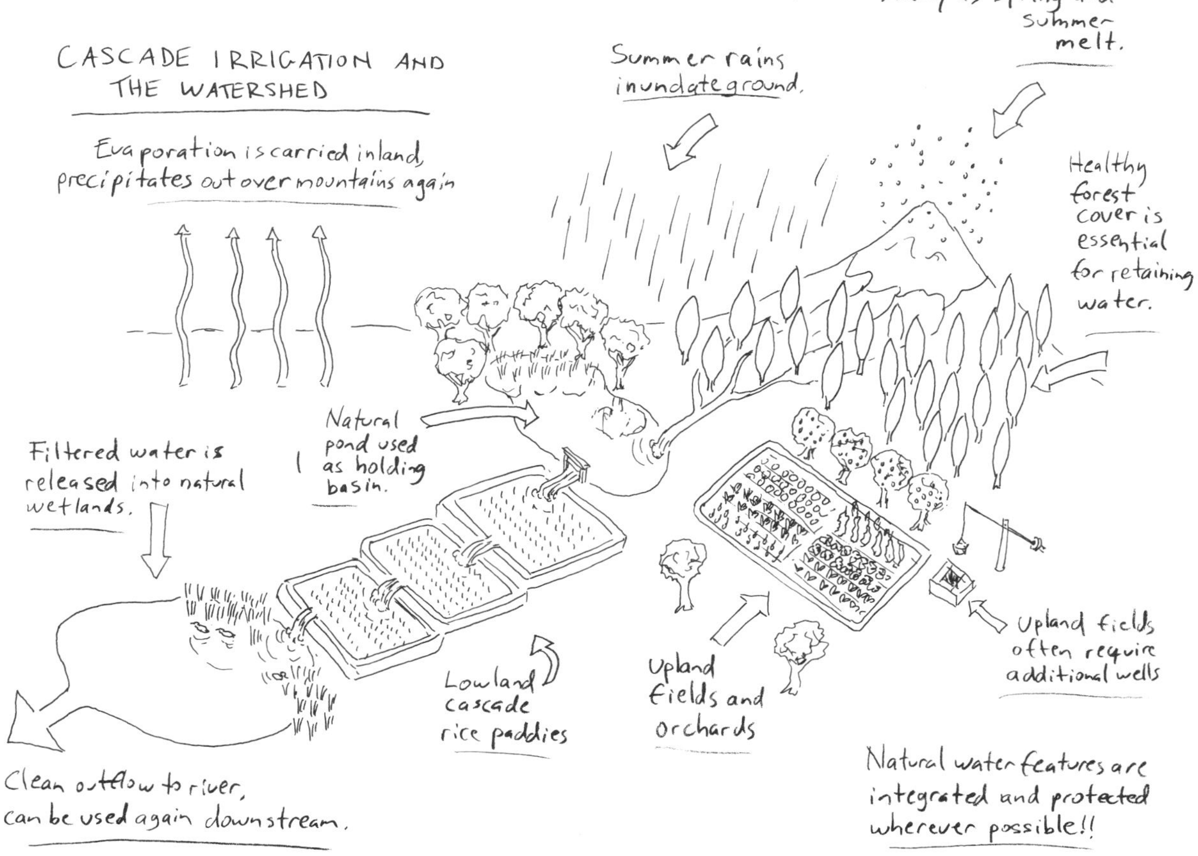

CASCADE IRRIGATION AND THE WATERSHED

Evaporation is carried inland, precipitates out over mountains again

Summer rains inundate ground.

Snowy peaks are the primary reservoir of water for the entire ecosystem. It is released slowly as spring and summer melt.

Healthy forest cover is essential for retaining water.

Filtered water is released into natural wetlands.

Natural pond used as holding basin.

Lowland cascade rice paddies

Upland fields and orchards

Upland fields often require additional wells

Clean outflow to river, can be used again downstream.

Natural water features are integrated and protected wherever possible!!

secondary effect whereby the paddies and other fields become ideal environments for other species, the farmers have developed an agricultural ecology that replicates the purely natural one in several of its most essential aspects. The balance has been altered, true, but humans are being supported in large numbers without degrading their environment.

Irrigation is a major undertaking. Waterworks in general have achieved a high degree of technical sophistication, with well-engineered aqueducts supplying major urban areas and ambitious river works easing navigation and lumber transport. Rice field irrigation is similarly sophisticated and well engineered, while often using simpler technical means; it is implemented with the same attention to social cooperation and environmental monitoring that distinguishes forest gathering activities. A new rice paddy cannot be built unless its impact on the shared water supply is acceptable to all concerned, and the actual construction of the dams and dikes is a cooperative effort. The farmers manage their water supply precisely and with foresight.

Gravity is made to do the work of moving water from source to destination

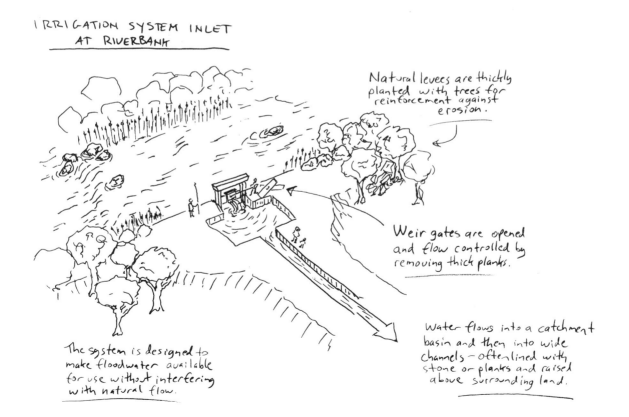

IRRIGATION SYSTEM INLET
AT RIVERBANK

Natural levees are thickly planted with trees for reinforcement against erosion.

Weir gates are opened and flow controlled by removing thick planks.

The system is designed to make floodwater available for use without interfering with natural flow.

Water flows into a catchment basin and then into wide channels - often lined with stone or planks and raised above surrounding land.

wherever possible. While in some cases the geography makes this relatively easy, more often than not the choice is between expending resources and energy to construct an aqueduct to provide a gravity-fed water supply from a distant source, or to implement a system of human-powered pumps and lift systems to bring water from a low-lying source to paddies above. The former is a vastly preferred solution. The earliest irrigation systems in Japan, developed shortly after the beginning of paddy agriculture around 400 BC, utilized catchment basins to collect water until it was needed to flood the paddies, and this method is still widely practiced. Although in some situations it is necessary to dig artificial ponds for this purpose, for the most part naturally occurring ponds can be made to serve beautifully with the addition of weirs, sluices, and gates.

In cold parts of the country, sun shining on the pond water warms it to the optimal temperature for use before it is released to the crop; in other cases long, serpentine irrigation ditches serve an identical function. The design process is essentially one of augmentation—reinforcing and shaping naturally occurring features and forces. Natural ponds have the tremendous advantage of having evolved symbiotically with their watersheds and possess naturally occurring inflow sources as well as natural outflows; they are balanced with their local ecosystems in a way that is difficult to replicate through engineering alone. Larger projects such as levees and dikes, intended to limit damage from seasonal flooding, are usually based on similar principles. The meanders of the rivers are left untouched, but the riverbed is broadened, and low levees are built that allow natural flooding to pour into a wide catchment beyond.

One commonly used design that originated in nearby Koshu uses separate, discontinuous levees that are angled to the direction of flow to guide the floodwaters. They are planted with trees and bamboo to anchor and consolidate the earthwork and to encourage further natural growth. Riparian works like these undertaken during the previous century allowed a considerable increase in arable land through reclamation of otherwise dangerous flood plains, but there are few opportunities for similar gains now.

Although the dynamics of steeply terraced and lowland irrigation differ, in both cases the result is a gravity-fed cascade. From original sources such as rivers and streams, water flows into a catchment, and from there it is released into the paddies at prescribed intervals; it flows from one level to the next, and excess water can be released back into the waterways. This cascade captures sludge and organic matter and has a filtering and purifying effect on the water. For this reason it can be argued that these systems actually improve the local water supply, with benefits to those downstream.

It's not always possible to irrigate every field by gravity alone. This lightweight wooden paddlewheel pump can be easily transported from place to place as needed.

### sharing the wealth of water

At every step, from planning to construction and utilization, cascade irrigation requires very close cooperation among community members, and often among members of different communities. This is particularly true because—due to successive projects of clearing and reclamation as well as intermarriage and redistribution of assets—a single family's fields are likely to be scattered and interspersed with those belonging to others. Consequently, simply deciding the order in which fields will be flooded requires tremendous coordination and agreement, and the earthen dams separating one paddy from another must usually be considered assets shared by more than one family. The canals, ponds, sluices, and other major components of the irrigation system require the mediation and guidance of village headmen and possibly government representatives, and they are therefore assets shared by the village as a whole, under the jurisdiction of the village's *suiri kumiai*, or water-use association.

The effort expended on constructing, maintaining, and intensively farming the extensive rice paddies goes far beyond what would be needed for self-sufficiency on a local scale, and beyond what would be necessary to secure a good living through open-market sales, because the government has saddled the peasantry with a large tax burden. Officially discouraged from eating the rice they grow, the peasants surrender a third or more as tax, sell some, put some in communal emergency stores, and keep a portion for consumption despite the

CLIMBING CROPS
Include egg plants and melons (above) and Soybeans (left) (main source of protein in inland areas)

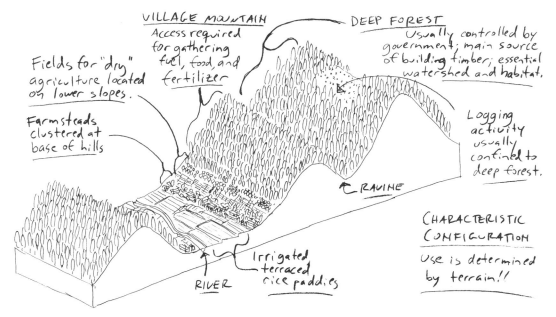

Fields for "dry" agriculture located on lower slopes.

Farmsteads clustered at base of hills

VILLAGE MOUNTAIN
Access required for gathering fuel, food, and fertilizer

DEEP FOREST
Usually controlled by government; main source of building timber; essential watershed and habitat.

Logging activity usually confined to deep forest.

← RAVINE

CHARACTERISTIC CONFIGURATION
Use is determined by terrain!!

RIVER

Irrigated terraced rice paddies

prohibitions. Through their taxes, the 80 percent of the population that are farmers support the entire ruling class and subsidize the feeding of the remaining 10 percent who live in cities.

The lower slopes of many of the surrounding hills have been cleared for dry field agriculture, but they represent less than half of the total crop acreage. Although these proportions may be reversed in some areas where the market for cash crops is so well developed that tax liens can be paid from crop sales, by and large the lower hillsides are the only land that can be used for other crops once the premium land has been reclaimed for growing rice. Too steep to be terraced for paddies but not too steep to retain soil, the hillsides themselves are divided into two agricultural strata.

turnips, "daihon" radish, yams, are common ROOT CROPS

The lower level is devoted to vegetables, yams, grains such as wheat, millet, and barley, and fibers such as hemp and cotton, while the higher, steeper slopes can be used for orchards—apples, persimmons, peaches, *mikan*—as well as tea and mulberry bushes (to feed silkworms). These dry fields may be small enough to be considered family garden plots and satisfy subsistence and community needs alone, but where resources and market size allow, they may develop into truly commercial-scale activity. Many such crops can be grown with rainfall alone, but these fields must also be provided with a water supply, usually in the form of spring-fed ponds or additional wells (with the approval and assistance of the village well association, or *igumi*). In extreme cases, farmers resort to water lifting devices or buckets hauled by human power.

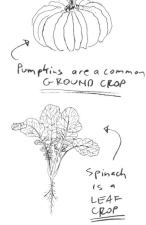

Pumpkins are a common GROUND CROP

Spinach is a LEAF CROP

The hundred or so houses of the village are grouped in loose clusters, with one cluster of about twenty houses here at one end of the valley, along both sides of the dirt road we are following as it descends from the hillside. Somewhat uniform in size and general configuration, they nevertheless present great variety in detail and in the particulars of their layout. While in some regions multistoried farmhouses are the norm, here they are all essentially single-storied buildings with occasional second-story additions and other modifications, sheltered under thick, steep thatch roofs.

ORCHARDS include "kaki" persimmons which ripen in autumn.

Homesteads consist of several related buildings arrayed around a roughly rectangular work yard. The largest structure, the house, is placed on the northern side of the yard, so that it will receive maximum southern exposure. The complex is not fully enclosed but is rather loosely delineated by the buildings themselves, some hedges, a few low walls and pathways, a small garden, a simply marked open gateway, as well as a line of *sugi* trees that appear to have been placed as a windbreak. It seems less of an architecturally designed unit than an incrementally evolved one, and in fact over the course of one hundred and fifty years it has undergone significant change and adjustment.

There is almost as much variety in the type, size, and placement of outbuildings among the various homesteads as there is among the houses themselves. Here as elsewhere, pragmatism and frugality rule. The wealthier farmers are likely to have a two-storied, whitewashed, fireproof storehouse for valuables and records. There is at least one family with a small, open-sided smithy, where others come to have tools repaired or hardware made. In some cases, home industries like weaving or brewing warrant the construction of extra work sheds and storage.

### the homestead of the first-born son

We are on our way to the house of a man named Shinichi. Like most peasants, Shinichi has no family name, and though this sometimes leads to confusion, each family has other identifiers: the location of their homestead—near the bamboo grove, along the river, uphill from the well; dominant features of their house—a large roof, board fence, big storehouse; or job identifiers—roofers, carvers, smiths. Shinichi's name means "Shin's first-born son," and there's only one person who fits this description in this village.

Shinichi's homestead is typically modest, with a simple open-sided shed for firewood, another for drying heaps of straw for household use, a green fertilizer shed, one for composting night soil, a small shed for ashes, and another for storing the bales of rice that represent a year's ration for the family. There are simple roofed storage racks for ladders and bamboo poles, for buckets, lumber, and miscellany. Other homesteads may have special storage buildings for soy sauce and miso, for cotton or other cottage industries, or special work sheds. These outbuildings are usually dirt-floored.

Noticeably absent are large barns or separate stables. Very little meat is consumed, and no dairy products, and the use of draft animals as aids to farm labor has gradually declined to the point where it is extremely uncommon, largely because acreage cannot be spared for growing feed. Stable space for those families that pos-

FARMSTEAD
LAYOUT

1. Forested mountainside
2. Bamboo grove
3. Large trees
4. Farmhouse
5. Farmyard
6. Sheds for storage, fertilizer, ash, work, etc.
7. Pond and well
8. Vegetable garden
9. Gateway
10. Irrigation channel
11. Rice paddy
12. Path to upper fields

sess a horse or an ox (about 10 percent of the total population) is often integrated into the main house, but a stable may also be combined with one or more of the other work functions.

Shinichi's young son spots us and runs to announce our arrival. His father emerges from the house, wiping his hands on his short cotton tunic. His legs are bare because it is summer and, like most of the men and boys in the village, he wears only a loincloth under the tunic.

He welcomes us with excitement, and with his wife, Misaki, leads us to the well. She draws a bucket of water and hands us a wooden dipper. The water is clear and nearly ice cold, and we all express our appreciation and compliments, exchanging a moment of social ritual that establishes good will and gratitude for natural abundance. As Misaki hurries back into the house to prepare tea, we sit outside on a rough bench with our host.

The well we have drunk from is a roofed structure, with room for three or four people to haul water, wash vegetables, or fill tubs. A shallow wooden splash basin catches runoff, which drains into a simple stone-lined channel leading to a small pond. This pond, partly functional, partly ornamental, is manmade, and it is carefully sited to collect drainwater from the entire site, though many farmhouses are sited to take advantage of existing natural ponds.

Considering the heavy rainfall that Japan experiences, providing adequate drainage is high on the list of farm design requirements. The homestead is therefore provided with two sources of water, one potable (the well), and one for general use (the pond). Wastewater is collected to become part of the general use.

THE WELL

Is like an outdoor room for water work.

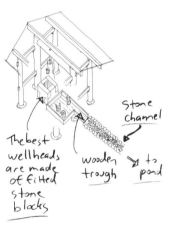

The best wellheads are made of fitted stone blocks

Stone channel

wooden trough

to pond

The FARMHOUSE

front elevation

side elevation

## ROOF

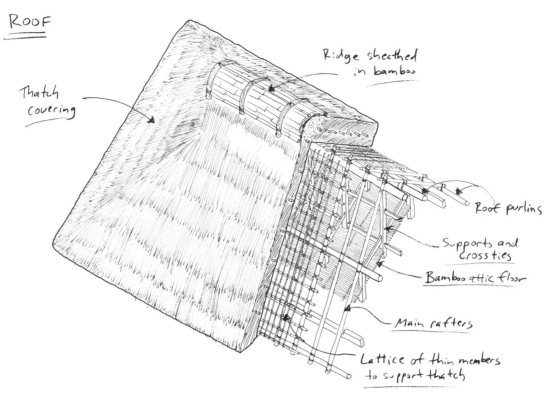

Thatch
covering

Ridge sheathed
in bamboo

Roof purlins

Supports and
cross ties

Bamboo attic floor

Main rafters

Lattice of thin members
to support thatch

## MAIN BEAMS

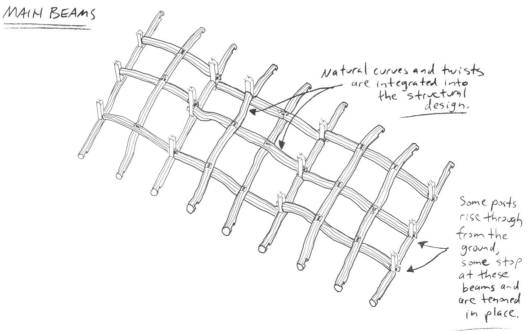

Natural curves and twists
are integrated into
the structural
design.

Some posts
rise through
from the
ground,
some stop
at these
beams and
are tenoned
in place.

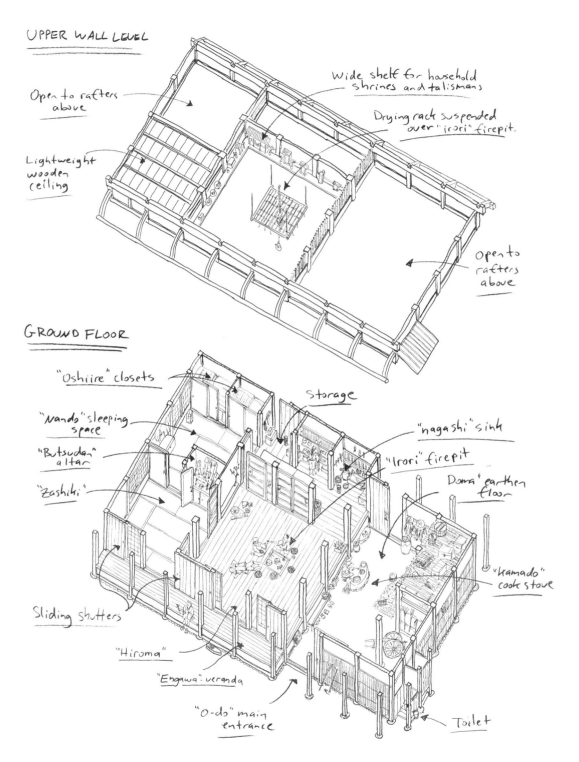

## UPPER WALL LEVEL

Open to rafters above

Lightweight wooden ceiling

Wide shelf for household shrines and talismans

Drying rack suspended over "irori" firepit.

Open to rafters above

## GROUND FLOOR

"Oshiire" closets

"Nando" sleeping space

"Butsudan" altar

"Zashiki"

Sliding shutters

"Hiroma"

"Engawa" veranda

"O-do" main entrance

Storage

"nagashi" sink

"Irori" firepit

"Doma" earthen floor

"kamado" cook stove

Toilet

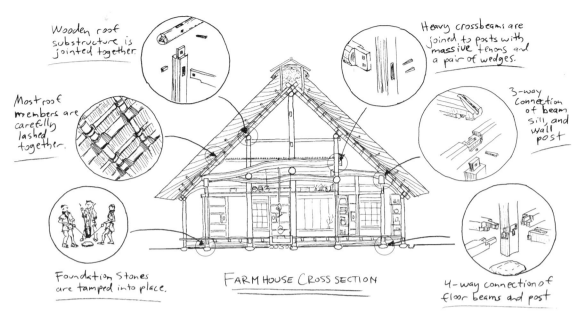

Wooden roof substructure is jointed together.

Most roof members are carefully lashed together.

Foundation stones are tamped into place.

Heavy crossbeams are joined to posts with massive tenons and a pair of wedges.

3-way connection of beam, sill, and wall post

4-way connection of floor beams and post

FARM HOUSE CROSS SECTION

ROOF STRUCTURE VARIATIONS

"Sasu-gumi" – no bracing.

"Oodachi-gumi" – tall bracing

"Sasu-oodachi" hybrid

"Wa-goya" – complex bracing

Some villages have the additional benefit of nearby natural rivers and streams or engineered water supplies, use of which may be approved for households. Many villages have communal washing streams, and it is not uncommon to see baskets suspended in the irrigation culverts running alongside homes, to cool and preserve vegetables. But unlike the communal systems, household water supplies must be provided and maintained by each individual family.

The dirt-floored work yard occupies a little more ground area than the main house. It is a true multipurpose space for almost any farm activity that is better done outdoors. We see wash hung out to dry and racks of vegetables drying in the sun. This is also where carpentry and repairs take place. One end of the yard is devoted to a small kitchen garden and a compost heap for mulch. In particular, though, the area must be large enough for threshing and winnowing large quantities of rice after harvest.

The house is over one hundred years old, and it bears its age handsomely. Venerable and spacious, in materials and coloration it is fully of a piece with its surroundings. The thick thatch roof is massive and enveloping. Its eaves descend almost to eye level, providing a generous roofed space all around the exterior of the building. This intermediate space, the *dobisashi*, is ample enough for many kinds of work and shelters a variety of implements from the elements—fruits and vegetables can easily be strung up to dry here as well. For part of its length it shelters the *engawa*, the raised veranda, and the depth of the eaves allows someone seated there to converse easily with someone outside while both are sheltered from sun or rain. It is a simple arrangement, beautiful in its function and accommodation, and perhaps unique in the world.

Farmhouse walls come in many types. The materials used on the exterior surfaces are chosen for local cost and availability, appropriateness to local climate and weather, and the durability required at that particular location on the house. The lower walls of the large farmhouses in the mountainous, snowbound Hida region, for example, are usually covered in cryptomeria bark, giving them a moisture-resistant and easily replaceable surface. Vertically battened wood siding is common in several regions as well, and in the Akita region of the far north, the walls are thatched like the roofs for extra insulation from the cold. But the most common wall treatment by far is a mixture of clay and straw that is applied between exposed half-timbers as wattle and daub, and this is how Shinichi's house is made.

From time to time one sees farmhouses that have a layer of hard white plaster added over the clay undercoat, resulting in a strikingly contrasting patterned wall like those of temple residences, and the homes of samurai and wealthy townsmen. But Shinichi's farmhouse presents a face of earth to the world—sandy ochre expanses framed by tough structural timbers, all beautifully aged and eroded by time and patched with use. The walls of the few work areas under the eaves have been reinforced with panels of split bamboo, but even with this third material there is a wonderful harmony of earthen hues.

A simple wood-paneled sliding door gives access to a single generous ground-level opening, the *o-do*, and it is only in the details of its frame, as well as in the carved brackets that lend extra support to the eaves, that we see any truly decorative embellishment. On the other hand, the tight and skillful ropework visible on the underside of the eaves, binding the poles and purlins of the roof to other, smaller elements, expresses a design spirit rooted in logic and economy but allowed to elaborate into an almost luxurious care and finish. Everything about the exterior of the house demonstrates a similar decisiveness, appropriateness, and awareness. Shinichi leads us inside.

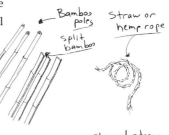

WALL CONSTRUCTION

Bamboo poles
split bamboo
Straw or hemp rope

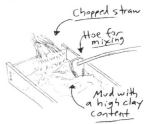

Chopped straw
Hoe for mixing
Mud with a high clay content

Sturdy bamboo framework
Lattice of thin bamboos wrapped w/ rope

The most common wall material is wattle-and-daub ("tsuchi-kabe" or "arakabe"). These earthen walls are easily made, easily patched, and easily removed and recycled. Pretty good insulation too!!

Mud applied in layers

Wood-paneled walls are desirable in some climates and for some uses.

A view of the "doma" and "hiruma" from inside the main entry.

### inside a remarkable place

We find ourselves in a large, dark, earthen-floored space. Smoke wafts from a partly visible firepit to the apex of the roof high above, and the entire space is steeped in the smoky aroma. The atmosphere is damp and quite cool, even now at the height of summer. Sounds are muted by the earth beneath our feet.

We are in the *doma*, the earth-floored vestibule, starkly functional and ancient in spirit. This is a workspace, and the implements of farming life are arrayed on the wall like emblems: rakes, scythes, baskets, strainers, ropes, boxes, pestles, overshoes, hats. There is ample storage space for tools and food. A few of the larger farm contraptions like pumps and looms take up some floor space, but almost everything else finds a place off the floor. Rakes, ropes, tools, baskets, and racks are in nooks and crannies to our right. Straight ahead are an earthen stove and a back door, with assorted storage shelves and containers nearby. To the left is a raised, floored space with a suspended ceiling made of thin bamboo poles. Massive, squared wooden posts flanks the raised floor, but no wall or other divider separates it from the doma.

The floor of the doma is more carefully constructed than it appears, and it

about 2~3m

The "dobisashi" is a dirt-floored outdoor work space sheltered by the eaves

## The ENGAWA

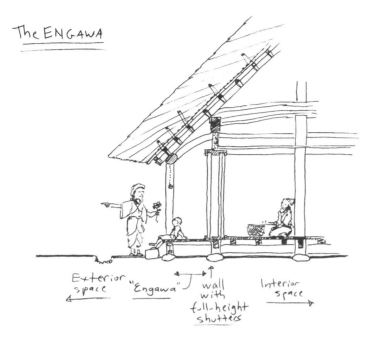

The "engawa" is a versatile intermediate space. In farmhouses it is usually nestled under the protective eaves, and opens to the wood and tatami-floored interior rooms. It allows a comfortable degree of separation that nonetheless encourages conversation.

Exterior space ← | "Engawa" | wall with full-height shutters | Interior space →

is very durable. Layer upon layer of clay mixed with lime have been laboriously pounded down and allowed to cure, leaving a surface more like concrete than plain earth. It is easy to clean and sheds water well, and after years of use the surface has taken on a pebbled texture, soothing to the eye and soft underfoot. This texture is all the more apparent because the only significant natural light comes through the wide door through which we have entered, a low-raking light that is diffused upward by the sheen of the floor and that puts its irregularities in high relief.

The Japanese have used these pounded earth floors since they began to build three thousand years ago, and the firepits and lashed and thatched roofs bear an identical pedigree. In fact, the doma sometimes goes by the name of *niwa*, "garden" or "courtyard," implying that it began as a truly outdoor space. This degree of continuity, with design solutions being continually refined but surviving from neolithic times into the early modern period in clearly recognizable form, is remarkable and probably unprecedented among literate civilizations.

Shinichi seems to be proud and a bit self-conscious of his doma, which takes up nearly half of the overall interior area: proud because it is ample and generous and speaks of generations of hard work; self-conscious perhaps because it is nevertheless cluttered and worn.

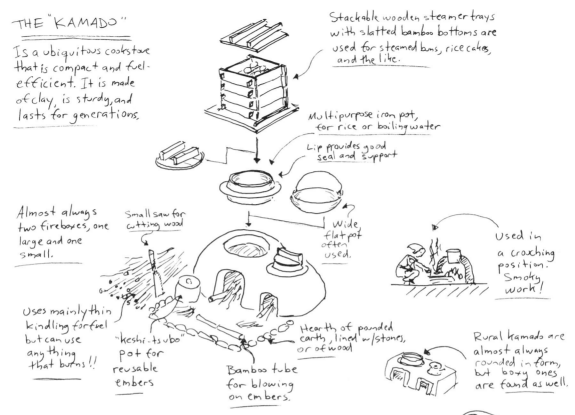

## THE "KAMADO"

Is a ubiquitous cookstove that is compact and fuel-efficient. It is made of clay, is sturdy, and lasts for generations.

Stackable wooden steamer trays with slatted bamboo bottoms are used for steamed buns, rice cakes, and the like.

Multipurpose iron pot, for rice or boiling water

Lip provides good seal and support

Almost always two fireboxes, one large and one small.

Small saw for cutting wood

Wide, flat pot often used.

Used in a crouching position. Smoky work!

Uses mainly thin kindling for fuel but can use anything that burns!!

"keshi-tsubo" pot for reusable embers

Bamboo tube for blowing on embers.

Hearth of pounded earth, lined w/stones, or of wood

Rural kamado are almost always rounded in form, but boxy ones are found as well.

← 2 m →

"Maga-tama"

Large and prosperous households might have kamado with many fireboxes.

The kitchen functions are divided between those performed in one corner of the doma and those done on the raised floor. A short step away from the raised floor is a plastered clay stove, or *kamado*. It is a model of fuel efficiency, built in place by specialized craftsmen out of adobe clay and made to order in any size, shape, or capacity. Shinichi's stove is a fairly standard-sized one that has been in use for over fifty years. Shaped somewhat like a bean when seen from above, it is about knee high and is used in a crouching position.

This one has two fireboxes, one large and one small, each custom-fitted with a lidded iron pot. The largest is for rice, and while the others can be used for rice, they are more often used for vegetables and stews, as well as for steamed items. Each is independently fueled using scavenged wood and fallen branches. Straw, broken wooden implements, cloth, and charcoal can be used as well, but for the most part cooking with one of these stoves involves close monitoring of the fire, feeding it new sticks and twigs at frequent intervals. The time and attention required are more than compensated for by the economy of fuel use.

Very large ones can be made for cottage industries like dyeing.

The other kitchen area is tucked against the rear wall of the raised floor area. Its main feature is a wooden sink, built into the floor and used from a seated position. The sink, set in front of a small, slatted window, is made of wooden planks carefully fitted together with joints tight enough to prevent leakage. Shinichi's mother crouches over it, scrubbing a large white radish. She takes water from a large earthenware jug, fitted with a lightweight wooden lid. The water is drawn out with a wooden ladle, and the jug is replenished as needed from the well outside. A drain spout protrudes from one corner of the sink through the exterior wall below the window; from there it drips into a narrow, stone-lined channel and, like overflow from the well, flows as waste-water into the pond. This wastewater contains dirt and organic matter from vegetables and other foodstuffs, but nothing in the way of soap or toxic chemi-cals. Little that resembles soap is used, in fact, with rice hulls and other gentle abrasives being preferred for most purposes, so the wastewater is fairly clean.

The kitchen is equipped with a variety of storage shelves, but there are only a few dishes and cooking implements. Good durable dishes must be purchased from specialized craftsmen, such as potters and woodturners, and like most farm families, Shinichi's tries to use only what they can make themselves, min-imizing cash expenditures. Each family member has a bowl, a cup, homemade spoons and chopsticks, and little else. On the other hand, durable storage jars are considered worth the expense of purchase.

The family eats very little meat or poultry, and they consume their vegeta-bles either fresh or preserved by drying or pickling in brine. Indeed, the variety of pickling techniques is awe inspiring. The kitchen has several large, lidded pickling jars, each containing a different item: radishes, plums, cucumbers, cabbage, and more. A number of these have been actually buried in the floor with just the lids protruding in order to take advantage of natural cooling. There are similar but smaller jars for miso, soy sauce, and cooking oil. Rice for daily use is stored in a finely constructed oblong wooden box with a close-fitting lid.

## from the unclean to the clean

A low, thick beam called the *agarikamachi*, or "stepping-up sill," marks the edge of the raised floor. Polished and worn from generations of physical contact, it is the ideal height for sitting, and it forms a clear demarcation line between the "unclean" doma, where outdoor footwear is worn, and the "clean" house proper, where wearing shoes is taboo. Our initial impression of the *hiroma*, or "big room," is one of dark wood and bamboo. Open at the entrance, the hiroma is bounded to our right by the kitchen wall and shelves,

"Kojin-sama"

The kamado is so important, a small altar is always maintained nearby. The kamado itself is honored during New Year's celebrations!

and to the left by wide sliding doors that open onto the veranda. The far wall is a solid one, framed with smoke-blackened wooden boards. We slip off our footwear, and follow Shinichi in stepping up onto the floor.

The floor is made of thick, wide hardwood planks. No coating was applied as a finish, but generations of hand rubbing and contact with bare and slippered feet have rendered them black and shiny, and we can clearly see the light from the wide sliding doors reflected in the floor. The hiroma of many houses have no ceilings and are bound overhead only by the roughly hewn crisscrossed logs that serve as roof beams. But the bamboo ceiling of this particular room lends it a rustic dignity and delicacy, almost as if a simple lean-to has been erected inside the house. Transformed as it has been by long exposure to smoke, the bamboo reflects a warm russet light. This room is stark, resonant, robust, cool, and aromatic.

It is also well appointed. What appear at first glance to be solid walls are in fact sliding panels concealing capacious storage space, and upon closer inspection we can see that a few of these are actually movable, modular storage units

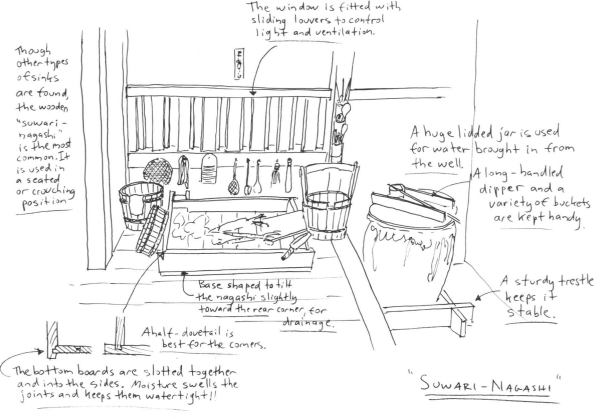

The window is fitted with sliding louvers to control light and ventilation.

Though other types of sinks are found, the wooden "suwari-nagashi" is the most common. It is used in a seated or crouching position

A huge lidded jar is used for water brought in from the well.

A long-handled dipper and a variety of buckets are kept handy.

Base shaped to tilt the nagashi slightly toward the rear corner, for drainage.

A sturdy trestle keeps it stable.

A half-dovetail is best for the corners.

The bottom boards are slotted together and into the sides. Moisture swells the joints and keeps them watertight!!

"SUWARI-NAGASHI"

that fit perfectly into wall openings and recesses. The thick, horizontal framing that surrounds the room at the height of the doorways supports shelves of various widths, upon which are stacked containers and household implements, boxes and baskets.

The most prominent shelf is a spiritual one: the *kami-dana*, or "god-shelf," that bears a miniature Shinto shrine as well as votives and offerings for the gods of nature. There is also a simple, large recess in the wall in front of us, the *oshi-ita*, which is decorated with paper talismans. Together the kami-dana and oshi-ita transform the entire space into a place of devotion and spiritual significance, a place in which residents and visitors are constantly reminded that nature and the spirits by whose will all was created are the true center of life, and man is allowed to dwell here only with their permission.

The center of life in the house is the unassuming firepit, the *irori*—a square recess in the floor of this main room. It serves as a cooking facility, where pots of stew or gruel can be hung to cook, and fish and vegetables can be roasted on skewers. Other treats can be toasted over this fire as well, though rice and most rice dishes are better prepared on the kamado. The firepit is the information and communication center of the house. It commands a view of the doma as well, allowing someone seated here, usually the matron of the household, to witness all comings and goings and to monitor and direct all activity. We've arrived just as Shinichi and his family are finishing their midday meal. The cast-iron stew pot has been replaced by one for boiling water for tea, suspended over the embers by an adjustable hook. As Misaki and her mother-in-law bustle about the kitchen area, other members of the household lounge comfortably on woven straw mats, some sprawled on the cool floor in hopes of catching a short nap. All told, there are six people, an average number for a farm of this size.

Shinichi is the head of the household and is in his thirties. He grew up in this house, which was built by his grandfather on land obtained by his great-grandfather. As his name indicates, he is the eldest son of his deceased father, Shin. His wife, Misaki, who is a few years younger, grew up in a neighboring village; their marriage was an arranged one. The matron of the household, however, is Shinichi's mother, who is over fifty years old and therefore quite elderly. Though she defers to her daughter-in-law in many matters, this is her domain and the place where she spends most of her day.

The couple has two children, the boy of twelve who had first noticed our arrival, and a girl of ten. Misaki was pregnant twice since, and while both came to term, they were "sent back" by the midwife at birth. While not explicitly prohibited, large families are strongly discouraged by social norms, and adequate

*Wastewater from the kitchen sink flows outside to a trough, and then to the pond for further use. (Sometimes bamboo pipes are used for long distances!)*

*Crouching or sitting to work is more comfortable than standing for long periods.*

resources for all can only be provided if the population growth of the village is inhibited. This is also the reason the sixth member of the household, Shinichi's younger brother Tsuyoshi, has never married and lives here in his brother's house.

More prosperous families with much larger landholdings might be able to consider allowing a second or even a third son to build a house and start a family, and many are taken into childless households or those with only daughters as adopted heirs. But the second son's lot is assumed to be a solitary, if not strictly celibate, one. This value system definitely sacrifices a large measure of personal liberty for the greater common good. It may seem unfair, and some aspects of it, such as infanticide (*dataimabiki*, or literally "thinning out"), even extreme. But the voluntary limitation of birthrate and family size has led to a stable population nationwide for nearly two hundred years, to the benefit of all.

From where we sit we can see most of the rest of the house. Beyond the hiroma lie several other modest rooms, all opening onto each other and to the hiroma itself by large sliding doors. In inclement or cold weather, each room can be individually closed, shuttered, and independently heated with small braziers if needed. But on warm days like today everything is opened to the breeze, and it is possible to look from the doma all the way through to the other end of the house and into the garden beyond, a free-flowing enfilade of subtly differentiated living space.

Nearest the hiroma is the *zashiki*, a tatami-matted space that is less purely utilitarian but nonetheless well suited to many kinds of work as well as to the comfortable reception of guests. It is the most formal room of the house, and is where the third spiritual space, the *butsudan*, or Buddhist family altar, is located, concealed behind sliding or folding doors. Funerals are held in this room, as are the periodic devotional observances dictated by the faith that require the presence of a Buddhist priest.

The design and features of the zashiki provide a good indication of the prosperity of the household—and perhaps of the community as a whole. It also serves as a barometer for the broad cultural shift in which aspects of the aristocratic lifestyle have gradually percolated through society and become available to nearly everyone, even average families like Shinichi's. There are many communities around the country where a zashiki with tatami mats would be considered an unnecessary luxury. In those areas, the zashiki would be nearly identical to the hiroma in terms of walls and flooring, and it would most likely not have a ceiling. Large straw mats might be placed on the floor as a kind of proto-tatami (for in fact tatami evolved from rougher, thinner woven mats).

But Shinichi's zashiki is representative in its construction. It has a ceiling of

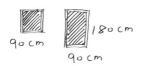

90 cm / 90 cm / 180 cm

Square irori are most common, but larger rectangular ones are often found.

CUSTOMARY SEATING

Main pillar "daikoku-bashira"

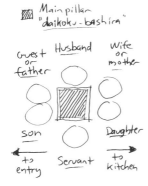

Guest or father / Husband / Wife or mother

son / Daughter

to entry / Servant / to kitchen

Large woven straw mats can be used for seating, as can small round ones.

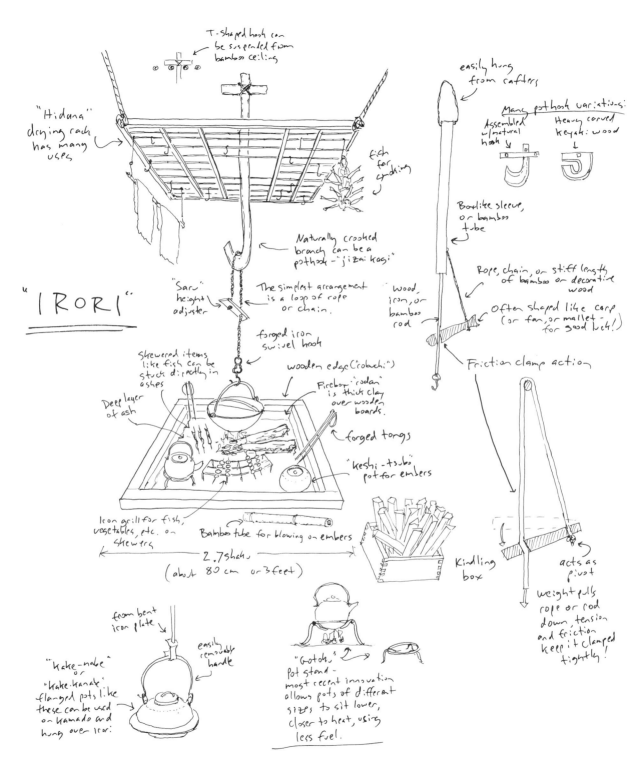

T-shaped hook can be suspended from bamboo ceiling

"Hidana" drying rack has many uses

easily hung from rafters

Many pothook variations:

Assembled w/natural hook

Heavy carved keyaki wood

fish for smoking

"IRORI"

Naturally crooked branch can be a pothook - "jizai kagi"

Barklike sleeve, or bamboo tube

"Saru" height adjuster

The simplest arrangement is a loop of rope or chain.

Rope, chain, or stiff length of bamboo or decorative wood

Wood, iron, or bamboo rod

Often shaped like carp (or fan, or mallet - for good luck!)

forged iron swivel hook

Skewered items like fish can be stuck directly in ashes

wooden edge ("robuchi")

Firebox "robori" is thick clay over wooden boards.

Friction clamp action

Deep layer of ash

forged tongs

"keshi-tsubo" pot for embers

Iron grill for fish, vegetables, etc. on skewers

Bamboo tube for blowing on embers

2.7 shaku (about 80 cm or 3 feet)

Kindling box

acts as pivot

weight pulls rope or rod down, tension and friction keep it clamped tightly!

from bent iron plate

easily removable handle

"kake-nabe" or "kake-banabe" flanged pots like these can be used on kamado and hung over irori

"Gotoku" pot stand - most recent innovation allows pots of different sizes to sit lower, closer to heat, using less fuel.

lightweight battens and boards that is suspended from the beams above, requiring the services of a good carpenter. It has sliding doors as well as *shoji* made of rice paper over a fine wood framework, and although they were a bit pricey initially, they have proven to be quite durable and easily re-covered when the paper gets ragged. But these all require specialized craftsmen (like the "door and window man" who did the work here) and materials like paper—which cannot be made by most families at home, and so they represent a step away from true self-sufficiency and into the wider cash economy. At the same time, the design is simple to the point of austerity, is unembellished, and relies primarily on the harmonies and counterpoints of unadorned natural materials for its beauty.

## a beautiful extension of space

The zashiki is also located to take best advantage of the engawa. With the exterior shutters open, the space under the eaves becomes a beautiful extension of the tatami room. The deep, low eaves shade the interior and modulate its light, and the shoji may be closed fully or partially to control the light even further. The engawa is an intermediate zone, and people can remain in that part where they are most comfortable at the moment or that part best suited to what they happen to be doing, without needing to break off conversation. It also allows visitors to drop by and chat very informally, standing under the eaves or sitting on the edge of the veranda.

To enter the house proper by removing one's shoes and stepping up to the hiroma implies a long visit and, consequently, the expectation of further hospitality in the form of food and drink. The intermediate space of the engawa, however, with its "here but not really here" ambiguity, enables both parties to end conversation easily and return to what they were doing.

Tucked most deeply inside the house is the *nando*, or sleeping room. Like the zashiki, the nando has changed over the course of recent decades due to technical and economic developments. From time immemorial, it seems, the nando was a small, wood-floored room with a deep sill into which straw would be thrown as bedding for the entire household. Cotton futon bedding was unavailable, and actual bedding of any sort was only available to the wealthiest classes. Commoners slept in their one set of daily clothes, covering themselves with piles of loose straw and huddling together for warmth. It was uncomfortable and not particularly warm or hygienic.

The early eighteenth century witnessed an agricultural revolution, however, when cotton was grown on a large scale with the encouragement and support of the government. From the point of view of the government, cotton textiles present obvious advantages for outfitting armies because of their durability and strength when compared to hemp, the most commonly used fiber until then. (Silk, of course, is a superior fiber in these regards, but it remains a luxury item.) As cotton has become more widely available, it has declined in cost to the point where even commoners can afford more than one set of clothes as well as bedding, and everything can be repeatedly washed at high temperatures. Mortality records show that the overall health of peasants has improved with the introduction of cotton.

Like the zashiki, the nando of Shinichi's house is floored with tatami—as is a small anteroom—and it has the deep closets for bedding storage that have started to become common around this time. It is still a fairly small room, however in which the whole family sleeps together, clean, warm, and comfortable.

We ask to use the toilet and are led there by Shinichi's daughter. This is the smallest room in the house, and while located close to the entrance, it is an

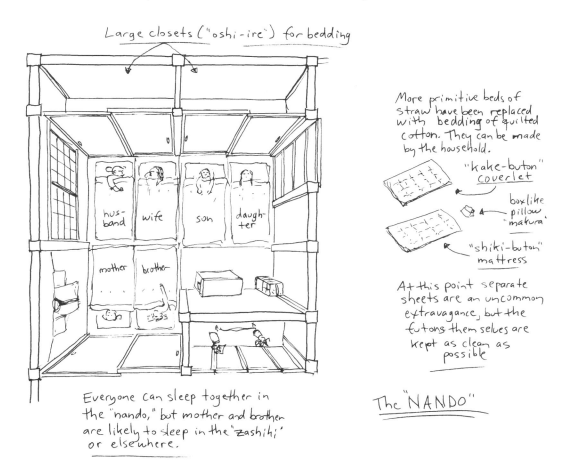

Large closets ("oshi-ire") for bedding

hus-band | wife | son | daugh-ter

mother | brother

More primitive beds of straw have been replaced with bedding of quilted cotton. They can be made by the household.

"kake-buton" coverlet

boxlike pillow "makura"

"shiki-buton" mattress

At this point separate sheets are an uncommon extravagance, but the futons themselves are kept as clean as possible

The "NANDO"

Everyone can sleep together in the "nando," but mother and brother are likely to sleep in the "zashiki" or elsewhere.

almost separate structure. It consists of two cubicles: one an open urinal for men, another just large enough for a wooden-floored squat toilet. The latter has a lightweight wooden door and latch, though there is no separation by gender, age, or status. It is simple and easy to clean, and though no one would consider it a pleasant place, it is made less offensive by incense and flowers. To the user, the toilet serves its purpose well. It is well ventilated (and consequently quite cold in winter), and a concern for hygiene is clear from the nearby hand-washing basin, which is found even in the poorest homes.

To the household, the toilet has an essential and positive economic value. Human waste, or night soil, has become an irreplaceable fertilizer, and considerable ingenuity has been expended on toilet design to allow these waste products to be easily collected and processed. The toilets are built over large wooden casks or earthenware jars sunken into the ground, with lids easily accessible from the ground level outdoors. The provision of a separate urinal is not purely for the convenience of the user; solids and liquids are processed differently before they are ready for the fields, and the underground holding tanks are also separate. From time to time, one sees outdoor urinals built directly over tanks, conveniently located for men working outdoors and intended to encourage them to deposit their waste fluids into the collection system rather than in the open field. Farmers also build toilets and urinals along well-traveled roads for public use, in the hopes of increasing their yields of fertilizer.

In fact, human waste has become a big business, and farmers go to great lengths to secure contracts to collect and transport night soil from the cities to use on their fields. In Europe, this waste is being dumped into rivers, polluting the water supply and leading to outbreaks of cholera, but here the frequent collection and efforts to minimize leakage and loss have positive health benefits for all.

The practice of bathing regularly also has tremendous health benefits. Whereas privately operated public baths have become very common in cities, where the density of the population can support the business on a large scale, bathing is a household affair in villages (unless there is a natural hot spring nearby). Although rapid development in bath facility design is taking place, including improvements in the construction of bathtubs and the design of water heating and drainage systems, few of these advances benefit peasants like Shinichi directly, and it will be over one hundred years before the average farmhouse is equipped with an actual bathroom, tub, and water heater.

At Shinichi's household, once a week a large tub is dragged either into the doma or outside, filled with water heated on the kamado and over the irori, and everyone, including the neighbors, takes turns washing themselves and soaking.

Waste is carried to the manure pile in a tall narrow bucket with a tight lid.

## TOILET

Usually attached to the main house, near the entrance and accessible from outside. But freestanding outhouses are not uncommon.

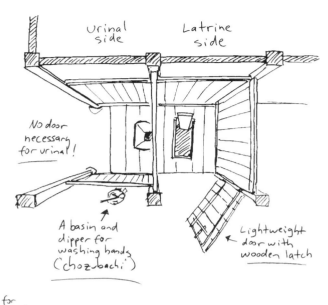

urinal side    Latrine side

No door necessary for urinal!

A basin and dipper for washing hands ("chozubachi")

Lightweight door with wooden latch

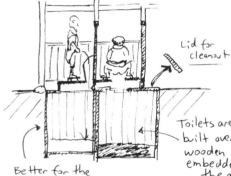

Lid for cleanout

Better for the urinal to have its own cask.

Toilets are usually built over large wooden casks embedded in the ground.

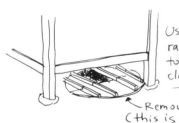

Usually a raised floor to give easier cleanout access

Removable lid (this is a nice arrangement — often more basic!)

Typical urinal for men, made of thin wooden boards in "morning glory" shape.

The main thing is to make it so convenient to use people won't be tempted to go in the bushes when working outside...

A wide-mouthed jar embedded in the ground under the eaves can be used by both sexes as a urinal!!

Bathers scrub themselves with small cloth pouches filled with rice bran, which provide the perfect amount of abrasion. Because no soap is used, the waste-water may be safely collected and sent to the pond. Heating this much water is laborious and consumes as much fuel as a day's worth of meals, and consequently it is difficult to justify bathing more frequently.

There are bathing methods that use less energy, the most common being the steam bath. Often little more than a shuttered cabinet barely large enough for two people and fitted with a small charcoal brazier and a pan of water, the steam bath provides several intense cleansing minutes of pore-opening and sweating. After scrubbing and rinsing with cool water, one feels very clean and refreshed. In summer months, solar energy is used to save fuel. A large jar of water is placed outside directly in the sun, and over the course of the day, it becomes warm enough to be used for the evening bath. Water similarly warmed may also be used to jump-start the heating of water for tea, also saving fuel.

Over time, a variety of bathing arrangements have appeared, from the cook pot-like iron *goemon-buro* tub to small rooms that have no tubs but are equipped with drains in the floor. But the key component of the bath remains hot water, and the respect and value accorded it reflects an awareness that the benefits come with a significant cost in fuel and therefore in environmental impact. This drive to economize on hot bathwater will prove to be an enduring value (and continue to influence bath design) in later centuries as well.

"TAWASHI"
Rice bran ("nuka") sewn into a bag of scrap cloth....

... and used as a scrubber! (no soap)

A large cask provides the best bath, but takes lots of hot water

In order to heat enough water quickly, several pots and kettles will be used at once.

Even an average bath consumes a lot of fuel.

A hot bath is a bit of an extravagance in terms of energy use, but provides measurable health benefits.

A shallow cask may be all that is available for bathing, and will serve well.

THE "OFURO"

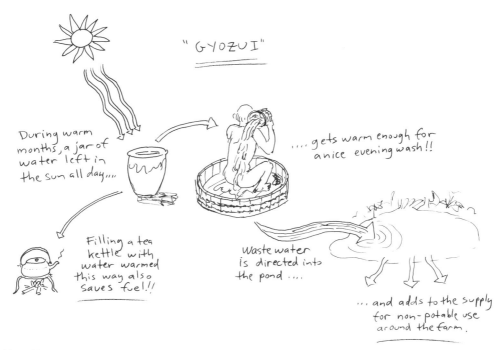

"GYOZUI"

During warm months, a jar of water left in the sun all day....

....gets warm enough for a nice evening wash!!

Filling a tea kettle with water warmed this way also saves fuel!!

Waste water is directed into the pond ....

... and adds to the supply for non-potable use around the farm.

## self-sufficiency as a way of life

Life in the village is marked by self-sufficiency on several different scales. Shinichi's household, like all the others, is nearly self-sufficient in food, producing enough rice for itself and for government levy and enough vegetables. Each household has at least a few fruit trees, can gather its share of forest foodstuffs, and can fish in the rivers. They press their own oil and ferment miso from soybeans. Unavoidably, temporary surpluses and deficits occur for each family, but more often than not, these can be remedied by the informal exchange that characterizes social interaction: one may receive a bushel of persimmons from a relative and reciprocate with a basket of fish. Unusual food items, perhaps for special occasions such as entertaining visitors, may only be obtainable by purchase, but this is infrequent.

Similarly, each household is self-sufficient in energy. Shinichi's household uses only the fuel it can gather, which is never more than a fair share of the village's supply. It has its own water supply in the form of the well. The house and work yards are designed to take advantage of solar energy, and the agricultural process would be unthinkable without it. The house is designed and oriented in conjunction with plantings to maximize natural shade and cooling breezes. Water power is used on a modest scale for pressing oil, grinding grain, and pulverizing minerals, but except for a handful of draft animals in the village, humans power nearly everything.

Shinichi's family makes most of their tools and implements and produces their own clothes—from spinning and weaving fabric all the way to actually cutting and assembling garments. But here an individual household may begin to rely upon the resources of the village as a whole: it may need to supplement its own cotton with some grown nearby; it may prefer to obtain more expertly woven and dyed fabric; it may need expert metalwork for a particular tool; it needs pottery, tatami mats, and paper for shoji. In all of these areas, while each family may not be truly self-sufficient, the village in general is. In fact, the only essential item likely to be obtainable only from outside the village is salt. Other items are imported, of course, and itinerant peddlers are allowed to sell an increasingly wide variety of items to peasants—seaweed, tea, oil, wooden water dippers, pans, rice pots, paper, fans, rulers. Luxuries and status items are available, like better sake, better cabinetry, finer pottery, ornaments, and accessories, and this attests to the peasants' increasing standard of living and integration with the wider cash economy. But the essentials are all locally sourced.

There is an incredible amount of recycling going on as well. Agricultural waste—what little there is, since most plants, from root to stalk, are fully utilized in some way—becomes compost and mulch. Similarly, fireplace ash is recycled into the fertilizer mix, as are worn-out woven rush and straw items. Metal (predominantly iron) is successively reworked. A broken cooking pot may be converted into several sickle blades, for instance, and broken blades beaten into straps and hooks.

Wood has a particularly long life cycle: a broken plow frame can become an axe handle, a broken axe handle refitted to a scoop, a broken scoop added to the firewood pile (and its ashes finding their way to the fields again as fertilizer). Clothing can be endlessly reworked, taken apart, remade, with the most intact portions of a worn-out jacket, for example, being carefully salvaged and worked into another as patchwork, which is eventually recycled into carrying pouches, and then as cleaning cloths. Old cleaning cloths can be cut into narrow strips and woven into indoor sandals or small mats, and when these are worn out, they will find their way to the compost heap or end up helping to heat water. In the village, this recycling takes place mostly at the level of households like Shinichi's, but, in fact, it has been institutionalized and commercialized throughout the country.

Beyond being self-sufficient, most households are able to generate a surplus of some nonagricultural items, which eventually evolve into cottage industries. Though raising food for the nation is their primary purpose and responsibility as mandated by Shogun Ieyasu at the beginning of the era in 1603, in 1649

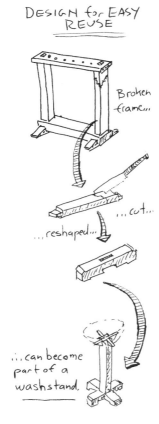

DESIGN for EASY REUSE

Broken frame...

...cut...

...reshaped...

...can become part of a washstand.

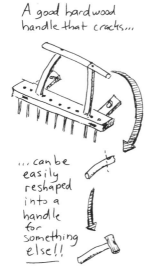

A good hardwood handle that cracks...

...can be easily reshaped into a handle for something else!!

the government decreed that after their day's labor is done, peasants should spend their evenings industriously working at crafts that can supplement their income. This is seasonal work as well, much of it ideally suited to occupying the winter months. It also provides a way of efficiently utilizing labor, since all hands are not always required for every agricultural task, and some can be better employed at other industries.

Among the most common cottage industries are straw work, basketry, and textiles. Straw work is incredibly wide in application since the rice straw (*wara*) from the harvest is the most readily available material for a great number of household necessities and is a prolifically renewable resource From their own leftover straw. Shinichi's family weaves mats of all sorts, from large floor mats to small ones for seating to "hot pads" and decorative items. Large mats require a specialized weaving frame, usually homemade, and the technique is really that of textile weaving. They also weave pouches and carrying bags from straw, either rough and open weave for heavy-duty work or close and finely woven with decorative patterns for more presentable occasions.

They weave a number of clothing items from straw as well, primarily footwear, aprons, and foul-weather gear. Straw footwear ranges from lightweight

An iron pot that's too broken to repair...

...can be refashioned into a number of iron tools!

Rice Straw is used for just about everything around the farm. Straw work can be extremely robust, very fine, or both!

"Mushiro" mats, both indoor and outdoor

"Enza" - round floor cushions

"Wara-nawa" - straw rope

"Mino" - rain cloak

"Mae-kake" - apron

"Ejikko" - straw rope bag

"Kya-han" - gaiters

"Waraji" - sandals

sandals to heavy snow boots, as well as gaiters and overshoes. In fact, straw overshoes are even made for horses. Straw aprons are mainly for outdoor use, and because they require flexibility, they are usually very finely and decoratively woven. Raincoats and cloaks are made thick and bulky to minimize the amount of moisture that can penetrate, but they are surprisingly lightweight; their collars and neck closures are comfortably thin and flexible. Many kinds of hoods and hats, as well as mittens, can be made from rice straw, and when twisted into rope, its uses are multiplied.

They make bales in which to package and transport rice, as well as brooms, brushes, and even toys from rice straw. It is durable enough to last a season or a year, but most straw items need to be replaced regularly. (There is a particularly high built-in demand for new footwear.) Finally, of course, Shinichi's family can easily recycle straw items into mulch or fuel, resulting in a zero-waste cycle of use.

They use woven reeds and bamboo strips for more durable items such as basketry and hats. Because of its resiliency, bamboo is particularly appropriate where stiffness and flexibility are desired, and it is fashioned into a variety of implements such as strainers, sieves, funnels, lids, dividers, as well as boxes, tubs, and even ceilings—all using basket-weaving techniques. Bamboo is extremely hardy, prolific, and fast growing, and like straw is easily recycled. It is an irreplaceable feature of Japan's technical and material culture.

## green cottage industries

There are many kinds of textiles that lend themselves to cottage industry, and some have evolved into mass production. True textiles include bast fibers (hemp and ramie), cotton, and silk. Of these, hemp is technically the most ancient and also the easiest to produce, and Shinichi's family produces enough for its own use. Silk was introduced from China in about 300 AD as a labor-intensive elite good, but Shinichi's household does not produce it. Cotton, though introduced from Korea and China initially in the twelfth century, was not produced on a large scale until the late seventeenth century, making it the most recent textile fiber. Shinichi's household does not grow cotton, but weaves and dyes cotton they obtain from relatives.

All of these cottage industries involve trade-offs between resource allocation, environmental impact and the value and utility of the finished products. Examined in this light, straw work represents a nearly ideal process, while devoting farmland to cotton instead of less-productive textile plants represents environmentally sound judgment. Until the dyeing step, the textile processes are

HOMEMADE BAMBOO BASKETS

Large basket for heavy items – can be mounted on a back-frame.

Box and lid

Large openwork basket

Carrying basket

Strainer

Funnel – tight weave!

Winnow – open weave!

COTTON ("wata") used in cotton fabric ("momen")

Almost every rural family weaves its own cotton cloth for home use.

TEXTILE CROPS

cotton boll

Cotton production began in earnest only in the 17th century. It is now a major cash crop, and cotton textile production a major industry.

nonpolluting in general, their products reusable and recyclable. The finishing steps are essentially indoor activities, and as such they allow the architectural space to be efficiently used for other purposes as well.

Brewing and fermentation at the cottage-industry scale do not consume large quantities of either fuel or freshwater, and their intermediate products are consumable or compostable. The equipment required is primarily wooden barrels and earthenware jars, both of which can be used for years if not decades; these activities do not significantly increase the household's environmental footprint. Making charcoal for sale is a special case because it involves the direct consumption of limited forest resources, transforming wood from a highly efficient heat source into a less efficient but more easily transported one. It is essentially a gathering activity, and it provides the fuel supply for city dwellers, a large fraction of the population.

Of the industries described above, only silk production embodies extravagance in several areas: acres devoted to mulberry trees, large architectural structures for raising the worms and, consequently, large consumption of building timber for the purpose, a several-fold increase in fuel consumption for heat, and a large outlay of human labor.

HEMP ("asa")

The stalk contains long, tough fibers that are woven into fabric.

SILK ("kinu")

requires mulberry leaves ("kuwa")

Silkworm (Bombyx mori) is actually a caterpillar

Mulberry is essential to silk production because the leaves are the preferred food of the silkworm. The silk fibers used in textiles are unwound from their cocoons.

(Fibers from the stalk of the mulberry are used in making "washi" paper.)

Two additional cottage industries should be considered from the standpoint of fuel and resource use, namely smithing and pottery. At the home-industry scale, these activities require several times the amount of fuel a typical household uses, and so their presence decreases the share available to all. Smiths require an intense charcoal fire to be kept burning at all times, while potters consume vast amounts of firewood every few weeks when the clay is fired. Both industries depend upon nonrenewable primary materials, namely iron and potters' clay. It may be surprising to think of clay as nonrenewable, but extracting clay is in fact a mining operation, albeit with shovels and relatively shallow pits. Sources of suitable quality are relatively rare and rights of access and use are contentious issues.

Good-quality pig iron must usually be transported great distances and has a high initial cost, but full use is made of its easy recyclability. Though many repairs to iron implements can be improvised at home, villagers require access to a smith, even if he devotes part of his day to farming as well. Having a local potter is less essential except in cases where the local economy and other cottage industries depend upon having a ready supply, and it is not surprising that potters tend to form specialized villages close to good sources of clay.

Many villages are too small to support full-time potters or smiths, so the need is met by farmers who do it part-time

POTTERY ("tougei" or "yakimono")
Adequate clay is readily available, but particularly high-quality sources may be fought over. Kiln design is continuously refined to maximize the efficiency of fuel combustion.

Big wood piles!!

A small kiln. Large ones can be 10 times this size!!

Forge

Water for quenching

Large fuel supply

Master

Assistant

SMITHY ("kaji")
Requires a constant source of high-heat (charcoal is used). In the case of most village smiths, fuel consumption is mitigated by the part-time nature of the work.

TREE CENSUS

## into the forest

Shinichi and the other residents of Aoyagi Village spend most of their time in and around their homesteads and fields, some of which occupy the lower hillsides. They frequently spend days a bit deeper in the mountains gathering food and fuel. But the villagers also participate periodically in logging activities that take them even deeper into the forest. While some of their farming activities provide for local needs, most of their rice finds its way to Edo and the other large cities. Similarly, the lumber they help produce is intended almost entirely for the urban market, linking the well-being of the city to the environmental health of the countryside even more closely.

In forestry, as in farming, an ethic of conservation and husbandry prevails. The forests around Shinichi's village are farmed for lumber products in a way that satisfies both the subsistence needs of the farmers themselves and the cities' voracious appetite for timber products.

Man has altered the balance of natural species in the archipelago, and the forest shows human influence clearly. Even at this point, very little is left in a virgin state, and the climax stands of sugi and hinoki trees that are so highly valued were mostly cut in the time of Shinichi's distant ancestors. The culture and the economy prefer these straight, aromatic, close-grained, and easy-to-work

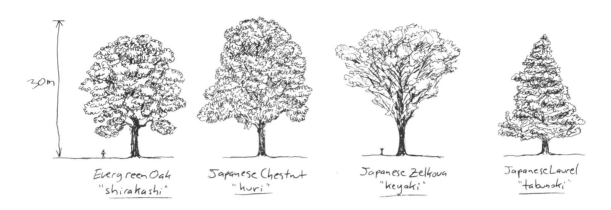

30m — Evergreen Oak "shirakashi" • Japanese Chestnut "kuri" • Japanese Zelkova "keyaki" • Japanese Laurel "tabunoki"

conifers for building material, and so much of the effort of forestry has involved finding and nurturing the best ones, cutting and extracting them, and planting more in their stead. Other species are not ignored, however, and they have their uses and so are valuable and marketable. But sugi is the new king of the forest.

Natural forest growth is a cycle of succession, where grassland sponsors scrub, which gives way to broadleaf species, and, possibly, conifers. Prior to man's arrival and for long thereafter, the native forests of central Japan were a mixture of deciduous broadleaf and conifer, and where broadleafs with their broad crowns dominated—chestnuts, oaks, laurel, beech—the understory, which received ample sunlight, was rich in grasses, shrubs, and other plants, while also providing niches for abundant fauna.

The broadleaf forest is by nature varied. Sugi and hinoki are taller and narrower than broadleaf trees, however, and grow more closely together, so the dark floor of a climax conifer forest is usually awash in fallen needles and ferns and little else. At higher elevations and in colder regions very little else will thrive, but when man first arrived in central Japan he found mostly broadleaf forests, liberally interspersed with stands of conifers.

Japan first experienced localized deforestation and its ill effects long ago, when the rulers of the eighth, ninth, and tenth centuries virtually stripped the surrounding valleys to build their capitals at Nara (Heijo-kyo) and Kyoto (Heian-kyo). Their buildings were vast and luxurious and squandered immense quantities of first-growth timber, while gigantic bronze sculptures like the Great Buddha at Todaiji consumed entire hardwood forests for smelting. In aggregate, at this time and ever since, the commoners in towns and peasants in rural

Before being modified by humans, the natural forests of Japan were dominated by broadleaf species such as these, and their associated plant communities. All are extremely useful to humans, either for food and material, or as habitat for animals who play an important role in maintaining the health of the ecosystem.

## KINGS of the FOREST — CONIFERS

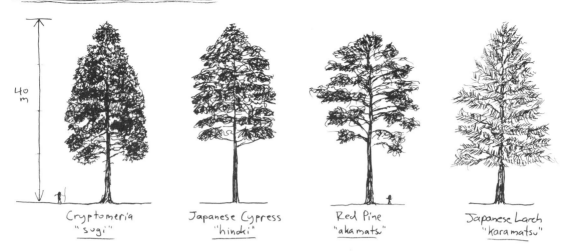

40 m

Cryptomeria "sugi"    Japanese Cypress "hinoki"    Red Pine "akamats"    Japanese Larch "karamatsu"

areas consumed more of the forest for their subsistence needs than did the ruling classes, but government-directed "command" forest clear-cutting regularly pushed the woodland environment beyond its ability to rebound healthily.

In many cases, the clear-cutting of coniferous woodland allowed healthier, more useful replacement growth to appear, as the natural replacement cycle leads to fast-growing broadleafs. These provide good fuel, their stumps and roots hinder erosion, and new shoots quickly emerge from the stumps, that can in time themselves be harvested. The undergrowth of this kind of replacement forest is ecologically rich and varied.

Unfortunately, because of overexploitation, and particularly the cutting of forests to make new farmland, in previous centuries this positive balance was rarely allowed to emerge. The needs of the peasants like Shinichi's grandfather—who didn't require many high-quality conifers but did need hardwood for fuel and forest litter for fertilizer as well as a variety of wild foods—began to collide head on with those of the rulers, who needed prime lumber. The government increasingly felt the need to close forests to peasant use, and it implemented prohibitions and penalties limiting harvesting, transportation, and consumption in clumsy attempts to conserve the resources.

A single hillside is expected to provide a large population with timber, firewood, fertilizer, and arable land, and though one can envision satisfying any two of these biomass needs reasonably, or three with difficulty, to meet all four would seem impossible. Now, however, the forests are producing more than ever before, and everyone, peasant and ruler alike, is getting pretty much what they need. Arrangements that allow long-term mixed use, with clearly defined

Natively, conifers dominated only the higer elevations of Japanese mantains, but through human cultivation have come to cover most mountainsides. Though each possesses several desirable characteristics and has many uses, they are primarily valued as building material.

rights and juridical recourse, have been implemented. Replacement silviculture techniques have been developed and widely disseminated. Conflicts between loggers and farmers over river use have been minimized. And consumption is limited by regulation, taste, the deeply held ethic of conservation, and a variety of technical factors. The new regime of forest management involves the villagers as essential shareholders, utilizes their knowledge and expertise, and provides them with clear economic benefit.

Much of the management and reforesting is made possibly by extensive and detailed tree censuses begun in the mid-seventeenth century, including actual stem counts and descriptions of stands of trees and bamboo. These have evolved into periodically updated forest registers, a key database that government officials, forest wardens, and entrepreneurs can use to plan and coordinate their activity. Similarly, these registers are essential resources for the policy-makers and scholars who write and publish the forestry guidebooks through which the new regenerative forestry methods are disseminated.

The government still reserves extensive forestland for itself, in the form of *ohayashi*, or "lord's forests." These include the best stands of construction-grade timber, the conifer woodlands on the upper slopes. There are mountainsides near Aoyagi that the peasants are forbidden to enter for any purpose without permission, though it is usually granted for cutting and collecting undergrowth, cutting lumber for dams and other irrigation works, and other clearly essential needs. Often villagers are required to pay fees for access, however, and to report dead or fallen trees and violations by others.

The government has become more understanding of villagers' needs than in Shinichi's grandfather's time, but it still feels it must tightly regulate access. Most years, Shinichi and his neighbors are allowed to scavenge nearby logging sites for usable material after logging has been completed, after which the forest will be closed for years to allow regrowth. Villagers are sometimes granted access to forests in return for replanting. Enterprising villagers have been known to obtain permission to replant clear-cut conifer forests in larch, whose needles fall in autumn and can be used as extra fertilizer for the fields, while providing openings for sunlight to reach the forest floor and encourage undergrowth.

Control of most lower forests, largely broadleaf woodland as well as bamboo forest and grassland, has also been granted to the villages. The greater portion is generally communal land, with access governed by the carefully worked-out rules of *iriai*. Shinichi and many of his neighbors hold forest land with primary rights of disposition, so they can use it as they see fit. But in reality the boundaries are often unclear. Other village households share use of nearby

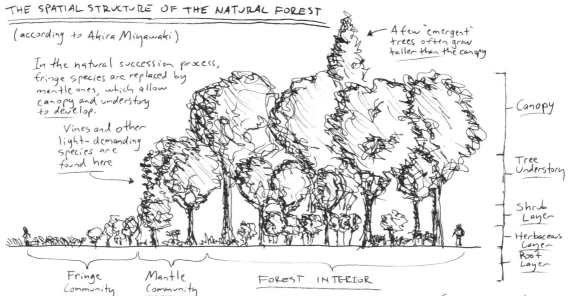

THE SPATIAL STRUCTURE OF THE NATURAL FOREST

(according to Akira Miyawaki)

In the natural succession process, fringe species are replaced by mantle ones, which allow canopy and understory to develop.

Vines and other light-demanding species are found here

A few "emergent" trees often grow taller than the canopy

Canopy

Tree Understory

Shrub Layer

Herbaceous Layer
Root Layer

Fringe Community       Mantle Community       FOREST INTERIOR

- Canopy - Natively, stands of naturally co-existing broadleafs whose crowns touch.
- The Understory below forms a darker and more humid micro-climate
- Tree Understory - Shade-tolerant species,
- Shrub layer - Woody shrubs and saplings
- Herbaceous layer - Short, leafy plants
- Root Layer - Tree roots as well as rhizomes and fungi
- Mantle - A buffer zone that protects the forest interior modulating light and wind.
- Fringe - Quickly propagating grasses and weeds that thrive in strong sunlight.

mountains in an arrangement called *wariyama*, extremely common but at times contentious. These agreements sometimes divide forest access equally among all parties, and sometimes on the basis of the arable land area each household tills, while others stipulate different types of access for different purposes at different times. It is very confusing, and despite the existence of written records, disagreements arise that require arbitration by the other village elders.

Nevertheless, much of the woodland around the village is managed by the villagers themselves, and it meets their needs. Shinichi has standing permission to fell trees for home use or special needs and to gather undergrowth from village land. All of the villagers require more firewood than building timber, and they have standing needs for fertilizer material and forest foodstuffs, so not much tree cutting is initiated by them.

Regardless of the basic forest rights that villagers enjoy, the government designates particularly desirable trees as *tomeki*, or reserved trees, which can't be cut by villagers no matter where they stand. In fact, an outstanding tall, straight hinoki about two hundred years old has shaded Shinichi's work yard since long before his grandfather's time. This is a tomeki, and though it has stood in place for generations, Shinichi knows that at any time it could be cut and carted away, with no compensation to him or his family. Seen overall, the rights to forest products are basically zoned and divided geographically, but often in shades of gray, with much overlap. Satisfying the many conflicting needs requires adequate oversight.

## guardians of the forest

On forestry matters, Shinichi and the other villagers answer to Daisuke Ohbayashi, a forest overseer—*ohayashi mamori*—and one of the village elders of Aoyagi. This office was established a century ago, when the government was still attempting to insure adequate timber supplies for itself by prohibiting access to others. Peasant officials like Ohbayashi's grandfather acquired status and badges of office—the right to wear swords and to use a family name in public—and minor stipends paid in rice, so for all intents and purposes they became low-ranking samurai for their trouble. And trouble it was. They discovered that policing the lord's forest was nearly impossible, for villagers always found surreptitious means to gain access to what they understandably felt was their hereditary gathering ground.

The job included maintaining boundary markers and signs, preventing theft and unauthorized charcoal burning, and monitoring sanctioned logging activities. But when the official focus shifted from prohibitive conservation to large-scale replanting, the nature of the forest patrols changed as well, and Ohbayashi's job is now quite a bit easier than either his grandfather's or his father's. His forest patrols still keep an eye out for fire, storm damage, and

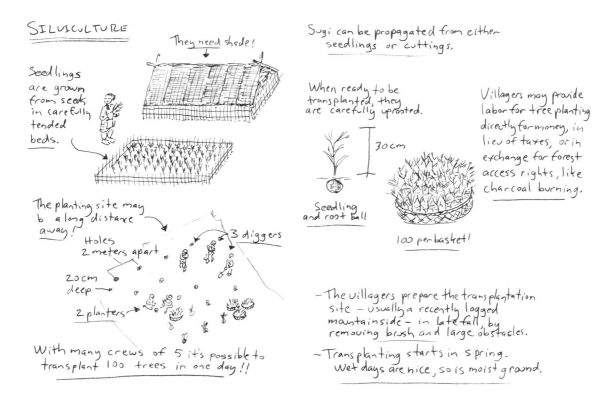

SILVICULTURE

They need shade!

Seedlings are grown from seeds in carefully tended beds.

Sugi can be propagated from either seedlings or cuttings.

When ready to be transplanted, they are carefully uprooted.

30cm

Seedling and root ball

Villagers may provide labor for tree planting directly for money, in lieu of taxes, or in exchange for forest access rights, like charcoal burning.

100 per basket!

The planting site may be a long distance away!

Holes 2 meters apart
20cm deep →
2 planters →
3 diggers

With many crews of 5 it's possible to transplant 100 trees in one day!!

— The villagers prepare the transplantation site — usually a recently logged mountainside — in late fall, by removing brush and large obstacles.

— Transplanting starts in spring. Wet days are nice, so is moist ground.

theft, but these activities are more likely to be performed communally by the villagers instead of by officials, who now take a more supervisory role. More importantly, through the forest patrols and by acting as paid woodsmen during their off season, the villagers like Shinichi and his neighbors take an active part in nurturing seedlings and maintaining the overall health of the forest.

Regenerative forestry as practiced so successfully relies on the application of agricultural knowledge, much of it derived from ancient practices refined over centuries and handed down by woodsmen, farmers, and gardeners, collated and supplemented with new knowledge and recent experience, and disseminated through printed texts. It builds on existing awareness of the role of healthy forests in maintaining viable watersheds, and on experience in using silviculture to control rivers, limit erosion, and protect arable land. Though the main purpose is to produce large quantities of construction material, the degree to which timber forests, broadleaf forests, grassland, waterways, and arable land form an integral whole whose parts must be kept in balance is reflected in the techniques adopted for germinating, nurturing, harvesting, and transporting the timber. It is an ongoing process of incremental adjustment, monitoring, accommodation, and readjustment, with ample provision for feedback from many

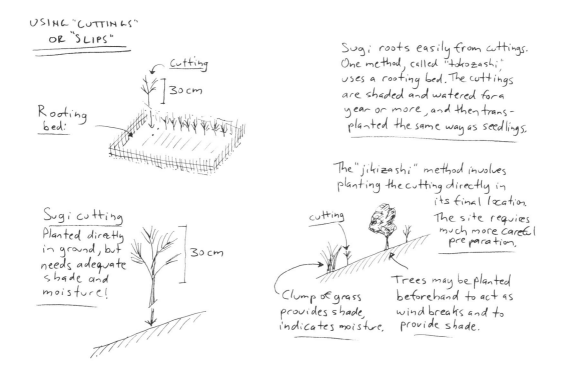

USING "CUTTINGS" OR "SLIPS"

Cutting

30 cm

Rooting bed:

Sugi roots easily from cuttings. One method, called "tokozashi", uses a rooting bed. The cuttings are shaded and watered for a year or more, and then transplanted the same way as seedlings.

The "jikizashi" method involves planting the cutting directly in its final location. The site requires much more careful preparation.

Sugi cutting
Planted directly in ground, but needs adequate shade and moisture!

30 cm

cutting

Clump of grass provides shade, indicates moisture.

Trees may be planted beforehand to act as windbreaks and to provide shade.

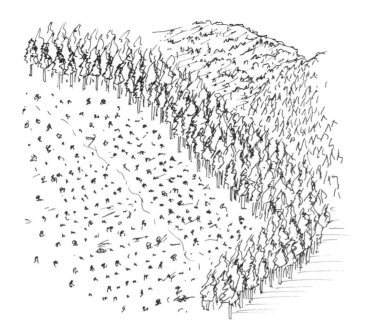

**A CLEARCUT FOREST**

Thousands of trees may be cut from a mountainside at once. If natural processes are allowed to function, it will eventually grow back as a "replacement" forest with a variety of species (though this may take the better part of a century!).
In most cases, however, the site is quickly replanted as a conifer plantation.

sources. And this process, difficult and imperfect though it is, plays a tremendous role supporting a high-quality life for city dwellers and peasants alike.

Late-eighteenth-century Japanese silviculture involves the heavy cultivation of a few species, the moderate cultivation of several others, and the exploitation of uncultivated stands of almost anything useful. By far the most intensively cultivated species is sugi, followed by hinoki, both of them highly desirable for both structural and finish building material, and so extremely valuable. Sugi is grown on large, single-species plantations established by entrepreneurs who provide material for government projects on contract and sell to others on the open market. In recent decades they have overtaken government forestry concerns (usually finance ministries) as major providers of lumber. Headquartered

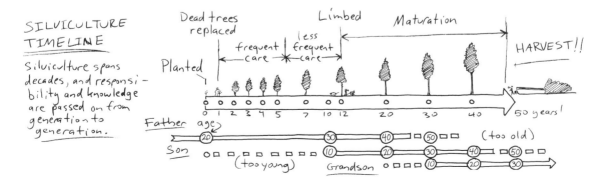

**SILVICULTURE TIMELINE**

Silviculture spans decades, and responsibility and knowledge are passed on from generation to generation.

in the major cities that constitute their primary markets, they operate through labyrinthine networks of brokers, woodlot owners, transporters, and laborers, extending from the cities into the deepest woodland valleys, with government oversight nearly every step of the way. Only about 5 percent of Japanese woodland is plantation, but this is very productive; in addition many practices have been established to maximize the yield from naturally seeded stands.

Silviculture, whether by seedling or cutting, has a high failure rate, which can be partly mitigated by adequate aftercare, including providing replacements for trees that fail to survive the first couple of years. This activity brings Shinichi and his son into the deep mountains several times a year. A year after planting, they help replace dead trees, and the stand must be patrolled and tended for five more years, including weeding and straightening trees bent by heavy snow.

After twelve years or so Shinichi's son will help limb the trees to encourage crown growth and minimize the size of knots on the most usable part of the trunk. More densely planted stands might require periodic thinning, both to enable the healthiest growth and to simplify felling. All in all, the care of a single stand of plantation trees will span about fifty years, during which time knowledge of the trees themselves and familiarity with the particulars of the locale are passed from generation to generation in the village, from Shinichi to his son and his future grandson. The government or the entrepreneurs who own the trees must wait that long to reap a profit as well. It is a very farsighted form of agriculture.

Logging Camp: Woodsmen live in rough, temporary bunkhouses erected deep in the mountains.

## the communal life of elite woodsmen

Occasionally, Shinichi crosses paths with lumberjacks deep in the mountains. Naoki is one of them, though Shinichi doesn't know him by name; their social spheres are quite separate and other than passing the time of day they wouldn't have much to say to each other. In reality, lumberjacks are some of the most isolated people in Japan, but their speech is full of bluster and they carry themselves with a swagger. They are a close-knit group, and they consider themselves to be an elite.

Naoki lives in a small village far up the hillside of a deep valley, several kilometers from Aoyagi. All of his relatives and neighbors make their livelihoods from lumber, and they are expert axmen. They tend small farm plots, because the hillside is too steep for anything bigger. Logging-related activities

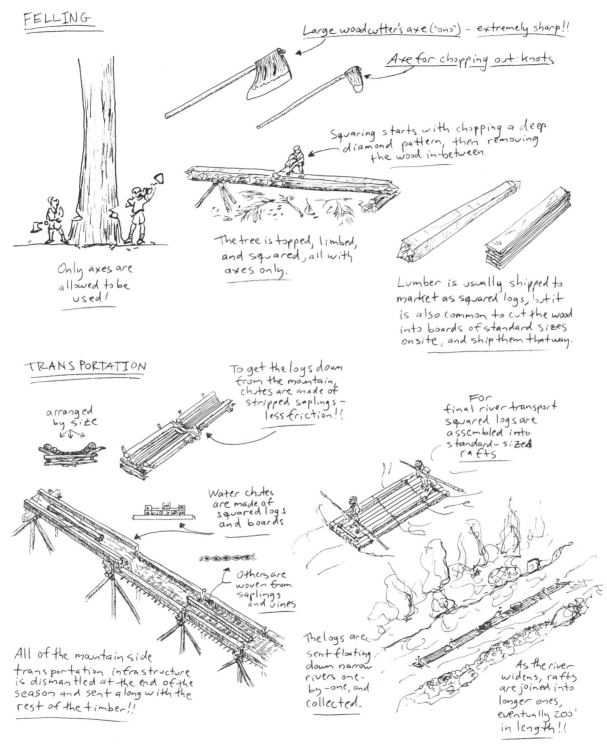

FELLING

Large woodcutter's axe ("ono") - extremely sharp!!

Axe for chopping out knots

Only axes are allowed to be used!

Squaring starts with chopping a deep diamond pattern, then removing the wood in-between.

The tree is topped, limbed, and squared, all with axes only.

Lumber is usually shipped to market as squared logs, but it is also common to cut the wood into boards of standard sizes onsite, and ship them that way.

TRANSPORTATION

arranged by size

To get the logs down from the mountain, chutes are made of stripped saplings - less friction!!

For final river transport squared logs are assembled into standard-sized rafts

Water chutes are made of squared logs and boards

Others are woven from saplings and vines

All of the mountainside transportation infrastructure is dismantled at the end of the season and sent along with the rest of the timber!!

The logs are sent floating down narrow rivers one-by-one, and collected.

As the river widens, rafts are joined into longer ones, eventually 200' in length!!

keep them busy for most of the year, but their busiest time is during the winter, when most of the actual harvesting is done. The men move to logging camps then, living together for months in rough, temporary bunkhouses, taking their meals communally in front of immense, blazing hearths.

The tree harvest involves complicated logistics, far-flung coordination, consideration, and supervision, and both skilled and unskilled labor. The deep forest is made accessible by sluices, chutes, trestles, dams, booms, bunkhouses, and transport vessels built en masse and on a large scale, but with few exceptions they are designed to be temporary and so are rapidly dismantled when a particular patch is logged. In most cases the structures are built of the logs themselves, which are then shipped downriver as lumber, so the industrial infrastructure largely vanishes without a trace. The river-opening work is a set of permanent but localized modifications to the rocky riverbed that alter the character of its flow, and it is difficult to quantify the long-term effects. But nothing is done that alters the natural functioning of the watershed.

From the forest to the end user, the lumber industry is highly organized and specialized, and it is characterized by interlocking webs of long-term obligations, contracts, and rivalries. In Edo, the end of the line for Naoki's felled lumber, there are over five hundred lumber brokers and several wholesalers' guilds that handle specific goods from specific regions. In every large city, individual lumberyards tend to specialize in a particular product, and the wood is likely to be processed into its final form before being sent down the mountain.

## big government vs. the local community

In the early 1600s, Shogun Tokugawa Ieyasu decreed that villages should have four hundred households, but in reality they range in size from fifty or fewer to over one thousand—and most lie in the hundred- to four-hundred household range. This size is ideal for an autonomous community, as it is large enough to allow pooling of labor and resources for large projects, yet small enough to enable good communication and coordination among the constituent parts. It is large enough to maintain and repair its local environment, but too small to do widespread environmental damage.

Community relations influence every aspect of village activity, promoting good farming practices, encouraging the sharing of information and responsibility, while discouraging wasteful use of resources. Planning is largely collective, and effective systems of mutual support and assistance serve to strengthen social bonds and keep households afloat in times of distress. Politically and economically, each village is fairly autonomous. While under the jurisdiction of the provincial government (to whom taxes must be paid), most decisions affecting daily life are in the hands of the villagers themselves, who form a self-governing unit called a *kumi*. In this sense, government rule is largely "hands off," its presence being felt mainly at tax time and when conflicts must be resolved.

The tax levies are paid in rice, collected from each household by the village officials and tallied in the presence of a government representative (usually a mid-level functionary, one of several who make the rounds through the province at tax time). The assessments themselves are carried out infrequently and are often the source of contention, particularly in years of bad harvest. Villagers like Shinichi can expect to surrender one-fourth to one-half of their yearly harvest to the government, to keep one-fourth for their own use, and to be able to sell the rest. In times of bad harvest, the tax levies may be reduced a nominal amount, but the difference must be usually made up from the farmers' household allotments. While this itself is rarely the cause of starvation, and the government will distribute its own grain to the people in times of real famine, the financial burden is heavy.

The collected rice is sold by government agents on the open market, with the profits going to support government functions. The peasants, therefore, are both feeding the nation and supporting it financially, and the samurai classes, from the highest lords to the lowliest foot soldiers, benefit the most directly. All receive government stipends for their livelihood, which, in effect, comes from the sale of rice surrendered by the peasants. Craftspeople and merchants suffer no similar tax burden, and this system is already showing signs of strain.

The government has the right to demand corvee labor from the villagers as well. Each community is usually responsible for providing workers on a recurring basis for tasks such as public works (roads and canals, for instance) and forestry. In most cases these workers are away from home for a few weeks or months, and so responsibility is rotated among the households. For special projects, such as defensive works and other large construction projects, the government requests additional labor. There are cases where a local lord will accept labor in lieu of rice as tax payment, the most famous being the carpenters of Hida, whose skills are valued very highly for castle construction.

The government's presence is also felt in its gathering and dissemination of information. Surveys and censuses are carried out periodically, and the government requires village headmen to make fairly detailed reports of economic and environmental conditions: the condition of forests and rivers, factors affecting agricultural productivity, unusual weather. The government also issues proclamations of which all villagers must be made aware, such as the closure of forests to logging, restricted consumption of particular resources, or increased

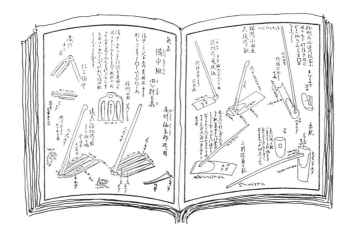

Farm Manuals ("no-sho") are extremely detailed and readily available. They provide information on every agricultural topic, from plant varieties, to tool design and fabrication, to climate and health.

production of others. When the system works well, which is most of the time, the government makes good use of the feedback it receives from the villages to gain insight into overall trends and deficiencies and to help formulate a coordinated response. All in all, the relationship between government and the villages has transformed agriculture into a very information-intensive activity.

This can be seen quite clearly in the use of government-supported farming manuals. There are quite a few of these highly illustrated printed manuals in widespread circulation, and they are the result of on-the-ground observation, academic research, and the accumulation and collation of peasant wisdom. The best contain botanical descriptions of species, analyses of soil conditions, advice on fertilizer and irrigation, almanacs, illustrated instructions on how to make tools, and general advice on health and farm economy. Some discuss forestry and hydraulic works. Not all are government sponsored, but many are (and quite a few are derivative or plagiarized). The fact is that, because the government has an interest in improving farm productivity, it tries to put the most reliable information in the hands of those who can use it.

This is made easier by the high literacy rate among peasants, which has quite a bit of regional variation but hovers around 60 percent. Village officials are usually highly literate, including in mathematics and the use of the abacus. In general they are on par with the samurai class, with whom they must exchange frequent written communications. In practice, this means that meetings are held at which the headman reads a manual, for example, to the other villagers. It can be passed around or lent, and the illustrations are usually clear enough that even the unlettered can absorb both gist and details. Some credit the circulation of similar manuals, such as the famous *Nogyo Zensho* of 1697, with enabling the rapid spread of cotton cultivation decades earlier, teaching double cropping and improving nutrition by introducing a wide variety of foreign vegetables, like potatoes, corn, carrots, green beans, pumpkins, and red peppers.

The social structure of the village is both hierarchical and egalitarian, with built-in asymmetries of power and influence, but also marriage- and merit-based mobility. The core members of the village are the *honbyakusho* like Shinichi, who own enough paddy land—about 1 *cho*, or 1 hectare—to be economically self-sufficient. They possess a homestead with a house and outbuildings, and they own the tools they use. They are usually nuclear families, a couple with children and possibly a surviving parent. They have the right to give their voice at village assemblies and the responsibility to serve on one or more village associations, such as those for water use or festival planning. Families like Shinichi's are likely to have occupied the same homestead for several generations; they expect to continue doing so indefinitely and assume their neighbors will do so as well. This has far-ranging effects on relationships among households.

There are a smaller number of households of the *mizunomi* ("water drinkers"), who own either little or no land, and so work as tenant farmers or for

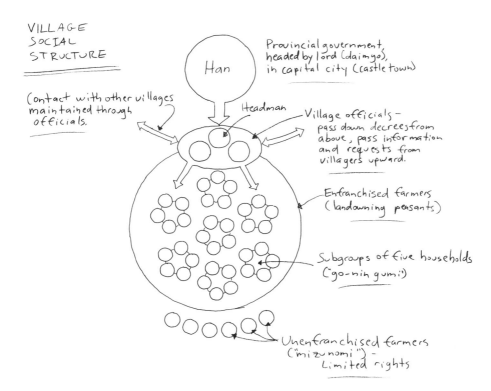

VILLAGE
SOCIAL
STRUCTURE

Han

Provincial government, headed by lord (daimyo), in capital city (castle town)

Contact with other villages maintained through officials.

Headman

Village officials — pass down decrees from above, pass information and requests from villagers upward.

Enfranchised farmers (landowning peasants)

Subgroups of five households ("go-nin gumi")

Unenfranchised farmers ("mizunomi") — limited rights

wages. There are also indentured peasants. Neither group has full rights in the village, but mizunomi in particular can improve their status through financial success or good marriage.

The shogunate has instituted a policy of mutual aid and responsibility called the *go-nin gumi* (five-person group), which acts as a political and social unit between the household and the village. Many cooperative activities, including planting, harvesting, clearing irrigation ditches, and major home maintenance, are organized at the go-nin-gumi level. Each group also selects a representative for the various other associations, and it is expected to be self-policing; in fact, members are expected to snitch on each other, since the entire group will be punished for the transgressions of a single member.

In practice, the mutual assistance the kumi provides, institutionalizing a dual labor system that benefits from having both a household and a communal workforce to rely upon, has an extremely significant positive effect, and most exist for generations without their police function ever being exercised. Shinichi's father and grandfather were particularly respected community members, and Shinichi himself benefits from generations of good relations with the neighboring families. Their discussions are candid and sincere, and as none of the families is particularly striving or avaricious, there is very little competition among them, but a lot of good-natured cooperation. Shinichi hopes his son will be able to continue these positive relations, and he often sends him to help his neighbors even before he is asked.

Shinichi belongs to a cooperatively run association known as a *ko*, which provides financial assistance and loans by pooling contributions from members and making sums available to those in need. Before he was married, he was a member of the *wakamono-gumi*, or "young men's association," that mobilizes unmarried adult males for service as night watchmen, firefighters, festival organizers, and other activities. Independent and egalitarian, the wakamono-gumi has its own buildings, tools, and other belongings. The wakamono live communally for set periods. Through participation, the young men acquire intimate understanding of village politics, farming techniques, and other valuable knowledge. They also act as a direct conduit to younger generations.

Village association meetings are held several set times a year and also in cases of emergency. Decisions reached by the honbyakusho at these meetings, whether written down or simply absorbed into village custom, become the regulations of the village. In this sense, the horizontal, egalitarian aspect of village rule is allowed strong expression.

At the same time, the village meetings are where government decrees are handed down to the villagers, so they also represent the endpoint of the vertical, authoritarian power axis, backed with the implicit threat of force. As in many authoritarian societies, subjects are allowed to exercise a large degree of autonomy and even have legal recourse when this is interfered with, but they have no real fundamental rights other than those granted by the rulers. Village meetings provide the venue for peasant subjects to read the ruling winds and plot their collective course.

## celebrating the community

The new year is an auspicious and celebratory time, ideal for large social gatherings. It is also the time of the most important annual meeting, because plans for the entire year are up for discussion. The meetings are likely to be held at a shrine or temple, not necessarily for their spiritual significance but because there is rarely any other building large enough to hold the entire community.

These buildings are scattered among the communities where they play an important role, since religious events like festivals and feast days are community events. But the religious institutions are linked to their brethren around the country through many networks of disparate sects, and because they are rarely able to act cohesively, they do not really exert significant political or economic force on the village level. On the other hand, the temple operates a school that is open to all regardless of status, and it is this widespread system that is credited with creating the high literacy rate.

The role of the "Three Village Officials"—the *murakata sanyaku*—is very important. These positions are hereditary, connected with the households rather than the individuals. The offices are headman, group leader, and peasant deputy, and they are both administrative positions carefully integrated into the ruling scheme and social positions that enable self-government to work. They are first among equals, and they are expected to work on behalf of the honbyakusho. The headman can be likened to a mayor; the group leader to a village foreman; and the peasant deputy to a constable. In reality their rights and roles overlap, and most leadership and coordination functions require them to work in concert.

The village officials cannot give orders or issue decrees themselves but merely pass on communications from above, and for this the headman's role is both ceremonial and actual. He is also the conduit through which the concerns and requests of the village as a whole are passed to the government. He helps arrange and approves marriages, land transfers, and the distribution of communal funds and supplies. He produces a tremendous amount of paperwork, keeping village records, passing information up the chain to the provincial government, copying decrees to keep on file in the village, producing budgets and invoices.

Village officials are usually the wealthiest farmers in the village. Their households have risen to positions of status because of success, prosperity, and the ability to help others, qualities that are taken to indicate superlative knowledge, virtue, and good management skills. Many are descended from samurai who chose to remain on their land when Ieyasu established the new social order; those who moved to the castle towns kept their samurai status and accrued new privileges, while the few who remained in the villages lost their status but benefited by becoming politically connected landholders.

Regardless of descent, officials keep a foot in both worlds: as farmers living off the land, with concerns identical to those of their neighbors; and as people who enjoy many of the privileges of the samurai. Sumptuary regulations are often relaxed for them, meaning they might be allowed to own silk clothing or fine lacquered furnishings, or even a tearoom; they might even be allowed to wear swords when acting in their official capacities—all of which would normally be prohibited to peasants.

The headman of Aoyagi Village is named Itagaki, a surname his family was granted two generations ago as a special honor for good service to the provincial lord. His house is the largest in the village, and his homestead is immediately identifiable by its large gatelike storage building where tax rice is collected and tallied. There is also a fine whitewashed, fireproof storehouse where village records are archived and valuable possessions are stored. Many features of Itagaki-san's home are ordained by the need to entertain samurai and other government officials during their official visits to the town.

In a society where decorum is one of the highest values, it is unseemly to force officials to enter the home through the doma, for instance, so a separate covered entrance with a formal low wooden step leading directly into the formal zashiki is provided. Proper reception of a samurai requires an appropriate room with a *tokonoma* and perhaps a desk, so extra reception rooms are necessary. Refreshments must be served on good trays and dishes; not ostentatious or elaborate, but of sober design and good quality. Sake is expected as well.

For all of these reasons Itagaki-san and the other officials are allowed—if not to say tacitly required—to have homes that embody a higher standard of living than those of their neighbors. Over time, many other prosperous families have been able to imitate some of these features in their own homes, and the law is likely to turn a blind eye to these expressions of lèse-majesté as long as social order is not threatened.

The Three Officials' social role among the villagers comes into play most visibly when conflicts arise, government intervention or assistance is desired, or planning is required for new fields or irrigation works. They, along with the monks and priests, are likely to be the most educated people in the village. They are the best informed of government workings and communication channels, are aware of longstanding grievances, alliances, and issues among the villagers, and are in frequent contact with the officials of neighboring villages and aware of their concerns. Their role is not to force decisions on the villagers, however, but to enable self-government to work by helping crystallize consensus. Itagaki-san is a skilled arbitrator, a force for compromise, and he and his colleagues must remain impartial if they are to continue to be respected. Corrupt officials are likely to find a revolt on their hands, with dire consequences for all if the government decides to step in. (In fact, revolt has become institutionalized as a nearly democratic check on poor government.)

As we've seen, much of the work in the village is cooperative and communal. On the one hand, decisions concerning forest access and gathering are made communally, but actual gathering is likely to be done by individual households like Shinichi's. Major works, including maintenance of the irrigation system, are both planned and performed communally. Other tasks that concern the village as a whole, like festival planning and preparation, are communal. All of these involve joint monitoring of the environment and sharing of information, as well as building a store of shared skills and understanding, that can be passed down to succeeding generations. Some of this will be specific to the village, but most will be widely applicable throughout the region. Among the best examples of *yui*, literally "knitting together," the frequently practiced communal labor in the form of mutual assistance, are rice planting and roof thatching.

We take our leave of Shinichi and his family, having gained a firsthand understanding of the sophistication of farming as he practices it, and of the society of which he is a part. We are particularly impressed with the body of knowledge in the form of the natural lore that underlies his farming practice, as well as the constant innovation in farming technique and infrastructure design, and the role that printed information and literacy play in the steady improvement of the quality of life. The efficiency of energy and resource use is unparalleled, and yet we rarely get the sense that the villagers are suffering from want.

They have transformed economy and efficiency into an aesthetic that touches every aspect of life, and zero-waste has become a habit that drives the design of everything they use. Both technically and in terms of the supporting capacity of their environment, they have achieved a sustainable form of agriculture. Finally, their self-sufficiency is extremely impressive, as is their close-knit and supportive social structure. We leave with the sense that if Shinichi and his peers were released from the unfortunate burden of heavy taxation, life would be extremely prosperous, generous, and good. As it is, they live well and reap ample benefit from their labors.

"CHINJU no MORI"

Though the native lowland forests were cleared for cultivation long ago, irrevocably altering the ecosystem, remnants continue to thrive among the rice paddies in the form of the wooded grounds which have been preserved around shrines and temples.

# RICE CULTIVATION

① <u>PREPARING the FIELDS</u>

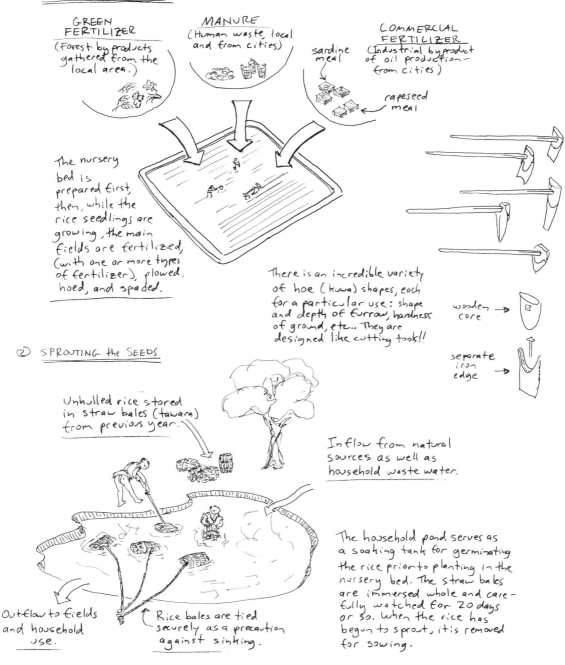

GREEN
FERTILIZER
(Forest by products
gathered from the
local area.)

MANURE
(Human waste, local
and from cities)

COMMERCIAL
FERTILIZER
(Industrial byproduct
of oil production—
from cities)

sardine
meal

rapeseed
meal

The nursery
bed is
prepared first,
then, while the
rice seedlings are
growing, the main
fields are fertilized,
(with one or more types
of fertilizer), plowed,
hoed, and spaded.

There is an incredible variety
of hoe (kuwa) shapes, each
for a particular use: shape
and depth of furrow, hardness
of ground, etc... They are
designed like cutting tools!!

wooden → core

separate
iron →
edge

② <u>SPROUTING the SEEDS</u>

Unhulled rice stored
in straw bales (tawara)
from previous year.

Inflow from natural
sources as well as
household waste water.

The household pond serves as
a soaking tank for germinating
the rice prior to planting in the
nursery bed. The straw bales
are immersed whole and carefully watched for 20 days
or so. When the rice has
begun to sprout, it is removed
for sowing.

Outflow to fields
and household
use.

Rice bales are tied
securely as a precaution
against sinking.

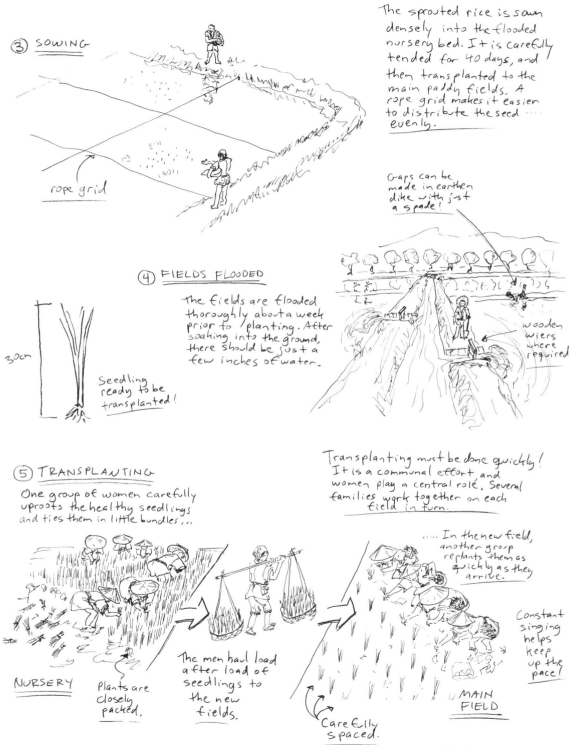

③ SOWING

rope grid

The sprouted rice is sown densely into the flooded nursery bed. It is carefully tended for 40 days, and then transplanted to the main paddy fields. A rope grid makes it easier to distribute the seed evenly.

Gaps can be made in earthen dike with just a spade!

④ FIELDS FLOODED

The fields are flooded thoroughly about a week prior to planting. After soaking into the ground, there should be just a few inches of water.

30cm

Seedling ready to be transplanted!

wooden wiers where required

⑤ TRANSPLANTING

One group of women carefully uproots the healthy seedlings and ties them in little bundles...

Transplanting must be done quickly! It is a communal effort and women play a central role. Several families work together on each field in turn.

..... In the new field, another group replants them as quickly as they arrive.

NURSERY

Plants are closely packed.

The men haul load after load of seedlings to the new fields.

Carefully spaced.

Constant singing helps keep up the pace!

MAIN FIELD

# ⑥ GROWTH

Seagulls sometimes make it far inland to feed.

Hawks and falcons circle overhead.

Swallows ("tsubame") feed on mosquitoes and other flying insects.

Dragonflies feast on mosquitoes.

fireflies

Soybeans planted on earthen embankments

Frequent inflow of fresh water

Small freshwater fish arrive via the irrigation system, or are introduced.

Frog eggs adhere to rice stalks, leading to many tadpoles and adult frogs!

Egrets, herons, and other large striding birds come to feed.

Ducks are frequent visitors, even nesting in paddies.

Snails, water striders, mosquito larvae all thrive!

During the late summer, warm water in irrigation ditches can be used to soak flax and hemp stalks to the point of decomposition, so the useful fibers can be easily separated out.

During the growth phase of the rice, the paddies become a diverse and extensive artificial wetland. The composition and animal populations change over the course of the year, but the habitat is particularly thriving in July and August.

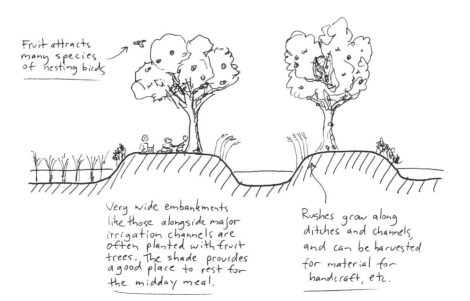

Fruit attracts many species of nesting birds

Very wide embankments like those alongside major irrigation channels are often planted with fruit trees. The shade provides a good place to rest for the midday meal.

Rushes grow along ditches and channels, and can be harvested for material for handcraft, etc.

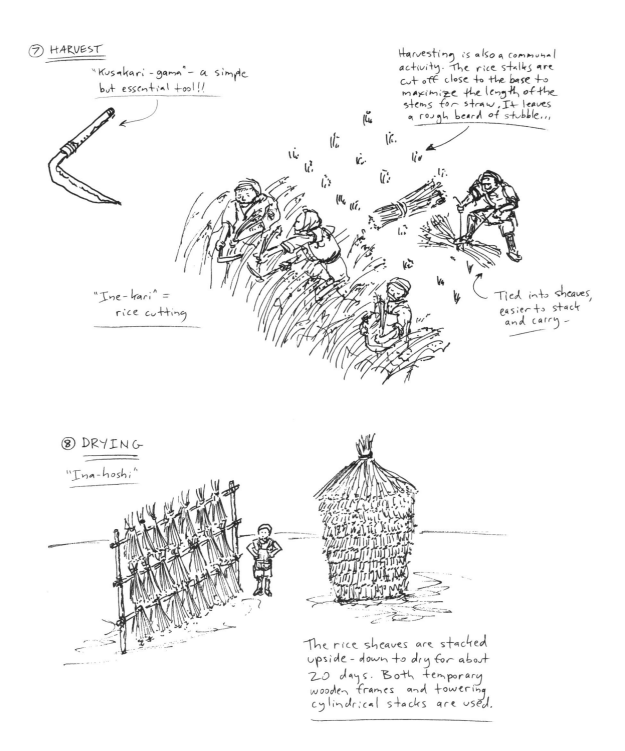

⑦ HARVEST

"Kusakari-gama" – a simple but essential tool!!

Harvesting is also a communal activity. The rice stalks are cut off close to the base to maximize the length of the stems for straw. It leaves a rough beard of stubble...

"Ine-kari" = rice cutting

Tied into sheaves, easier to stack and carry –

⑧ DRYING

"Ina-hoshi"

The rice sheaves are stacked upside-down to dry for about 20 days. Both temporary wooden frames and towering cylindrical stacks are used.

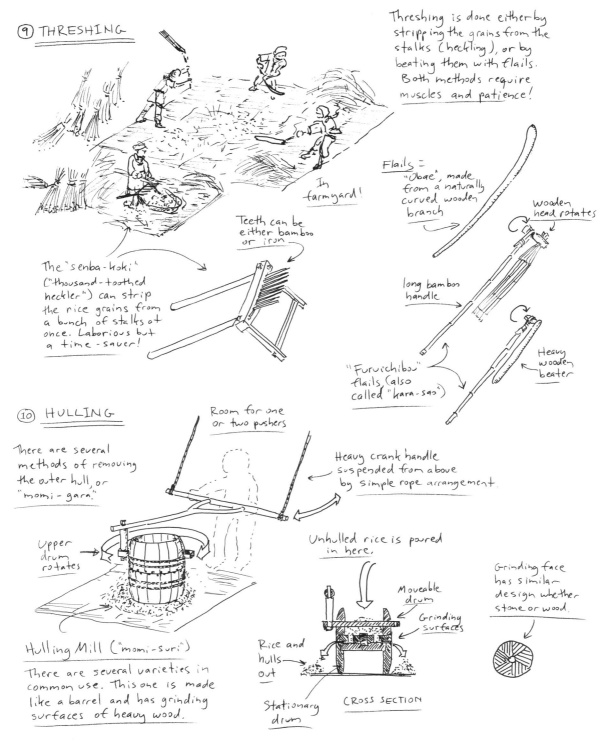

## ⑨ THRESHING

Threshing is done either by stripping the grains from the stalks (heckling), or by beating them with flails. Both methods require muscles and patience!

In farmyard!

Flails = "Obae", made from a naturally curved wooden branch

wooden head rotates

Teeth can be either bamboo or iron

The "senba-koki" ("thousand-toothed heckler") can strip the rice grains from a bunch of stalks at once. Laborious but a time-saver!

long bamboo handle

"Furuichibou" flails (also called "kara-sao")

Heavy wooden beater

## ⑩ HULLING

Room for one or two pushers

There are several methods of removing the outer hull, or "momi-gara."

Heavy crank handle suspended from above by simple rope arrangement.

Upper drum rotates

Unhulled rice is poured in here.

Grinding face has similar design whether stone or wood.

Moveable drum

Grinding surfaces

Rice and hulls out

Hulling Mill ("momi-suri")

There are several varieties in common use. This one is made like a barrel and has grinding surfaces of heavy wood.

Stationary drum

CROSS SECTION

# ⑪ WINNOWING

This is an incredibly useful basket design, and serves many purposes — gathering, carrying, pouring, etc..

The simplest way to winnow rice is to pour it out of a basket onto a straw mat, and let the wind blow the hulls away —

"Furui" — a simple sieve of bent wood and bamboo, suspended from above and shaken vigorously! (Rice falls through, hulls are blown away)

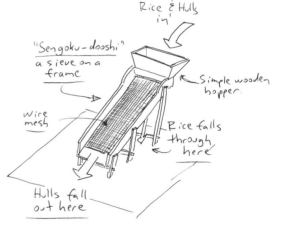

Rice & Hulls in

"Sengoku-dooshi" a sieve on a frame

Simple wooden hopper.

Wire mesh

Rice falls through here

Hulls fall out here

The "mangoku" winnower is a lightweight hand-cranked device that uses a strong air current to separate rice from hulls. The most mechanically advanced device in common use on farms, it is too expensive for many households.

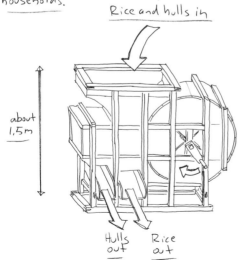

Rice and hulls in

about 1.5 m

Hulls out

Rice out

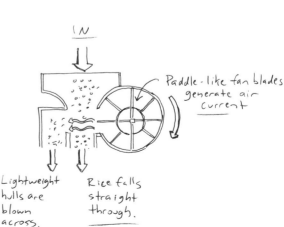

IN

Paddle-like fan blades generate air current

Lightweight hulls are blown across.

Rice falls straight through.

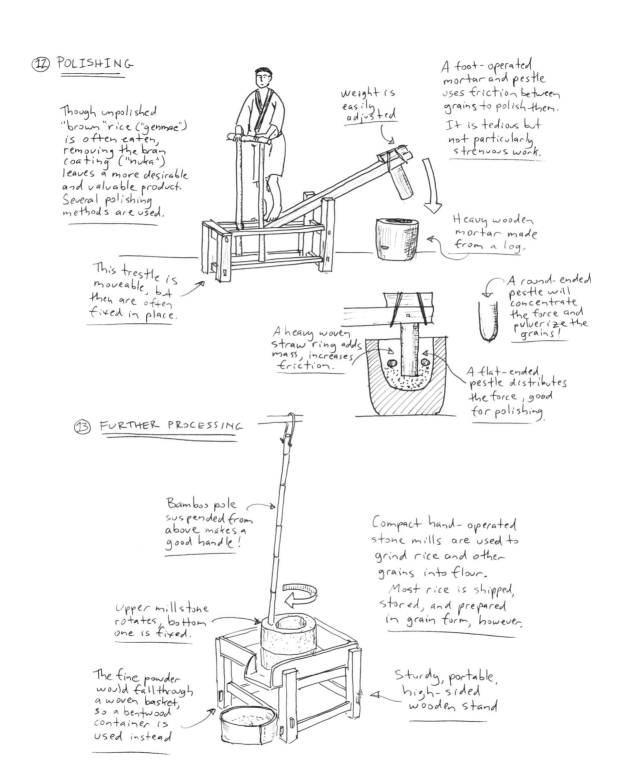

## 12 POLISHING

Though unpolished "brown" rice ("genmae") is often eaten, removing the bran coating ("nuka") leaves a more desirable and valuable product. Several polishing methods are used.

Weight is easily adjusted

A foot-operated mortar and pestle uses friction between grains to polish them.
It is tedious but not particularly strenuous work.

Heavy wooden mortar made from a log.

This trestle is moveable, but they are often fixed in place.

A heavy woven straw ring adds mass, increases friction.

A round-ended pestle will concentrate the force and pulverize the grains!

A flat-ended pestle distributes the force, good for polishing.

## 13 FURTHER PROCESSING

Bamboo pole suspended from above makes a good handle!

Compact hand-operated stone mills are used to grind rice and other grains into flour.
Most rice is shipped, stored, and prepared in grain form, however.

Upper millstone rotates, bottom one is fixed.

The fine powder would fall through a woven basket, so a bentwood container is used instead

Sturdy, portable, high-sided wooden stand

## (14) PACKING

The hulled and winnowed rice (polished or un-polished) is carefully measured and packed into large woven-straw bales ("tawara"). The portion due the government is collected at the village headman's house and inspected, the rest stored for sale and consumption.

Heavy but manageable by one person!

Certified-capacity measuring box

woven basketwork funnel

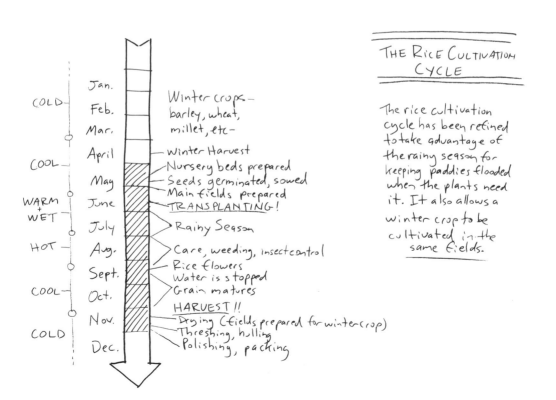

| | | |
|---|---|---|
| COLD | Jan. | |
| | Feb. | Winter crops— barley, wheat, millet, etc— |
| | Mar. | |
| COOL | April | Winter Harvest |
| | | Nursery beds prepared |
| | May | Seeds germinated, sowed |
| WARM + WET | June | Main fields prepared |
| | | TRANSPLANTING! |
| | July | Rainy Season |
| HOT | Aug. | Care, weeding, insect control |
| | Sept. | Rice flowers |
| | | Water is stopped |
| COOL | Oct. | Grain matures |
| | Nov. | HARVEST!! |
| COLD | | Drying (fields prepared for winter crop) |
| | Dec. | Threshing, hulling |
| | | Polishing, packing |

## THE RICE CULTIVATION CYCLE

The rice cultivation cycle has been refined to take advantage of the rainy season for keeping paddies flooded when the plants need it. It also allows a winter crop to be cultivated in the same fields.

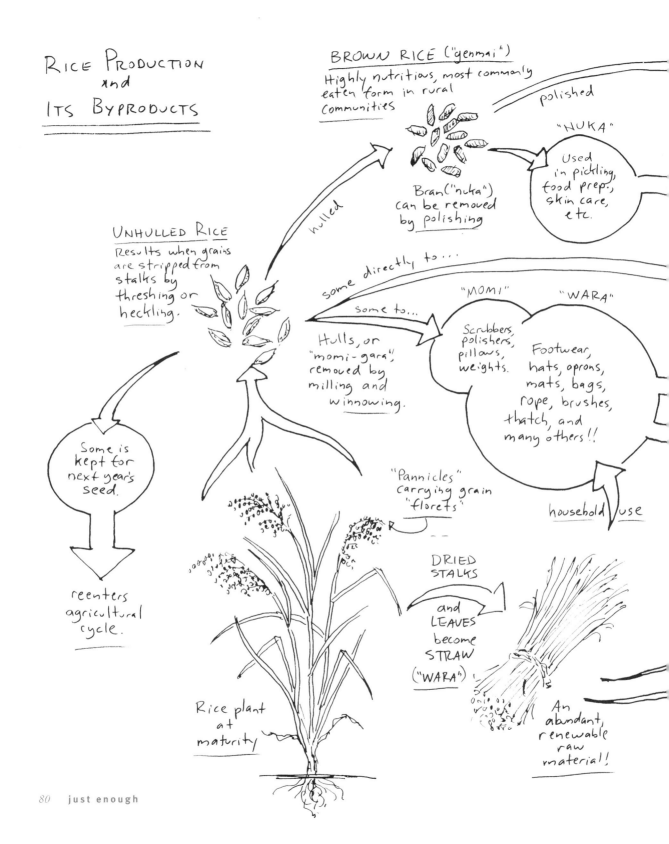

# Rice Production and Its Byproducts

**BROWN RICE ("genmai")**
Highly nutritious, most commonly eaten form in rural communities

*polished*

Bran("nuka") can be removed by polishing

**"NUKA"**
Used in pickling, food prep., skin care, etc.

*hulled*

**UNHULLED RICE**
Results when grains are stripped from stalks by threshing or heckling.

*some directly to...*

*some to...*

Hulls, or "momi-gara", removed by milling and winnowing.

**"MOMI"**
Scrubbers, polishers, pillows, weights.

**"WARA"**
Footwear, hats, aprons, mats, bags, rope, brushes, thatch, and many others!!

*household use*

Some is kept for next year's seed.

reenters agricultural cycle.

"Pannicles" carrying grain "florets"

Rice plant at maturity

**DRIED STALKS**
and LEAVES become STRAW ("WARA")

An abundant, renewable raw material!

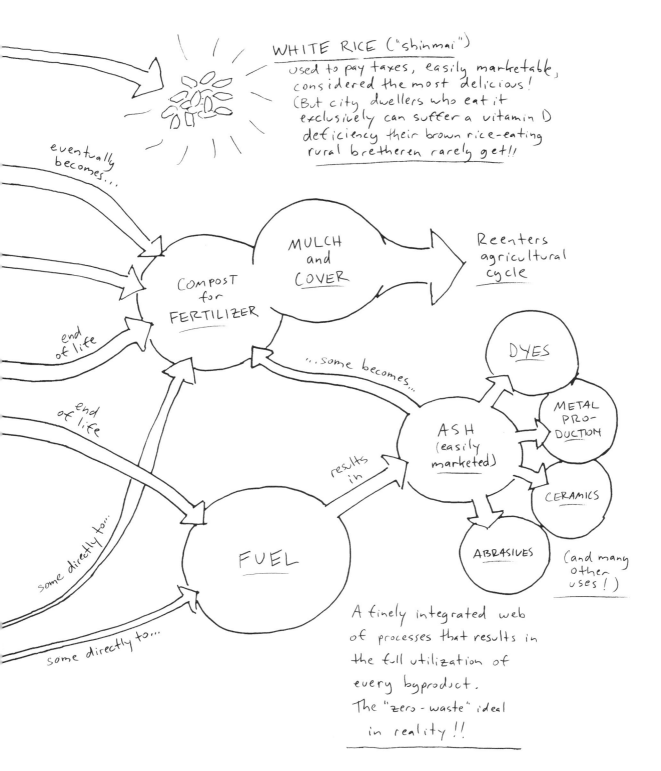

WHITE RICE ("shinmai")
used to pay taxes, easily marketable, considered the most delicious! (But city dwellers who eat it exclusively can suffer a vitamin D deficiency their brown rice-eating rural bretheren rarely get!!

eventually becomes...

MULCH and COVER

Reenters agricultural cycle

COMPOST for FERTILIZER

end of life

end of life

...some becomes...

DYES

METAL PRO-DUCTION

ASH (easily marketed)

CERAMICS

results in

some directly to...

FUEL

ABRASIVES

(and many other uses!)

some directly to...

A finely integrated web of processes that results in the full utilization of every byproduct. The "zero-waste" ideal in reality!!

# THATCHING a ROOF

While in some regions farmhouse roofs may commonly be made of boards, shingles, or bark, by far most are made of thatch. Thatch roofs can be easily patched, but will require replacement every 20 years or so. This large undertaking involves the entire community, and is a prime example of communal cooperation, or "yui".

Because the communal thatch reed field usually produces enough material to cover one house per year, the community decides in advance whose house gets rethatched when, allocates materials, and divides the labor. In its design provisioning, constructional details, and the way the work is carried out, the Japanese thatched roof is a microcosm of village society and its values. Material is largely free for the labor, the labor is cooperative, and the process involves extensive reuse and zero-waste. And each roof expresses both community tradition and household identity.

## ① GATHERING MATERIAL

2-2.5 m.

Bulky but light for its volume!

The most common material for thatch is "yoshi" - ditch reed, which grows 2 to 2.5 m. in one growing season. Other grasses, like miscanthus and "sasa," as well as straw, are used also.

Thatch fields are set aside and supervised, but don't require much attention. Otherwise unusable hillsides are best for "yoshi" and other roofing grasses, but it grows easily in many locations. Free for the gathering, and requires no energy besides the sun and human labor!!

Starting at the bottom of the hill, the reeds are cut, bundled, and rolled downhill. Gravity power!

Besides thatch, other materials must be prepared in large quantities: bamboo, wooden poles, rope and vines, and bark.

## ② DRYING

Because the entire house will be exposed to the elements while roofing work is done, the warm, dry summer months are best. The thatch is cut well in advance and allowed to dry for a few months.

**"To-gai cho-zo" – Haystacks**

Most thatch is stacked to dry in large conical haystacks, as near the house as possible.

Thatch cut in the fall is often stored in the farmhouse loft to dry over the winter. Hearth smoke helps season it, and it adds insulation to the living space!!

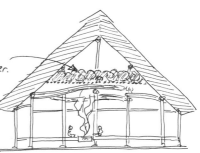

## ③ CLEANING and REPAIRS

The old thatch is removed from the roof and sorted to find what is reusable (usually women's work). This is rebundled, while the rest goes to mulch, fertilizer, and fuel.

The roof structure is cleaned with short brooms, and the wooden and bamboo poles are replaced and re-lashed where necessary.

Lashing is a very ancient skill, and predates most tools!!

# ④ LAYING the THATCH

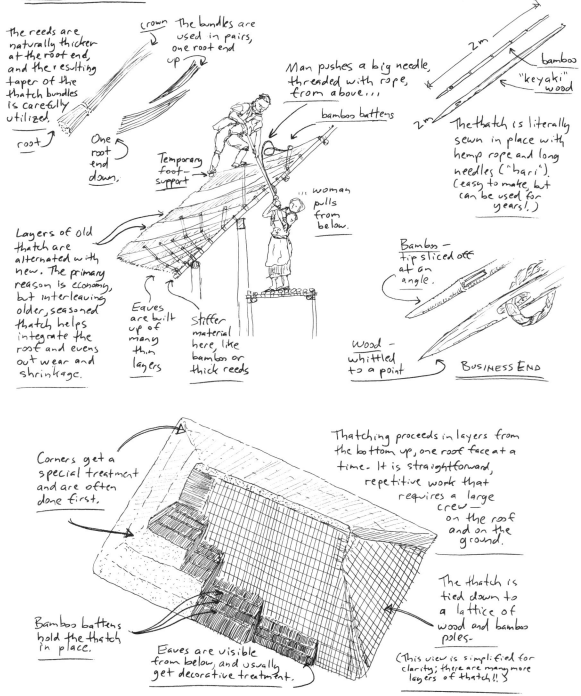

the reeds are naturally thicker at the root end, and the resulting taper of the thatch bundles is carefully utilized.

root

crown The bundles are used in pairs, one root end up.

One root end down.

Man pushes a big needle, threaded with rope, from above...

bamboo battens

2m

bamboo

"keyaki" wood

2m

The thatch is literally sewn in place with hemp rope and long needles ("hari"). (easy to make, but can be used for years!)

Temporary foot-support

...woman pulls from below.

Layers of old thatch are alternated with new. The primary reason is economy, but interleaving older, seasoned thatch helps integrate the roof and evens out wear and shrinkage.

Eaves are built up of many thin layers

Stiffer material here, like bamboo or thick reeds

Bamboo - tip sliced off at an angle.

Wood - whittled to a point

BUSINESS END

Corners get a special treatment and are often done first.

Thatching proceeds in layers from the bottom up, one roof face at a time. It is straightforward, repetitive work that requires a large crew — on the roof and on the ground.

The thatch is tied down to a lattice of wood and bamboo poles.

(This view is simplified for clarity; there are many more layers of thatch!!)

Bamboo battens hold the thatch in place.

Eaves are visible from below, and usually get decorative treatment.

## ⑤ TRIMMING

When the thatch is all laid up, workers start at the top and groom it.

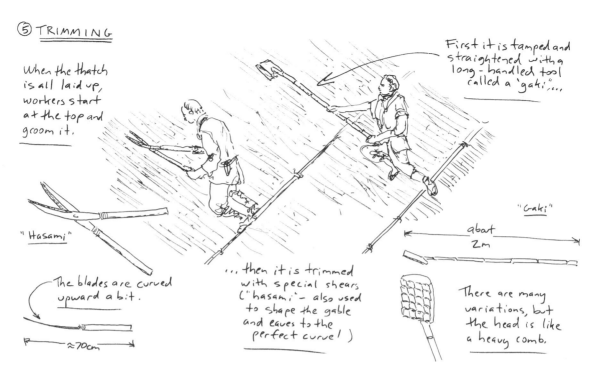

First it is tamped and straightened with a long-handled tool called a 'gaki'...

"Hasami"

The blades are curved upward a bit.

≈70cm

...then it is trimmed with special shears ("hasami" — also used to shape the gable and eaves to the perfect curve!)

"Gaki"

about 2m

There are many variations, but the head is like a heavy comb.

## ⑥ RIDGE

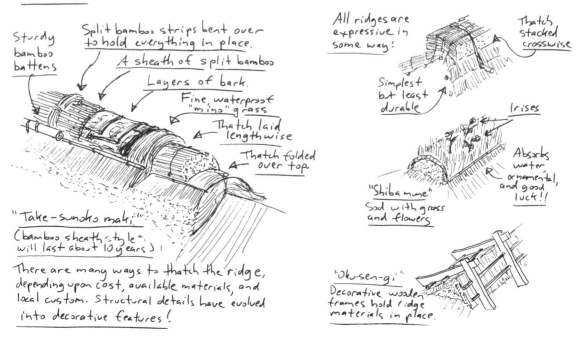

Sturdy bamboo battens

Split bamboo strips bent over to hold everything in place.

A sheath of split bamboo

Layers of bark.

Fine, waterproof "mino" grass

Thatch laid lengthwise

Thatch folded over top.

"Take-sundro maki"
(bamboo sheath-style — will last about 10 years)

There are many ways to thatch the ridge, depending upon cost, available materials, and local custom. Structural details have evolved into decorative features!

All ridges are expressive in some way!

Thatch stacked crosswise

Simplest but least durable

Irises

Absorbs water, ornamental, and good luck!!

"Shiba mune" Sod with grass and flowers

"Okusen-gi" Decorative wooden frames hold ridge materials in place.

# BUILDING MATERIALS AND THEIR VIRTUES

| MATERIAL | primary uses | availability of natural sources | possibility of large-scale cultivation and/ or production | special techniques required | durability |
|---|---|---|---|---|---|
| **wood** | Large-dimension timber for primary structure | Useful species grow wild; some hardwood species can only be found in natural stands. | Several species cultivated on timber plantations, also large-scale harvesting of natural stands. | Cutting, transporting, shaping, and assembly skills. | Extremely durable, can last for centuries. |
| | Wide boards for flooring, etc. | Useful species grow wild. | Usually requires hardwood species not easily grown on plantations. | Special skills for cutting and installing boards. | Extremely durable, but often used in areas that receive high wear. |
| | Scantling and thin pieces for smaller elements | Useful species grow wild, some useful supply readily available. | Lumber industry produces wood cut to suitable dimensions. | Many uses require great skill, but purely functional items can be made by semiskilled workers. | Lasts at least a generation; longer if skillfully made and not subject to excessive wear. |
| | Poles for roofing, etc. | | | Can usually be shaped and assembled by semiskilled workers. | |
| **bamboo** | For roof structure, walls, occasionally floors, incidental structural and decorative uses | Grows wild and prolifically. | Usually not cultivated, but areas are set aside for natural growth. Certain decorative species may be cultivated. | Can usually be shaped and assembled by semiskilled workers. | Usually lasts a generation or more, depending upon area of use. |
| **mud, clay** | Walls, floors, stoves | Only natural sources. An adequate supply for household use can be extracted by occasional quarrying. | Cannot be grown or quantity increased by human effort, but large-scale quarries are active. | Most processes can be carried out by unskilled or semiskilled labor, but high-quality work requires great skill. | Moderately durable depending upon use, but requires frequent maintenance and renewal. |
| | Tile | | | Tile making and tile setting are technically demanding. | Extremely durable, can last for centuries. |
| **plaster** | Fireproof walls for storehouses, etc. | Lime for plaster can occasionally be obtained from nearby natural sources and produced on a household scale. | Limestone and seashells are the natural sources of lime for plaster, but most lime production is industrial in scale. | Both production and application require great skill. | Durable, can last several generations, especially with frequent maintenance. |
| **rush** | Tatami mats for flooring | Can be found in the wild. | Fields set aside, require minimal attention. | Raw material production is essentially an agricultural process easily mastered by farmers; making and finishing tatami require great skill. | Not very durable, several years of use at most. |
| **thatch (pampas grass, etc.)** | Roofs | Grows wild. | Communal fields maintained to insure adequate supply require minimal attention. | Raw material production is essentially an agricultural process easily mastered by farmers; roofing requires some skilled workers but many more semiskilled and unskilled. | 20 years on average, 50 years maximum. |
| **hemp, straw** | Rope | Grows wild. | Hemp is grown agriculturally for several uses; straw is a byproduct of rice production. | Raw material production is essentially an agricultural process easily mastered by farmers; making rope requires semiskilled and unskilled labor; can be done as a cottage industry or on a large scale. | Moderately durable depending upon use; 50 years maximum. |
| **paper (mulberry)** | *Shoji* doors and *fusuma* screens, etc. | Grows wild. | Mulberry and other required species are grown agriculturally. | Raw material production is essentially an agricultural process easily mastered by farmers; paper-making requires great skill. | Not very durable, several years of use at most. |

| recyclable and/or reusable | environmental impact | costs and constraints | useful byproducts | renewability |
|---|---|---|---|---|
| Can be reused, reshaped many times; eventually useful as fuel and source of ash. | Overcutting threatens watershed, habitat, and other aspects of environmental balance. Replacement growth takes generations. | Availability limited by government regulations; high initial costs. | Bark, shavings, leaves, sawdust, nuts, seeds, fruit, fibers, sap, etc. | Yes, over long run and with careful management. |
| | | Requires large, mature hardwood trees; availability limited by nature and by government regulation. | | |
| | Adequate supply can often be obtained from trees thinned out to promote overall health of forest, so carefully regulated use can actually be beneficial. | Relatively low cost, inexpensive to transport. Use is monitored by government but rarely restricted. | | Yes, both over long run and also quickly through coppicing and other wise forestry practices. |
| When initial use is complete, it is usually too weakened or brittle for reuse, but it can be composted or burned. | Due to fast growth, little negative impact from harvesting and use. It is an almost ideal material in environmental terms, but some species are invasive and require effort to control. | Very low costs and no constraints upon use besides the limits of human ingenuity. | Leaves, edible shoots, useful fibers. | Yes, extremely rapidly. |
| Once dried out, not easy to reuse for walls etc., but it can be returned to soil. | Relatively low impact except around large quarries. Extracted material degrades readily into earth. | Almost free for the cost of digging and transportation. Prized types, however, may be monopolized and expensive to acquire. | Few if any byproducts, but the mud itself can be put to many additional uses. | No, but an ample supply for succeeding generations appears to be available. |
| Very easy to reuse for same purpose, or as decoration, gravel for garden and farm fields, etc. | Large impact from tile-making, particularly the amount of fuel needed and some localized air pollution from smoke. Tile does not biodegrade but is inert. | High initial cost. For fire prevention, government requires use of tile on urban roofs but not rural. | Ash from fuel used in tilemaking. | |
| Not easily recyclable, but it can be pulverized and mixed in with soil. | Lime-making kilns require a lot of fuel, cause localized pollution. Limestone quarrying may damage environment as well. | Moderate initial cost for materials, high cost for labor. No constraints on use. | Ash from fuel used in kilns, chemicals. | No, but an ample supply for succeeding generations appears to be available. |
| Recyclable as mulch or fuel. | Low environmental impact in production, use, and at end of life. | Low cost for materials, moderate cost for labor. No constraints on use. | Useful ash at end of life; product itself is an example of full utilization. | Yes, rapidly. |
| Old thatch can be reused in new roofs and eventually as compost, mulch, and fuel. | Low environmental impact. | Low cost for materials, low cost for labor, which is communal. No constraints on use but coordination required with community. | Useful ash at end of life; product itself is an example of full utilization. | Yes, rapidly. |
| Can often be reused for similar purposes; eventually compost, mulch, or fuel. | Very low environmental impact. | Low cost for materials, low cost for labor. No constraints on use. | Hemp produces useful leaves, seeds, and fibers. Straw itself is a byproduct and an excellent example of full utilization. | Yes, rapidly. |
| Can be recycled into new paper, used in other processes; eventually as compost, mulch, and fuel. | Low environmental impact. | Can be used freely, no constraints on use. | Leaves, adhesives. | Yes, but requires effort. |

# learning from
# field and forest

## ■ understand the importance of how ecosystems change

Ecosystems change over time even without human influence. But human habitation necessarily alters the environment to a different degree, and some species benefit or suffer as the direct result of our planning and activity. It is important to observe, understand, and record what happens—deeply, broadly, and over time—when humans do attempt to influence things directly. Most of our current environmental difficulties are events we have set in motion ourselves, and we must ask questions: Which species have become scarce? Which new species have appeared? What has eroded? What has become infertile? Though records on such issues were rarely kept in earlier centuries, and cultural memory itself can disappear rapidly, answers to these questions often survive in the form of stories, songs, and literature. Luckily, many tools, including alluvial geology, archaeology, and paleobotany, are providing windows into how our forebears influenced their environments.

## ■ a healthy balance does not necessarily mean restoration

It is doubtful that natural environments that have hosted centuries of human populations can be restored to their prior states. It may be less important for us to restore the prior balance and mix of species in a particular area than to design a sustainable and healthy emergent system using natural elements to replicate the essential aspects and functions of a natural ecology. This means limiting our activities to those not exceeding the earth's regenerative capacity and redesigning our patterns of occupation and use so that they remain within sustainable yield limits.

This also means recognizing the degree to which our civilization is dependent upon services its ecosystems provide, such as water purification, flood control, soil conservation, pollination, and critically, carbon sequestration. Degraded ecosystems will ultimately prove incapable of supporting human life. Maintaining a "healthy balance" means, first, reversing the present degradation, and subsequently, avoiding placing demands upon them that will degrade them further.

### ■ gathering is learning

Food- and fuel-gathering activities involving regular forays into the wild are important means of information gathering. These activities require observation and interaction of the sort that is essential for monitoring the health of the environment, for maintaining certain species, and especially for learning and passing on first-hand knowledge to younger generations. It is an inherently creative activity, and it can provide the basis for design and policy proposals.

Sudden changes in the environment or in species behavior can forewarn of larger changes afoot, so information gathering also works as an early-warning system. Through it we learn which species can thrive unattended and serve as emergency sustenance. As we see in the case of traditional Japan, the extensive and frequent gathering activities undertaken by the rural population made up the first crucial stage in broad channels of feedback, and the new information it provided, coupled with knowledge gained through generations of experience, provided essential guidance for self-regulation. Gathering provides an opportunity for continued husbandry of the environment.

### ■ strive for closed-loop agricultural systems

Green fertilization as practiced in the Edo period placed inherent limits both on the human population the agricultural system could support and also on the maximum agricultural productivity

## the satoyama initiative

Forest areas near human settlements have traditionally been referred to in Japan as *satoyama*, and in earlier centuries they were carefully monitored and maintained. Besides being sources for fuel and foodstuffs, satoyama were important indicators of the health of the overall ecosystem and of man's impact upon it. But, as industrial development led to decreasing dependence on nature for essential energy and sustenance, awareness of the environment—and the satoyama—declined. In many respects, the environmental damage witnessed during the twentieth century may have been noticed earlier and halted if people had not stopped paying close attention to what was happening in their satoyama areas.

Recently, through efforts such as the "Satoyama Initiative," public awareness of them is growing. The goal of this government-supported plan is to recover the nation's ecosystem, restore its biodiversity and watersheds, and develop sustainable agriculture that coexists with forest areas in a mutually reinforcing manner by the end of the current century. Three hundred important satoyama have been targeted for attention in the initial phase currently under way, and educational programs have begun. It is a far-reaching and ambitious initiative, and its proponents are enthusiastic about the inspiration gained from traditional Edo-period practices. As more and more satoyama areas are placed under protection, and as local residents, companies, and other organizations recognize the stakes they hold in maintaining the health of their mountain ecosystems, the Satoyama Initiative is likely to have a widespread, positive effect.

it could sustain—and both of these could be exceeded only with unacceptable environmental cost.

This closed-loop system remains an excellent instructive model for agricultural production. Recent data indicate that the use of industrial fertilizers represents approximately 20 percent of the energy used on farms in the United States, including the energy used to produce, transport, and apply the fertilizer. They have proven very effective, of course, so much so that it is difficult to imagine efficient and productive large-scale agriculture without them. Populations in developed countries resist the reintroduction of human manure as farm fertilizer, and this resistance is not likely to end soon. The problem of completing the biological nutrient cycle remains.

In contemporary terms, green fertilizer is essentially plant matter applied to the soil as either compost or mulch. In most cases today, "green manures" are nitrogen-rich crops like rye, oats, and legumes that are grown as part of crop rotation and tilled back into the soil; this also helps control erosion and is well suited to large-scale farm production. As high transportation energy costs cause us to find ways to provide for our food needs without relying on long-distance shipping of fruits and vegetables, we can expect to witness a tremendous upsurge in small- and medium-scale urban farming. Mulching, composting, and other green fertilization methods will have a large role to play here.

Mulching, spreading a protective layer of plant material on the soil, is a simple and beneficial practice that reduces erosion, conserves ground moisture, minimizes compaction from heavy rains, inhibits the growth of weeds, and helps maintain even soil temperatures. Mulches decompose slowly and improve the soil by adding organic matter that aids aeration and water retention, and that provides an attractive environment for earthworms and other desirable organisms. For the Japanese, mulching was

an essential process that additionally provided a means of returning used straw, textile fibers, and other household items to the soil.

Compost, on the other hand, is a full-blown microbial farm that can use any organic matter to produce a rich fertilizer. Edo-period Japanese practiced both "hot" and "cold" composting. "Hot" composting uses a carefully controlled mixture of carbon-rich plant material and nitrogen-rich material to provide an environment in which the bacteria of decomposition can thrive. The end product is rich, evenly colored humus that can be easily mixed into the soil, keeping it loose and well aerated and releasing its nutrients slowly. Cold composting takes longer and requires less monitoring and attention. It does not provide the hygienic benefits of heat, but it results in excellent fertilizer as well. A scenario in which entire populations turn their kitchen waste (and perhaps even their own waste) into compost and mulch for local use, and where even textiles and other household items are designed to be composted when they reach the end of their usable lives, would undoubtedly be good for the environment and perhaps even for our well-being. The rate of topsoil loss to erosion and overexploitation around the globe began to exceed the rate of new soil formation at some point in the twentieth century, even in the developed world, with increasingly dire consequences; greater reliance on organic fertilizers and less on industrial-grade products could begin to increase the rate of soil formation once again, with benefits that could extend into the forest, the watershed, and our cities.

## ■ don't underestimate microclimates and ecological niches

One way to achieve more efficient and better use of natural resources is by better understanding and utilizing microclimates and ecological niches. Are there overlooked zones, such as alleyways, vertical faces, sandy soils, or shady areas, where can food be encouraged to grow?

How can different growth types be combined to mutual benefit? How can this approach be used to support other beneficial growth, improve the water supply, moderate the climate, etc.? An awareness of how microclimates interact should inform decisions about land use and building across the spectrum, and as we move into an era of widespread urban farming, this kind of knowledge will become more essential.

A microclimate can be distinguished from others nearby by small but detectable differences in ambient temperature, airflow, available light, and moisture. In addition, like the overall climate in any area, microclimates undergo fairly regular shifts over the course of the day and through the progression of seasons. Skilled gardeners develop an innate understanding of microclimates and learn to plant accordingly; in both agriculture and in ornamental gardens, the Japanese were masters of microclimate understanding and use. Perhaps you have noticed that, because of the chance adjacency of a tree and a wall, one corner of your garden is shadier and cooler than the rest through most of the year but several degrees warmer during the winter. Perhaps there is a passageway along one side of your house where water evaporates so slowly that green moss grows on the bricks with no encouragement. Perhaps your deck, which is just slightly elevated off of the ground, receives more sunlight than anywhere else, and more breeze as well. Each of these represents a microclimate with implications for what will more easily grow there. The difference between the north and south sides of a house can be immense, but in fact the natural environment is full of pockets and gradations, and the things we build can either reinforce these differences or serve to mitigate them.

Like the larger environmental zones of the natural world, every microclimate plugs into those adjacent; though they are maintained by various degrees of soft separation from their neighbors, they emerge through integration with them. In the natural world, the borders between them can be formed by elements such as rocks, bushes, pools, or trees; these can be augmented or replicated by careful planting and by structures such as berms, walls, trellises, pots, and canopies. As is usually the case, small and slow solutions are more likely to result in long-term success than attempts to alter chunks of the environment quickly. This is especially true on the home or community scale. Many prescient landscape designers are bringing an awareness of the function and benefits of well-maintained microclimates into the community planning process. Because this approach shows such tremendous promise for making more land available for urban agriculture, the benefits will become even more widespread.

## fruit trees everywhere

Japanese benefit today from the widespread planting of fruit trees their ancestors undertook—persimmon (*kaki*), pear (*nashi*), loquat (*biwa*), tangerine (*mikan*), apple (*ringo*), and others—trees that have relatively limited lifespans but propagate quite easily. Planting fruit trees in household yards and gardens is a habit that seems to have been passed down intact to present generations, as if the virtue of adding visual color and the scent of blossoms to the air and seasonal treats to the table needed no explanation.

## ■ practice natural pest control

Biological controls are the most effective means of regulating populations. In nature, every organism has predators that feed upon it and parasites that inhabit it, and natural pest control of the sort the Japanese practiced in their rice paddies relies upon an understanding of these dynamics and the careful nurturing of appropriate predator species. In fact, the loss of predator species over the course of the past century has led to many pest problems. Many fish feed on insect larvae, many birds are insectivorous, and bats consume so many nocturnal insects that they are probably the most significant biological control of all. Any actions we take to provide habitat for the natural predators of undesirable insect species—matching ponds to fish, building tree canopies for birds, and protecting bat roosts—will pay off in decreased use of insecticides, less groundwater contamination from them, and a more biologically diverse environment.

### ■ let gravity do the work

Though Japanese irrigation made frequent use of human-powered water lifting systems, for the most part it was gravity-fed and required no external power. Ultimately, the agricultural water supply came from precipitation that was naturally stored as masses of ice and snow on mountaintops, melting during warmer months in time to feed rivers during the drier months. Ideal irrigation systems avail themselves of this gravity-fed supply and base their detailed design on the functioning of natural water flows.

At present, however, this system is breaking down. The culprits are both overexploitation of water resources and the loss of mountain snow cover due to climate warming. In particular, an increased reliance on underground aquifers, including nonreplenishable fossil water aquifers, has meant that external energy—overwhelmingly fossil-fuels based—must be used to pump water from ever deeper wells, so we have lost the free ride that gravity formerly provided. In the United States, water pumping represents close to 19 percent of total farm energy expenditure, and in some parts of India over half of all electricity is consumed by agricultural water pumps. Use gravity wherever possible. It's free!

### ■ base water systems on what nature has given us

Water systems should be based on the natural features of the watershed wherever possible, and they should make use of existing ponds, streams, and dispersal areas. Riparian works may be unavoidable, but they should be limited in size, should not interfere with seasonal flow or aquatic life, and should be reversible and/or permeable. Irrigation and water-use systems should improve the quality of water downstream. The challenge is to insure that we have enough water for growing food while providing adequately for our other uses as well.

Our freshwater supplies are being stretched beyond their regenerative capacity. The bulk of our freshwater use—70 percent—is for irrigation, with 20 percent for industrial needs and only 10 percent for household consumption. While the tensions between urban and rural users of a diminishing water supply often erupt into political dispute and even violence, the fact is that all of our water uses require infrastructure in the form of dams, channels, pipelines, pumps, settling pools, and purification plants. While on the one hand these have achieved an unprecedented level of clean water delivery to uses of all types, too often the infrastructure relies on brawn and artificial intervention while failing to understand how nature performs similar functions.

In Japan, rice paddies have always functioned as manmade wetlands. Wetlands are the unsung heroes of nature's hydrological cycle, its water system. They are natural filters, extracting minerals and organic nutrients from the water flow, thereby purifying and protecting rivers and streams. They have an inherently flexible capacity, expanding to accommodate and store excess water during particularly wet times and shrinking during dry periods. They are habitat, of course, whose biological components—aquatic plants and grasses, water-loving trees, and the animals that complement them—are also resilient and have evolved to spring back into full activity after periodic dry, fallow seasons. A natural wetland is a reservoir that grows and shrinks as necessary, surrendering its periphery to drought-loving species when such times arrive and reclaiming it when the water returns. It is the principle of collecting when resources are abundant and reducing demand when they are not that we must learn from.

We should try to move from a "pump and isolate it" water management mindset to a "collect and share it" one, where wetlands can be nurtured and benefited from even in urban areas, and where the water system itself can be a driver of biological diversity, an essential component of urban climate control, all while using little or no external power.

### ■ understand that without cooperation, nothing happens

Nothing big can be done without cooperation. It can be enforced, coerced, or legislated, but it will obviously work best if the goals and benefits are clearly understood by all and the agreements are entered into willingly. Better yet if there is an existing network of social and economic interdependence and reliance of which a particular cooperative effort is only one part. It is hard to find a true community-wide

spirit of cooperation today, and in the West we are averse to legislated cooperative efforts. We should learn how to allow more ambitious cooperative environmental efforts to emerge from our existing institutions and be open to the possibility that new institutions may need to be allowed to appear.

### ■ envision "multiform" solutions

Allowing each element to perform several functions, and each function to be supported by several elements, is a fundamental design principle applicable to everything: interior design, architecture, town planning, agriculture, and ecosystem management for sure, but also to graphic design, system design, writing, and even cooking. Why are multiform solutions so rare then? The biggest reason is probably that we are overspecialized and are not taught to understand the functioning of complex interacting systems. Another is that we simply misstate design problems and goals, assuming that limiting the scope of the task will lead to a better solution. Finally, grasping "multiform" problems and their possible solutions requires creativity that is equal parts perception, vision, imagination, and intuition. Crucially, our failure to understand this connectedness—how stretching

## irrigation as culture

Rural Japan has been under cultivation for rice for centuries, so long that the landscape has been irrevocably altered. It may strike us as ironic to realize, then, that while it is difficult to find towns and cities where it is possible to experience historical vistas, when one gazes upon broad expanses of rice fields one is probably gazing upon history. In large part this is due to the fact that irrigation systems that were planned and established during the Edo period are so efficient that they are still in use all over the country. Just as road locations are often the oldest things in a Japanese city, irrigation channels are usually the oldest element of the rural landscape; in many cases the roads appeared much later! Most have been incrementally improved, expanded, or tweaked, and a few large new irrigation projects were implemented during the twentieth century, but by and large farmers are still using what their ancestors used to flood their rice paddies.

the ecosystem in one area can cause it to break in others—has led to the widespread disappearance of species. As Lester Brown of the Worldwatch Institute puts it, "We are in the early stage of the sixth great extinction," and this one is of human origin. Every element of the ecosystem provides services for the others, such as pollination, predator control, and provision of nutrients. The loss of a single species represents the loss of several ecological services, which we ourselves have been benefiting from in some important way. Much as an artist is trained to notice the "negative space" between the main elements of a picture, we need to train ourselves to immediately see the interactions upon which natural processes are based, and to better observe how the things we make interact with what is already there. Perhaps we can graduate as a species from the ecologically rickety approaches we have saddled ourselves with to something truly worthy of the name "environmental design." When the birds return in great numbers, we'll know we are on the right track.

### ■ look at the edges; they are where everything happens

Learn to recognize and understand the edges and boundaries of natural systems and how to take advantage of them without destroying them. Whereas the middle of a field of grass may be uniform and stable overall, each square meter sharing most characteristics with its neighbors, at the edge we will usually find tremendous diversity as the grass gives way to bushes, flowering plants, or trees, and this transitional zone will witness the most active interchange between species. Biological zones of influence overlap here, each species of plant and animal extending its normal range and habitat into the "edge" zone and sharing its resources. This "overlapping and interacting sphere" is an extremely informative model for human settlement and community design as well.

### ■ use our generous solar heat engine

Our biosphere is a vast solar-powered heat engine whose workings are getting better understood daily. We are utterly dependent on solar energy for all of our food and for the maintenance of our climate, but we still use it poorly. It is converted by plants through photosynthesis and stored as chemical energy, but plants only use part of the solar energy they absorb for growth and reproduction. The remainder can provide our nutrition and feed other plants and animals in the food chain. The fossilized organic matter we extract from the earth as coal and oil has stored the energy of the sun for millions of

## life on the edge

Much of the renewed awareness of the importance of edge conditions in agriculture and nature, and their inherent complexity and delicacy, can be credited to the Permaculture movement. It is interesting to note that permaculture ideas have a lot in common with traditional East Asian sustainable farming methods, including Japan's, and that a Natural Farming movement in Japan that anticipated many of the findings of permaculture began as early as the 1930s. All of which is to say that Permaculture has found a natural home in Japan, and the network of practitioners and advisers has been steadily expanding over the last few decades. Practitioners in other parts of the world are eager to learn from the Japanese experience, and an exposure to the experiences of natural farmers on other continents gives like-minded Japanese an important sense of context.

years. By burning it to obtain thermal energy, we set off a chain of unintended consequences, primarily by releasing not-easily-reabsorbed carbon back into the environment, but also by releasing a lot of excess heat—that ancient sunlight, in effect—into the environment as well. Basic thermodynamics and the law of the conservation of energy inform us that we can never obtain more heat from organic chemical sources like fossil fuels than those organisms obtained from the sun in the first place. We should get it directly from the sun ourselves.

### ■ rethink the meaning of "comfort"

Should we stop trying to be so comfortable all the time? Though strong arguments are made to the contrary, with some insisting that lifestyle and value change is not necessary and that technical solutions will allow us to solve our environmental problems without any inconvenience, in fact we probably should reexamine our notions of comfort and convenience first. At the very least we should pay attention to what we are doing on a day-to-day basis, decide to walk more often, stop sitting at home in a t-shirt with the heater on, and in general assume that energy is more precious than comfort. The fact is that we have as yet found no way to use energy on a mass scale without damaging the environment. There is a lot that we do in the name of comfort that we should do differently, or stop doing altogether.

What this entails is self-regulation. Our notions of comfort have led us to expend far too little physical energy in the course of our daily lives and to consume fuel for reasons that are difficult to justify on the basis of health or well-being. Walking and biking are healthier than driving or riding, and they consume little or no fuel. A simple increase in these activities, which would mean increasing the pedestrianization and bikeability of our communities, would go a long way toward reducing our already dangerous obesity levels. Allowing ourselves to become comfortable a few degrees warmer or cooler than usual and adjusting our thermostats accordingly could reduce overall fuel consumption significantly. Reconsidering our wardrobes, as the Japanese have begun to do in recent years, going so far as to abandon the wearing of business suits during the summer months, will help. We are not talking about instituting a spartan regime that will leave us either shivering or drenched in sweat, but about minor shifts in thermostat settings that will effect a marked cumulative reduction in fuel use and hence carbon emissions, and an increase in natural heating and cooling methods that consume little or no fuel whatsoever. It also means, perhaps, integrating our homes more closely with the natural environment in a manner that became instinctual for the Japanese, and allowing the outside in.

### ■ look for beauty in function

We should learn to see beauty less as the result of visible features than of things that are invisible. What something does can be a source of greater beauty than its surface appearance. Can our sense of beauty change as much as it needs to in order to fully recognize this? It has in the past, when machine-made forms were first embraced; in the late nineteenth century, machine forms were initially regarded as repellent or even frightening, but over the course of subsequent decades we discovered in their clarity and unambiguity and in their economy and purity of function a new kind of aesthetic pleasure that remains with us today. Perhaps a new "environmental functionalism" can show us the beauty in buildings and other designs that help maintain and restore environmental equilibrium. And perhaps our changing understanding and appreciation of the essential characteristics of Japanese architecture can serve as a model. It was disparaged by the first European visitors as insignificant in the sixteenth century, praised for its craftsmanship in the nineteenth, and

## the bamboo kitchen

Small things can be very significant, and the near ubiquity of bamboo kitchen utensils in Japan is a case in point. Most of the spoons, stirrers, ladles, paddles, holders, skewers, and chopsticks, as well as many kinds of strainers and baskets in use now would be instantly recognizable to Edo-period ancestors. Their designs have been refined over the course of centuries and perfected long ago; lightweight, easy on the hands, sturdy, efficient. Bamboo was used for these items back then because it was inexpensive, durable, and easy to shape, and it is used now for the same reasons, as well as being a highly renewable material. There are, of course, quite a few items that have been improved by being made from more durable materials like stainless steel, copper, and iron, but the continuity of the materials used in the Japanese kitchen is a living bit of cultural poetry.

served as a model for modern modular design in the twentieth. All of these appreciations were based on its appearance. We are now in a position to appreciate the "invisible" features of Japanese architecture, such as its sophistication in terms of material and energy use, in enabling a zero-waste lifestyle and in supporting human habitation without excessive negative influence on the natural environment.

### ■ use water more fully

Often the low price of water leads to the illusion of abundance. Adjusting the price of water so that it more accurately reflects its environmental value should encourage users to conserve it. In the case of traditional Japan, even though water was in fact abundant, it was never wasted, and it was usually put to multiple uses before being released back into the environment. The capture and diversion of well spillage and household wastewater to farmstead ponds, the capture and use of rainwater, the use of irrigation water channels as a source of water power, were all Japanese efforts at conserving a precious resource despite its ready availability. We should learn from this.

As William McDonough and Michael Braungart clearly illustrate in their influential 2002 book, *Cradle to Cradle: Remaking the Way We*

*Make Things*, industrial processes can be made much more water-efficient, as can household appliances. Our urban water systems are due for a redesign also, taking a hint from the Japanese here as well. The major issue is what happens to sewage and "gray water," that is, household wastewater. At present we use fresh-water profligately for washing, bathing, cleaning, flushing, etc., and along with our sewage this polluted effluent is returned to the watershed or to the ocean after barely being utilized. The initial step that should be taken is to prevent wastewater from becoming so toxic in the first place, by not allowing human waste into it and by redesigning our detergents and cleansers so that they are actually beneficial for the biosphere. (The Japanese of this period used rice husks and other mild abrasives for cleaning, all of which could be composted or mulched.) Then this already cleaner gray water should be treated and recycled so that it can be reused continuously. This may require the establishment of a two-tiered water supply that separates potable water from that intended for other uses. The technologies are already available and if they are implemented widely, even large urban populations would have a negligible negative impact on freshwater resources.

## ■ establish a "material mile" standard

The cost and availability of building materials has always been a primary consideration in what we use, and they have largely determined the design, appearance, and atmosphere of our built environment. During the past century our notion of availability has changed, and building materials are often transported great distances. In the case of lumber, transcontinental or even transoceanic shipment has become the norm. As long as the cost of transportation is relatively low, we have been willing to overlook the wider environmental costs. Considering the tremendous amount of energy used by the construction industry, a large portion of which is devoted to transporting building materials long distances, perhaps it is time to implement a "material mile" standard like the increasingly popular "food mile."

In every case, we must take the total embodied energy of building materials and the overall environmental impact into account. In some cases, the energy and impact involved in sourcing materials close to home may outweigh that of transporting the same items from a neighboring state or country. The people of the Edo period were forced to transport large quantities of timber long distances from their mountain forests to their cities, but by relying upon gravity and human power alone, and by inventing temporary transportation structures that would easily revert to nature, they kept the environmental damage of building material transport to a minimum. Though our methods will undoubtedly be different, we should aspire to similar goals.

## ■ design buildings for reuse

We should develop building material and construction systems that have easy reuse designed in. People will want to do this only if the building elements are extremely practical, extremely beautiful, or both.

Building construction consumes approximately 40 percent of all the raw materials pro-

duced globally. Not only does the production and transportation of these materials consume vast quantities of water and energy, but we have given little thought to what happens to the materials after buildings are demolished. Some, such as steel, is easily recycled and so usually find a subsequent use, but the rest usually becomes waste. The goal is to insure that all materials used in building can be repeatedly reused or recycled, thereby reducing the amount of energy and raw material production necessary to support new building activity. This entails designing structures that can be easily dismantled.

The Japanese were fortunate to have inherited a wood-frame building system based upon easily dismantled wooden joints, and to have been foresighted enough to refine it to a peak of beauty and efficiency over the centuries. Their architectural aesthetic was based on articulated, jointed frames, and the possibility of removal, reuse, and recycling was always kept in mind during the design and construction process. This was much less the case in the West, where masonry and brick were long preferred materials, and where jointed timber construction tended to aspire to permanence as well. In contrast with the solidity and permanence we expect from our buildings, prefabricated structures have generally struck us as poor and insubstantial substitutes.

This is changing, however. On the one hand, manufactured buildings (particularly in Japan) have developed to the point of being indistinguishable from conventional ones in quality of appearance and in solidity, though they can be easily disassembled for reuse. On the other, driven by the environmental concerns we discuss here, a lively, low-impact, energy-efficient "prefab" architectural design aesthetic has begun to blossom throughout the developed world and is being highlighted by the design and lifestyle press and through well-attended exhibitions. At present its impact is limited in terms of the number of buildings actually built, but both

## reviving materials

Doing things "the old way" is often a hard sell, where people are constantly reminded of how much their comfort level has risen over the past one hundred years and are easy to convince that it's mainly due to having better materials to work with. Nevertheless, if one observes homebuilding marketing and periodicals in Japan it is hard not to notice increasing space being devoted to high-quality "alternative" methods that are derived from traditional practice. In particular, it is becoming easier to find clay-based wall plaster and lime coatings of high quality and aesthetic variety, good tatami, tiles, shingles, handmade hardware and fittings, and *shoji* and *fusuma* that use papers and adhesives similar to those common long ago. Materials like these still represent a minor fraction of the overall house-building materials market in Japan at this point, but the increase in interest in this area points to an incipient broad shift in attitudes.

designers and the public are paying close attention. We can expect to see more widespread adoption of reusable/recyclable buildings, particularly homes, as the offerings become more technically refined and popular sensibility finds itself in alignment with the new aesthetic.

### ■ use dirt
Look for opportunities to use dirt as a floor, as either pounded earth or some other easily maintained and renewed form. When your building is gone, a garden should grow there.

### ■ make your own gadgets
Don't have more kitchen implements and household gadgets than you really need and use. See how many of them you can make yourself. We should try to develop more things whose parts and materials can be reused in some way, even if only as fuel or compost.

For most of us, kitchen implements and other gadgets are often purchased on impulse and not because they will serve a real need. From the outset we should separate those that consume power in their operation from those that don't. By now it should be clear that we should think long and hard before making a decision that will increase our energy consumption, particularly

if the reasons are frivolous. Who besides the disabled or infirm really needs an electric can opener?

There are many reasons to get into the habit of making things to use in one's daily life. It will usually be cheaper. It is gratifying and fun. But beyond this, it provides an opportunity for reflection and consideration, for thinking through implications of design and use, and for arriving at solutions ideally suited to oneself. The product of one's own hands is meaningful in a way that massproduced items cannot be. All of this was taken for granted by our forebears and contributed greatly to their well-being. But it is nearly lost to us now.

### ■ increase the use of unrefrigerated, uncooked foods
Find food that has been preserved without the use of external energy sources and make more use of it. Food preservation, packaging, and preparation are remarkably energy-intensive: one-fifth of the total energy devoted to getting food to the table goes into growing it, and the rest is used to transport, process, preserve, package, sell, and finally, prepare it in the kitchen. According to the Worldwatch Institute, "The most energy-intensive segment of the food

chain is the kitchen. Much more energy is used to refrigerate and prepare food in the home than is used to produce it in the first place." Despite technical advances that have improved energy efficiency, the home refrigerator remains the largest energy user in the food chain.

In addition to avoiding inefficiently grown and transported food, we should attempt to minimize our use of foods that require refrigeration. This may mean more fresh fruit and produce, less meat, and avoiding chilled drinks; it may mean more use of dried, salted, and pickled foods and a greater reliance on raw grains and flours that have a long shelf life. Many foods need not be refrigerated but can be kept cool enough for preservation in other ways—until recently, most homes had cellars or other cool spaces for storing food.

One remarkable aspect of the traditional Japanese diet is the degree to which it depended on raw and uncooked foods, on items served at room temperature, and on salting, smoking, and pickling, all of which lessened the need to consume fuel in order to feed the population. Alternate energy sources may eventually alleviate our most pressing concerns, as could solar cookers or extremely energy-efficient food coolers. But just as most of us have become comfortable with the idea of eating a salad for dinner, not to mention the idea of eating sushi, we should begin to alter our diet to be less energy-intensive in the preparation phase.

### ■ celebrate spiritual centers

To speak of the "spiritual center of a house" means having places where we are reminded to care about other things and people more than ourselves, and to feel continuity with the past, and where we can experience love. Every home needs one or more spiritual centers, as do communities, schools, even companies. Learn to recognize them and keep them functioning as a site for human communication; they might not look like what you'd expect. A kitchen table, a sofa, a watercooler or bulletin board where people post cartoons, a playground, or some steps somewhere might all be spiritual centers in disguise.

### ■ learn how houses speak

The design of homes and other buildings should let people know what to expect and tell us about who we are and our relationships to other people. The Japanese home was extremely hospitable but still very private, and this was accomplished through spatial cues, decoration, garden views, and other poetic gestures rather than with solid walls. Far too few contemporary homes exhibit this degree of legibility and identity; visitors are usually either left standing outside or must be invited directly into the family sphere, with very little in the way of intermediate space where strangers can experience an appropriate level of hospitality without an expectation of familiarity or intimacy.

### ■ put human waste to good use

We spend an incredible amount of energy and freshwater on getting rid of our digestive wastes, and the process is very polluting. We need to find a better way of making use of these waste products, either to restore the health of the environment or as a source of thermal or chemical energy.

As stated elsewhere, it is ludicrous, even insane, to dump our wastes into our freshwater supply, regardless of the sophistication of our purification systems. The main reasons we ended up with our "flush and forget" system were the "yuck" factor among the Victorians who developed it during the late nineteenth century and a serious concern for improved health and hygiene. There are several alternatives: using human waste for agricultural fertilizer, using it to generate energy, or transforming it into useful products such as building material. Some may retain a "yuck" factor, but the hygiene issues have been largely worked out.

Using human waste as fertilizer is extremely

## in with the old

Old wooden *minka* farmhouses and *machiya* townhouses are being given away, and many owners will even pay people to demolish them and cart them off. Demographics are partly to blame: as rural villages age and empty out, the vacant houses become unnecessary and unsafe. Part of it is the real-estate business, which has largely failed to recognize the inherent desirability of historic housing stock. But eventually one is forced to accept the fact that most Japanese simply do not want to live in old houses. The image is of something poor, out of date, and uncomfortable, and it requires them to answer too many probing questions from relatives and neighbors.

There are a number of individuals and organizations, however, who have devoted themselves to preserving, moving, and renovating old minka, though much of the support and enthusiasm comes from non-Japanese who are fascinated with these unique homes and often appreciative enough of them to pay a premium to live in or stay in one. Traditional environments have always been popular for eating, drinking, and entertainment, and historical houses of the embalmed sort one finds in farmhouse museums and in preservation districts get a steady stream of local tourists as well as those from overseas. But increasingly, younger Japanese are taking the time and effort to renovate old houses as residences for their own families. It's become a bit easier to find craftsmen who can do the work, and easier to find some of the materials. But above all, once they get past the naysayers, renovators often discover a wealth of ideas and techniques that have been tried and tested by others, and find themselves part of a far-flung community eager to share experience and information. As living in old homes becomes a more visible alternative, their value will be recognized and the trend will undoubtedly grow.

straightforward and has a long history; much has been written on the subject, and a grassroots movement has arisen to promote its renewed use. The key health concern has been the transmission of pathogens, but careful hot composting largely eliminates the problem. An important development is the dry composting toilet, which was sold commercially as far back as the 1970s and is now quite refined. By allowing natural composting heat to occur inside a well-ventilated compartment, these turn human waste into a dry, nearly odorless compound that looks and feels like peat moss. The Japanese separated urine from feces and processed them separately, mainly because of the high nitrogen content of urea, and recent composting-toilet designs divert urine from solids so they can be

separately processed as well. China is poised to be the global leader in composting toilets, partly because relatively few communities are served by the sewer infrastructure and the government is promoting these new designs as an attractive alternative that will help mitigate its freshwater problems as well.

Biogas production—that is, harnessing the methane gas emitted by hog and cow manure—is a proven technology, and there is no real reason that human waste cannot be a source of thermal energy as well. The agricultural infrastructure for collecting animal manure on farms was already well developed when biogas experiments began, and a similar system would have to be developed in order to harness human methane. Collection and harnessing on the household or neighborhood scale may prove to be the most effective and manageable.

Finally, attempts to transform human waste into building bricks or paving tile have met with technical success if not commercial viability. Animal dung is one of the most ancient building materials, and it is still used in many places in Africa and the Indian subcontinent. The key to using human dung for building is applying heat sufficient to sterilize it. After that, it is a matter of combining it with sand, plant fiber, and other compounds to improve structural performance and wear characteristics. There are no great technical barriers to be surmounted.

### ■ remember: hot water equals fuel consumption

A great deal of our household energy use is for hot water. If you are not using a solar hot water heater to supply all of your hot water needs, you should use hot water it as if it were expensive. Environmentally speaking, it is.

For Edo-period Japanese, although many geothermal sources of hot water were (and still are) utilized, even prized, for the most part heating water meant consuming fuel in the form of wood or charcoal, and fuel represented a considerable household expense and environmental impact. Bathing practices evolved to conserve and reuse bathwater once it was heated, and tea kettle and brazier design underwent continual refinement in order to produce more hot water with less fuel. Hot water is so valued it is even given an honorific: *o-yuu*.

In the present day, we are either heating water directly through solar or geothermal power, or using an electric- or gas-powered heating device of some sort. Rooftop solar water heaters are particularly attractive and have become extremely cost efficient in most areas; some can also be used to heat indoor space. If everyone had one square meter of solar collectors on their roof, the need to use fossil fuels to heat water would become negligible, many

coal-fired power plants could be closed, and natural gas use would decrease because of the reduced demand for electricity for heating, with many positive environmental effects. Anyone who uses water heated by fossil fuel should keep the environmental consequences in mind and use hot water sparingly. Those whose water is heated by the sun can use it with a bit more freedom of conscience.

### ■ embrace cottage industries

People of the Edo period embraced cottage industries for a variety of reasons. Most cottage industries were based upon tasks the households already performed to help provide for daily needs. Increasing the scale allowed them to sell the goods on the open market in order to supplement their income.

Many people today already work from home, and some industries, such as computer programming, writing, tutoring, and art, already largely depend upon such people. The recent resurgence of interest in handcrafts provides new opportunities both for people who want to earn money with their hands and for those who would like to teach others similar skills. Great satisfaction comes from doing creative work that is appreciated. One is brought into a wider network of practitioners, can learn from them and share ideas. Having a special skill can allow a person to become a more valued member of their local community, and to be sought out for input and advice. And there is the special quality of communication that comes from group handwork activities, and from teaching.

If one has even a small farm, such as the kind that are becoming known as "Micro Eco Farms," suitable for suburban or even urban areas, a host of other home business opportunities arise.

Starting a cottage business is a wonderful way to capitalize on knowledge gained from a hobby, and an opportunity to learn new skills. It's a way to become part of a positive social movement, and to pass on important knowledge.

# gray water washing machines

Many contemporary Japanese households have compact electrical pumps designed specifically for transferring used bathwater to the washing machine, thereby recycling the gray water for further use before sending it down the drain and into the wastewater system. Users are likely prompted as much by the significant decrease in their water bill that results as by the environmental considerations. The devices are easy to use in most Japanese households because of the customary practice of placing the laundry close to the bath—often a mere arm's length away—and are practical from a cleanliness standpoint because Japanese-style bathing does not call for washing in the tub, but for scrubbing and rinsing outside of it before climbing in for a relatively clean soak. Because of the pumps' popularity, refinements will undoubtedly appear and we can expect subsequent versions both to be more convenient and to consume less energy.

## ■ optimum sizes for self-sufficiency

Even in the past, self-sufficiency was difficult to attain on the household level, but it is progressively easier the larger the scale of the community considered. At present few countries are self-sufficient in energy, food, water, or materials. Our processes, our consumption patterns, and the things we use should be redesigned to make it easier to attain self-sufficiency in all essentials for increasingly smaller population groups. With the use of photovoltaic panels, the individual household could easily become self-sufficient in energy today (and wind turbines, hydrogen fuel cells, and other technologies have the real potential to make it commonplace). Given adequate agricultural space, communities of one hundred or less can achieve food self-sufficiency; it can be done fairly easily by a community of a thousand; communities of ten thousand could conceivably produce all of the materials they require. Succeeding at any of these on an extensive scale would require the cooperation of hundreds of thousands if not millions in most countries, as our energy, food, transportation, material, and water systems are reconfigured. It will require both hitherto unapparent political motivation and the mobilization of market forces.

It will also require population control. Small families and stable populations both bring economic dividends. We must strive to achieve a worldwide population that maintains the fertility replacement level, an average of two children per couple. Some countries, such as Russia, Japan, Italy, and Germany, will undergo a decline in population over the next century; quite a few, including China and the United States, have reached replacement level and will probably have stable populations for the foreseeable future. But population is expected to double in many other countries, most of them developing nations whose environments are already stressed. The UN has studied several projections for global population growth and has determined that, in the most optimistic scenario, if population growth can be kept to 1.6 children per couple worldwide, the global population will peak at a bit less than 8 billion in 2041 and then start declining. This is an imperative goal, because further unchecked growth will hasten environmental disaster.

## ■ insure a free flow of information

Nothing that requires community cooperation can be done without a satisfactory flow of information and mutually accepted mechanisms for discussion and decision making. In every case where freedom of speech was inhibited by social or legal constraint, the Edo government was deprived of crucial feedback and was prone to disastrous decisions. Villagers enjoyed relative freedom of speech and were able to disseminate information rapidly and discuss its import, and this enabled rapid technical and economic development. The same is obviously true today. The only way to insure that we are receiving accurate feedback is to protect freedom of speech.

Freedom of speech and the free flow of information imply adequate education and literacy, particularly in developing areas, because printed materials that could prove lifesaving or lead to agricultural gains can only be effective in such a society. In particular, increasing education opportunities for girls leads to later marriage, smaller families, and more control over their economic lives, allowing them to both participate in and benefit from the two-way flow of information.

## ■ educate, educate, educate

There is no substitute for education. An educated person should be able to make use of historical knowledge, to access technical information and apply it, and to design. He should be capable of creative work expressing individual and cultural identity. Finally, an educated person should be able to feed himself, build or make most of what he needs, monitor and improve his environment, and communicate and collaborate effectively with people of different backgrounds and who have different concerns. Current education systems do a poor job of helping us develop these essential skills. They are grossly inadequate to the tasks at hand.

## ■ build a community through group tasks involving hand labor

Because of the nature of how people communicate while performing group tasks that involve

hand labor, this type of activity has proven essential to building and maintaining vital communities since prehistoric times. Such activities provide an irreplaceable educational setting for all ages. Over the course of a long day spent preparing, teaching, discussing, complimenting and criticizing, forming subgroups, accepting direction, and eating, drinking, and resting together, group members learn a lot about essential skills and about each other, their community, its history, and its values. New relationships are forged across generational lines, and an individual can be both a teacher and a learner. It is an ideal situation in which to introduce a new member, to inform others of important life events, and to disseminate information and receive feedback. Our current social structures and technical methods provide almost no opportunity for these important group activities. Out of the segregation and limited-purpose social groups that currently proliferate, new better-integrated networks can arise, however; think of what has emerged in recent years with tinkerers and inventors, where formerly isolated hobbyists have coalesced into a far-flung network of "makers." Similar opportunities should be recognized and encouraged.

## ■ houses: location, location, location

The importance of siting houses to take advantage of the sun, prevailing breezes, and natural drainage was obvious to experienced builders all over the world until mechanized heating, cooling, and infrastructure systems began to offer what seemed to be a free ride. Consequently, well-sited houses are now a rare exception. Rather than taking advantage of the best ground, a well-sited house actually improves its immediate environment by making use of ground that is not much good for anything else; it should act as an important boundary zone and be designed to mediate between microclimates. Building codes should probably be revised to reflect the fact that houses that are not carefully

## back to the farm

Japan has been home to communes and counterculture groups since the 1960's, and many of these were drawn to rural life, to farming and self sufficiency. There have also been many households who owned farms but who lived and worked in cities, venturing out on weekends to plant and weed. But recently we have begun to see another kind of "occasional" farmer, the "half farmer," a person who learns to farm in order to help feed their family, but who may have other passions, life's work, or occupation. A popular book by Naoki Shiomi, *Half Farmer/Half* , which was published in 2003, points out the viability of the lifestyle, and suggests that in it lies a means to well-being and contentment. As the economy has worsened in recent years, more and more educated professionals are retiring early, dropping out, or abandoning job searches and moving to farming regions. This can only be a good thing, both in order to restore the nation's declining farming population and to increase awareness of and interest in farming among people of different backgrounds. Hard numbers are difficult to come by, but the "half farmer" movement in Japan is an identifiable positive trend.

sited in this respect have a damaging effect on the functioning of natural systems.

A well-sited house takes advantage of solar exposure, of course, but it also is integrated into the natural water cycle. Good use should be made of ponds to store water and thermal energy, of terraces and small manmade wetlands to filter contaminants from the roof or lawn, and of the soil to absorb water from heavy rains and lessen erosion. Finally, there are many good groundcovers to use besides grass, particularly in dry areas. One can easily find plants adapted to the particular moisture and light conditions of a site, most requiring less care and watering than grass lawns. In every case, the most important thing is to integrate the house into the existing site, rather than eradicating the existing life and replacing it with something that wasn't there before.

### ■ aim for zero-waste materials

Straw as used by the Japanese of the Edo period is a model zero-waste material. At this point, producing materials with similar virtues should be a major thrust of industrial development.

This effort will involve designers most of all, but also major paper, plastic, and fiber producers, and ultimately marketers and retailers. Consumers, on the other hand, should notice no decrease in quality, increase in cost, or problems in availability.

According to Lester Brown, "The challenge is to replace the throwaway economy with a reduce-reuse-recycle economy. Officials should worry less about what to do with garbage and think more about how to avoid producing it in the first place." And architect and theorist William McDonough observes, "Pollution is a symbol of design failure."

Many excellent thinkers and designers are developing ways to rethink the product design process to take better advantage of recycling and reuse. They have demonstrated the advantages of rethinking the way raw material is used and have suggested that all of our products should enable their raw materials to be fully recovered and put back into the technological material flow upon which industry depends, just as biological material returns to nature. Both Germany and Japan have passed ordinances requiring appliances to be easy to disassemble and recycle, the goal being to prevent products from ending up as landfill.

McDonough and Braungart observe in *Cradle to Cradle* that recycling usually delays the ultimate disposition of material into landfill or incineration, but it does not prevent it. They have begun the search for materials that can be fully "upcycled," that is, reused as raw materials to make identical high-quality products. Only then will the goal of zero-waste be attainable.

### ■ understand that trade-offs are inevitable

There are always trade-offs between resource allocation, environmental impact, and the value and utility of the finished products we use, but these considerations are often hidden from the end user because the market fails to take them into account. We must learn to recognize what environmental costs are involved in manufacturing, transporting, storing, utilizing, and disposing of the items we use, not simply as individuals but on the mass scale most manufacturing entails. At present the indirect costs of energy extraction and use—in ecosystem damage, pollution, and climate change—exceed the direct costs and possibly even the benefits. We should be prepared to sacrifice personal convenience for a greater good.

### ■ change the meaning of literacy

Getting information into the hands of the people who can best make use of it is the only way to implement improvements. In the case of Edo Japan, a system evolved that took advantage of high overall literacy and centralized government

## the veranda solution

In the old days, Japanese verandas, or *engawa*, were found in many contexts. In the farmhouse, they opened onto the workyard, in official buildings they overlooked formal courtyards. But it is the model provided by the aristocrat or warrior's house, the *shoin* and *sukiya* style house and garden unit, in which the engawa reached it's poetic design potential, and an intermediary space between the rooms of the house and the garden itself. And it is this model that inspires most Japanese architects today when they include an engawa in their designs. It is possible to make engawa of many sizes, to enclose them or leave them open, to detail them traditionally or make them out of glass and aluminum. An engawa allows a building or wing to work well with another as an ensemble, and helps define and shape the exterior space as well as the interior.

But it is essential that it lie between an important room and a garden, and that it is separated from the room itself by panels which allow most of the wall to open up. In fact, there are houses that are all engawa, like the aptly named "Engawa House" by Tezuka and Tezuka—a a forty-foot engawa whose backing wall disappears without a trace to join the entire interior of the house to the garden. Of the many traditional features from the Edo period that have continued in use in home designs until the present, such as shoji, tatami, and tokonoma, the engawa has proven to be especially adaptable to new styles and materials, and stimulating for architects to think about. It allows homes to be both contemporary and traditional at the same time, and to handsomely provide good natural air circulation and connection to the outdoors.

## back to thatch

While the use of thatch began to decline in urban areas in Japan during the Edo period, it remained the most common material for rural roofs until about a century ago. But its flammable properties and the availability of inexpensive alternatives like corrugated iron caused thatch roofs to almost disappear during the twentieth century, and the slowly evolved and refined craft techniques involved in thatching faded along with them. This is why it is heartening to observe an upsurge of interest in traditional thatching—*kayabuki*—and a gradual redissemination of knowledge and skill. The designation of the village of Shirakawa-go, in Gifu Prefecture, with its dozens of thatched-roof farmhouses, as a UN World Heritage Site in 1996 gave thatching in Japan a big boost. Expert thatchers were suddenly in demand, and as house after house was rethatched, a new generation of expert craftsmen was born. It is still an expensive way to roof, sufficient supplies of pampas grass or other appropriate material are a bit hard to come by, and the fire concerns that caused it to disappear in the first place remain, but the craft has undoubtedly experienced a rebirth.

information gathering, as well as sophisticated printing technology and skilled illustrators, to reach rural farmers quickly and efficiently. Our era is unparalleled in both information gathering and dissemination, and it is the most highly literate in history. So why doesn't change happen more quickly? One answer is vested interests who are able to exert undue influence on the flow of information in order to maintain advantageous political and market conditions. Another is quite simply the cacophony: the proliferation of competing voices, all claiming if not authority then validity, makes it difficult to reach confident conclusions. Parsing and evaluating the messages requires an ever-evolving literacy with media and the factors that influence it. The answer is to do all we can to improve essential literacy through basic education, while also teaching the skills necessary to critically interpret mass media.

### ■ look for symbiosis and pattern solutions

The symbiosis exhibited in traditional rice paddies, where fish and frogs thrive and act as natural pest control, is an excellent "pattern" system

that we should emulate in our own agricultural activity. Pattern solutions are not limited to agriculture but can suggest themselves in any environment. Home gardeners can rely upon biological pest control by providing attractive habitat for birds or even bats; there are many ways to handle rain runoff so that it improves habitat for other species, like frogs and fish, rather than being sent down the drain; trees can be placed so that they provide shade for other plants, and architectural elements like walls will automatically provide shade on one side and reflect light on another, improving the environment for species that thrive in one or the other.

### ■ use materials like thatch

The virtues of a thatched roof are many. It is renewable and the owners can make it themselves, but only with communal assistance, thereby providing an frequent opportunity for an important type of social interaction. This kind of roof is engineered to take advantage of small structural members ganged together and countless individual straw fibers in bundled form, so the relative cost of individual elements is very low. It is very efficient in terms of insulation and economical to maintain, and it makes use of a household effluent, smoke, to strengthen, season, and preserve it. When its useful life as roofing is over, it can be reused in other ways, even to provide energy. We should be searching for materials that possess similar virtues.

### ■ limit the use of livestock

The Japanese discovered very early on that farmland could be devoted to growing food for humans or for livestock, but not both. Faced with an acute shortage of arable land, they gradually phased livestock out of their agricultural system. We are currently facing similar environmental pressures and the conclusion is inescapable.

Cattle are not an efficient source of protein. It takes approximately seven kilograms of grain to produce one kilogram of beef, plus large quantities of water, since the water used to grow the feed as well as that consumed by the animals must be taken into account. Add to this the ecological damage caused by overgrazing—the desertification of western and northern China can largely be attributed to this—and the clear-cutting of rainforest in Brazil and elsewhere to provide grazing land, and the tremendous cumulative cost of livestock production can be glimpsed. It may be necessary to stop the growth of human and livestock populations in order to halt desertification. So what are the alternatives?

People in developed countries, where obesity is a problem and the diet has a large percentage of animal products, should shift their diet to include more items that are low on the food chain, like vegetables of course, but also poultry and seafood. Aquaculture shows great promise of becoming a major source of animal protein, because herbivorous fish are very efficient in converting feed into protein. The process will involve several steps: increasing the protein yield of livestock by increasing the use of soybean meal for feed; shifting human consumption from beef to other kinds of animal protein that are more efficient consumers of grain and water; and moving our diet down the food chain, at which point it may well resemble the traditional Japanese diet.

### ■ manage and monitor the forest

Tremendous strides have been made in forest

## the revitalized forest

Japan's breakthroughs in forest management during the Edo period were extremely positive developments. However, the vast monocultures of *hinoki* and *sugi* that have characterized Japan's managed forests since then, especially the replanting that followed World War II, was ecologically questionable, though very few voices were raised in question or opposition. That's why the gradual acceptance of the biologically and environmentally sound reforestation techniques of Akira Miyawaki are cause for hope. Now in his eighties, Miyawaki is an ecology pioneer who has refined techniques for restoring forests to their native state, in which broadleaf trees predominate and forests are diverse, multilayered, and self-regulating. Miyawaki has started a movement for replanting that has affected the thinking and practice of communities and organizations all over the globe, and he is an outstanding educator, scientist, and policy adviser. Look for his book, *The Healing Power of Forests: The Philosophy behind Restoring Earth's Balance with Native Trees* (in English, from Kosei Publishing Co.), for a clear and concise description of the principles that motivate his work.

management over the course of the past century, and despite the undeniable excesses of the lumber industry, forestry research and forest protection attract particularly devoted and environmentally aware individuals. No matter which continent one examines, there is very little room now for "unmanaged" forests; "management" can mean many things, ranging from the careful monitoring of an otherwise untouched forest environment to intensive human activity intended to shape and reinforce the character of the woodland. From this point forward, all of our forests will require careful planning, monitoring, and maintenance work in order to continue to provide a healthy and diverse environment for human use as well as for other species.

Maintaining the overall environmental balance of our forests and insuring their continued adequate functioning as moderators of the atmosphere and of our watersheds will undoubtedly mean increasing the size and number of forest preserves, periodic forest closures, and moratoria on timber cutting. Thinking in the scale of centuries rather than decades, we must apply what we have learned about the importance of allowing natural damage and predation to occur and propel the forest succession cycle, but on a larger scale. If successful, this should allow periods of intensive timber harvesting to continue as well.

### ■ understand how ecosystems work

Forest ecosystems are built on a complex balance of plants, animals, microorganisms, water, and soil, and they have a built-in elasticity and resiliency. In the course of natural development and succession, the physical configuration of the forest cover and the balance of species undergo constant change, accelerated or retarded by natural fires, shifts in climate, changes in the watershed, and geological activity, all the while remaining healthy. Man can take advantage of this natural resiliency to influence the balance of species, thereby increasing the number and accessibility of desired ones. But this resiliency has limits. History is full of examples of human communities that have ignored these limits or misjudged them with disastrous consequences.

### ■ institute a global tree census

It's probably time for a global tree census like the nationwide ones carried out by the Japanese from the seventeenth century onward. Identifying individual trees may be one way to insure that they are no longer taken for granted. The very scale of the project may be daunting, but if undertaken as part of logging, replanting, and monitoring activities, and by using a combination of eyes on the ground and imaging and biological identification technologies, it is achievable. Many of our forest challenges can only be met by mobilizing large numbers of people, by making them stakeholders in the survival of particular stands of trees. Involving them in a census would be an excellent first step.

### ■ use it to keep it

The past century has witnessed an alarming decrease in the variety of wood species in common use both in Japan and in the rest of the developed world. Local lumber use has been replaced by a global timber economy based on the industrialized silviculture and exploitation of a handful of species.

Paradoxically, the best way to increase the numbers of other species of wood in our forests is to nurture a market for them, so that they will be planted in great numbers once again. Bearing in mind that uncontrolled logging of tropical species like mahogany and rosewood has brought them to the brink of endangerment, the new multi-species forestry must be designed from the outset to be sustainable. Only mature trees should be cut, and on a selective basis. The result will be both inherently more diverse forests and a renewed familiarity with the beauties of many woods in our daily life.

## slip culture is a pattern solution

Slip culture—trees grown from cuttings—involves the intelligent combination of botanical species based on how they interact and the mutual reinforcement of desirable characteristics. Simply by carefully choosing where to root the cuttings based on what is growing nearby, the moisture they receive, as well as the shade and wind, can be controlled without the need for manmade infrastructure or augmentation. This is a prime example of visualizing a biological process as a symbiotic interaction among species, a pattern solution in which many different requirements are met with one gesture, requiring much less energy and inputs overall.

## post-harvest salvage should utilize forest byproducts

Currently, after a forest is logged and the equipment has moved out, what is left looks like a moonscape. In contrast to the old Japanese way, where anyone who wanted to was allowed into the site to gather offcuts, bark, roots, leaves, and anything else of potential utility they could salvage, freshly logged forests today are usually an impassable no-go zone, and no effort is made to recover byproducts. Logging practice should be reexamined and redesigned to recover and maximize the use of secondary products.

## rethink lumber transportation to use less energy and be less disruptive to the ecosystem

Traditional forestry practices made excellent use of gravity, mountain slopes, and natural river currents to provide most of the energy required to transport the cut timber great distances. This was true in Europe and America during the nineteenth century as well as in Japan. Compared to the massive wheeled and tracked vehicles currently used to bring wood out of the forest and down the mountain, the former systems may seem to lack flexibility and speed, but in fact they have the tremendous virtue of using energy that is nearly free. If lumber transportation were approached as a design problem in which the widespread environmental costs are factored into the economic calculations—carbon from fossil fuels, pollution, habitat disruption, erosion, pesticides, and weed control—relying on gravity and natural currents would be recognized as an extremely economical approach.

## green curtains

During summer months, Japanese often used lightweight, removable trellises covered with climbing vines to help shade the interiors of their homes. We might call them "green curtains," and they were often sources of food (beans and squash), or color (morning glories), as well as shade. Recently the "green curtain" idea has found renewed acceptance, and has been adapted for use on institutional buildings. One corporation has added them to five factories, using morning glories and edible bitter gourd plants to make living shade curtains over 140 meters in length. They found the added shade greatly reduced the need for air-conditioning in the factories, particularly in the morning.

Other groups have begun similar projects to add green curtains to schools and government buildings across the country, and have established curriculum guidelines that use the creation and upkeep of the curtains to teach environmental science to elementary and junior high school students. The idea is excellent, inexpensive, easily approachable, and rooted in tradition, and we can expect to see it spread soon to other sectors of society as well.

# II

# the sustainable city
## the carpenter of edo

W e are tired but elated as we enter the city of Edo. Like the vast majority of our fellow travelers, we are journeying on foot. Too frugal to hire a palanquin and too low in status to be allowed a horse, we have worn out two pairs of straw sandals in the past week alone. We passed through a toll barrier yesterday at the edge of the mountains, crowded with fellow travelers going in both directions. Our documentation was in order, and we were eventually allowed to pass with only a cursory search of our meager belongings, for we seemed unlikely to be smugglers of weapons, subversive publications, or contraband luxury goods.

This morning we have arrived at Naito Shinjuku, the bustling western gateway to the city. It is teeming with farmers toting shoulder loads of fresh vegetables and charcoal to sell door to door, and others hauling cartloads of human waste out of the city. Mounted samurai, foot soldiers, and palanquins with hidden occupants add to the throng, and the smell of cooking assails us from inns on both sides of this road that leads to the town center.

Edo can be approached from several directions. Commercial traffic and goods nearly always travel by boat, either coast-hugging cargo ships or river barges. People making the journey usually come by road, making as much use as possible of the five "great highways" that radiate outward from the city and link it with distant provinces.

The city lies in a vast alluvial plain, close by a protected bay, and while not entirely flat its ground can best be described as undulating rather than truly hilly. Though there are five distinct ridges that jut toward the bay like fingers, there are no great promontories from which the entire city can be regarded, and the mountains to the north, south, and west are a full day's journey away. One gets the sense of being gradually surrounded by the city the deeper one penetrates, as truly rural landscape gives way to farm fields interspersed with commercial neighborhoods. Eventually, even the fields disappear from view and all is buildings, bustle, and clamor.

Edo, which has its roots as a small farming and fishing village during the medieval period, was selected as the site for a castle in 1457. When the victorious warlord Tokugawa Ieyasu chose the city as his new capital in the beginning

Nearly everyone travels on foot. If they are not loaded down with goods for sale, they are likely to have a small travel pack slung over their shoulders.

KANASEDO ROAD

KANEJI TEMPLE

NIKKO ROAD

KANDA RIVER

KANDA

SUMIDA RIVER

NAITO SHINJUKU

YOTSUYA GATE

EDO CASTLE

DAIMYO KOJI

NIHOMBASHI

FUKAGAWA

KIBA

ZOJOJI TEMPLE

EDO BAY

TOKAIDO ROAD

Shinagawa

Takanawa gate

| | COMMONER | | OTHER SAMURAI |
| --- | --- | --- | --- |

| | TEMPLE | | FARMLAND |
| --- | --- | --- | --- |

| | DAIMYO |
| --- | --- |

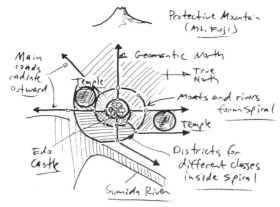

Protective Mountain (Mt. Fuji)

Main roads radiate outward

Geomantic North

True North

Temple

Moats and rivers form spiral

Temple

Edo Castle

Districts for different classes inside spiral

Sumida River

Edo was laid out according to geomantic principles of power and protection, with military and residential districts spiraling outward from the castle at the center. It has proved to be an excellent, flexible plan.

The huge disparity in land allocation meant that commoners lived in very crowded neighborhoods, most samurai had room for nice gardens, and lords ('daimyo') each had several large estates within the city limits (but to be fair, these estates also housed large garrisons of soldiers)

EDO POPULATION
Total: 1.3 ~ 1.4 million

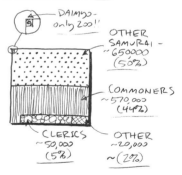

DAIMYO - only 200!!

OTHER SAMURAI - ~650000 (50%)

COMMONERS ~570,000 (44%)

CLERICS ~50,000 (5%)

OTHER ~20,000 ~(2%)

LAND USE

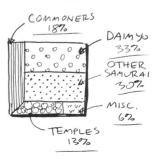

COMMONERS 18%

DAIMYO 33%

OTHER SAMURAI 30%

MISC. 6%

TEMPLES 13%

of the seventeenth century, he initiated an unprecedented period of growth, made possible by sophisticated civil engineering technology, economic where-withal, and concentrated political power. The plan was to be flexible, with growth in mind, and as it unfolded over the course of centuries the wisdom of the idea became evident.

From the start the landscape was both a benefit and a challenge. The plain in which the city sits was naturally marshy and easily flooded, and this land was gradually reclaimed by landfill. The radiating ridges, however, provided a basis for secure construction in the center of the city. The city planners took natural conditions into account with great foresight, so that the existing geology, watersheds and drainage, vegetation, and air currents would work to the city's benefit and allow an optimal balance between the manmade elements and water, hills, and trees. As a result, Edo presents an extremely varied city-scape, a network of places possessing strong individual identities.

The primary technique used in planning Edo is a grid that surrounds the castle, adjusted to fit local variations in topography. Axes exist, but unlike European cities the predominant organization is through irregular concentric rings that spiral outward, taking into account environmental, defensive, and economic needs, as well as spiritual beliefs.

The castle occupies the center, surrounded by a ring of warrior garrisons and residences, then loosely by temple grounds and shrines; beyond that are

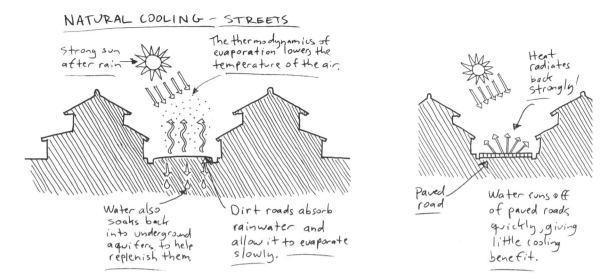

NATURAL COOLING - STREETS

Strong sun after rain

The thermodynamics of evaporation lowers the temperature of the air.

Water also soaks back into underground aquifers to help replenish them.

Dirt roads absorb rainwater and allow it to evaporate slowly.

Heat radiates back strongly!

Paved road

Water runs off of paved roads quickly, giving little cooling benefit.

commoners' districts, and finally farmland and the sea. Early on, canals and moats were used to augment rivers for protection and for the transportation of heavy building materials, like stone and timber, for the castle. This system has expanded along with the city, so that at this point Edo not only is heavily dependent on its waterways, it derives much of its character from them. Almost the entire commoners' city can be considered a port, extending deeply inland along the waterways, lending vitality to every district. There are over five hundred bridges in Edo, and many neighborhoods take their names from the bridges around which they have grown.

The five major highways that radiate outward from Edo were designed to take advantage of natural topography, and so they follow the hilly ridges that extend outward from the center of the city and coincide with the placement of the warrior districts. As a result, the expansive, green residences of *daimyo* and other samurai are usually easily accessible from these main roads, with narrower roads to the commoners' districts branching off downhill in many directions, reinforcing the topographically based zoning.

Thanks to the shogun's requirement that all daimyo and their families must spend alternate years in Edo, the city has an extremely fluid population and incredible inflow of wealth. Hundreds of daimyo and tens of thousands of samurai retainers travel back and forth between the city and their home provinces, resulting in a very large population of solitary males. That and the concentration of wealth (the daimyo are also required to surrender nearly half of their income to the central government) are incredible economic engines that have stimulated tremendous growth in the artisan and merchant populations whose

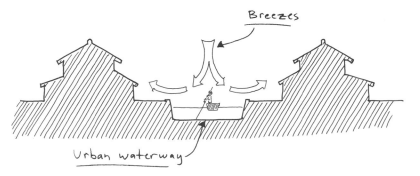

NATURAL COOLING - WATERWAYS

Breezes

Urban waterway

Edo's dense urban areas are laced with canals and rivers that channel and cool breezes.

livelihood ultimately depends upon providing the ruling classes with goods and services. Edo produces very little but consumes a lot.

## clean streets, green streets

We are on our way to visit a carpenter named Sadakichi. His home is in a back-alley rowhouse in Kanda, one of the livelier downtown neighborhoods to which commoners have been segregated. The easiest way to get there would be to hire one of the innumerable passenger boats plying the city's canals, but continuing by foot is cheaper and we get to pass through Nihombashi, the dense and vibrant commercial center.

Edo is divided into distinct neighborhoods both administratively and culturally. The most important and striking division is between the samurai districts and those set aside for commoners. The former are allotted property on the high ground of the city, the generosity of the plot being commensurate with the family's status. These are quiet, spacious neighborhoods, but they must really be considered housing for military personnel, domesticated garrisons. Edo now boasts a population of over 1,300,000, of which only 650,000, or 50 percent, are samurai (including daimyo), yet they are allowed to occupy 63 percent of the land, and the most desirable spots at that. There are about 50,000 monks and other religious, whose shrines and temples are allotted about 13 percent of the city's prime land area. The 600,000 commoners are forced to make do with 18 percent of the land, mostly reclaimed waterfront, as well as property straddling several major thoroughfares. This spatial confinement accounts for the

Urban Greenery  The city has many large areas that have been left in a natural state, particularly watershed features like the Tameike Pond.

high population density in the commoners' districts (68,807 persons per square kilometer) as well as for the city's commercial hustle and energy.

Business is good in Edo, and it is the commoners who benefit from it most of all. Nowhere is this more apparent than in Nihombashi, where block after block of shops, from simple stalls to gargantuan emporia, sell every possible necessity of life and innumerable specialties, a large proportion of which are imported from other parts of the country. Silk brocade from Kyoto, tea from Shikoku, lacquerware from Aizu, pottery from Aki—the size and dynamism of the marketplace makes fortunes for merchants around the country. And if one has the wherewithal, it is even possible to purchase luxuries, like fine worked leather, antiques, glassware, and woolen garments, imported from overseas.

Edo is a massive consumer, that draws its sustenance and supplies from the entire country. The necessity of supporting a large nonproducing overclass of samurai as well as a burgeoning commoner population has turned it into a gigantic marketplace. Our route is lined with shops, even in the hilly samurai districts, but it is nothing compared to the celebrated Tokaido "highway."

Travelers entering Edo on the Tokaido find markets, shops, warehouses, eateries—all commercial establishments—several blocks deep on either side all the way from the city limits to the Nihombashi terminus (a distance of roughly seven kilometers) and beyond. If one didn't stop to rest or windowshop, it might be possible to experience this one long arcade-like shopping street by devoting the better part of a day to it. Multiply this several fold to account for the other main shopping streets in town, like the one we are now on, and the true scale of Edo's commercially active population begins to sink in. This is the largest city in the world in terms of population, and its inhabitants are all being provided with food, water, fuel, and the necessary goods of life in a remarkably efficient and even aesthetically attractive manner.

The streets themselves are dirt, and they are devoid of sidewalks of any kind, but the scarcity of draft animals—only a few oxcarts, and no carriages or heavy wagons—means the traffic is overwhelmingly pedestrian. Oxcarts are used only for extremely heavy items like lumber and bales of rice, though both will be moved by other means if at all possible. There are many handcarts, however, as well as palanquins of varying degrees of dignity, and occasionally a daimyo and his retinue, including mounted horsemen, will pass through. Though they become a sea of mud after strong rains, Edo's streets are free of manure and don't present nearly the health hazards of their European counterparts. The dirt streets also absorb most rainfall, and during the peak of summer they are often sprinkled with water to cool the surrounding air. Unlike paved roads, these streets do not radiate stored summer heat back into the urban environment, and the cooling effect of the evaporating water is measurable.

Many parts of Edo are extremely green and wooded. This is particularly true of the large temple districts such as Zojoji in Shiba and Kaneiji in Ueno, whose beautiful grounds are open to all classes. Almost every neighborhood has one or more smaller temples or shrines whose trees provide shade and beauty as well. The samurai classes live in what can be called garden compounds, but movement through their neighborhoods is often restricted, so their greenery is not really a shared amenity. There are quite a few undeveloped places in town, usually marshy ground and ponds, that look absolutely bucolic. The many riverbanks are well planted, particularly since Shogun Yoshimune began a city beautification project in 1721. His plan included planting *sakura* (cherry) trees along the rivers, tearing down some of the less essential castle walls to make

Townspeople don't have room for large gardens, but they have found many ways to adorn their surroundings with all manner of plants and flowers,

# URBAN VISTAS

Many streets and waterways are aligned
with distant landscape features, like Mt. Fuji

Suruga-cho shopping street

Many samurai neighborhoods have fine
views of the ocean

Kasumigaseki -
(after Shimizu + Fuse)

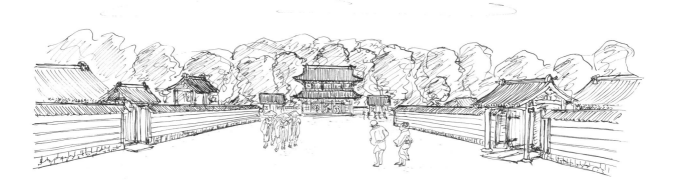

Zozoji Temple

Many streets are aligned with important gates and buildings.

Atago Hill

Hills and other urban landscape features are made part of the scenery

green space, and planting pines on the tops of others. He also established a few public parks.

The merchants' districts are primarily utilitarian. There are many trees on the streets but no tree-lined boulevards. We see trees behind garden walls and behind houses, but it is clear that where trees must vie with commerce for precious street frontage, commerce will usually win. On the other hand, gardening seems to be an incredibly popular pastime, for potted plants and flowers are tended with obvious care in front of nearly every house and establishment and on every balcony. Even the crowded backstreets with their narrow alleys and constant activity are full of tiny shrubs, bonsai trees, flowers, and herbs. Since the commoners' districts of Edo are built on landfill, the soil underfoot is of extremely poor quality with high clay content, but gardening is so popular that the sale of high-quality garden soil carted in from the rich farming areas to the north has become a major business. Edoites find ways to make their city green despite the extremely restricted space, and they have over time improved the quality of its soil.

Edo is also a city of views. From the beginning, the city planners considered both the nearby hills and distant landscape when laying out the major thoroughfares, and consequently many streets are aligned to provide urban vistas of Mount Fuji to the west, Mount Tsukuba to the north, and scenic hills and river views around town. These "borrowed" landscapes transform entire streetscapes into aesthetic experiences whose impact is celebrated in paintings and prints. Despite the relative paucity of tree-lined streets, nearly every avenue ends in a vista of green hills, distant mountains, or water, rendered more beautiful by contrast with the workaday.

Walking is a way to participate in community life, to learn, to observe and become part of one's surroundings. Walking is essential to fitness, and Edoites are nothing if not fit. Their city can be described as a network of connected places, each with a distinct identity and sense of belonging, but also a public face that welcomes interaction and interest. Wherever one turns, one finds places to eat, drink, rest, watch, learn, and discuss. For inhabitants and visitors alike it is an intellectual and creative powerhouse, and nowhere is this more evident than in Nihombashi.

## nihombashi: the ultimate marketplace

By midmorning, when we arrive, Nihombashi is thronged. Everyone is buying, selling, ordering, or delivering—and the din of commerce is deafening. The shop clerks and workers are very recognizable in their liveries: short

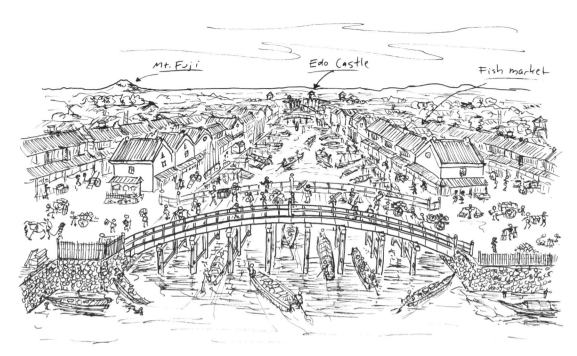

Mt. Fuji

Edo Castle

Fish market

*happi* jackets emblazoned with their employer's name or logo. Each shop has one or two clerks standing outside shouting or singing advertisements and greetings; peddlers pass back and forth along the street in great numbers selling everything from prepared food, housewares, and religious amulets to spices and sandals, adding their cries to the commercial din. The peddlers occasionally set their loads down to serve customers, their carrying crates instantly transformed into tiny shop stalls.

There are many porters whose sole job is to carry things for others: impossibly large stacks of boxes, buckets, baskets, brooms, books, or bolts of cloth. We find ourselves constantly having to dodge overloaded pushcarts whose sweating haulers can't always see beyond their loads.

The variety of people is equally dizzying. Shops employ many women, and quite a few are run by them. Children are frequently employed as well, both as shop labor and as runners. A lot of the customers are what we might call "commercial customers," making purchases and picking up goods on behalf of other businesses. There are many housewives, shopping alone if they live nearby, but otherwise accompanied by friends, servants, or male relatives. We see men taking a few minutes off from their own businesses to shop for clothing or tools, or even to indulge a hobby like poetry—there are hundreds of bookstores in Edo— or art—there are dozens of art dealers as well. And though we see a handful of samurai men (but few if any samurai women) who appear to be shopping for

NIHOM BASHI ("Japan-bridge")
Lies at the crossing of the major road (Tokaido) the major urban waterway (Nihombashi River)

themselves, most of them are making official purchases on behalf of the sho-gun or the daimyo households to which they are attached. We see them in small groups swaggering about the huge fish market that lines the Nihombashi River, picking out large numbers of the best specimens and barking, "Appropriated for the shogun's household!" Though the procurers are said to be fair, the par-ticular fishmonger thus honored may or may not receive just compensation.

For all the crowds and activity, the streets are fairly clean. In addition to the absence of animal waste, there are none of the heaps of rotting garbage so foully evident in the great cities of the West. What refuse we see is likely to be on a wagon being hauled away for composting, reuse, or recycling. True, the fish market smells like fish markets everywhere, and particular shops have their own odors and aromas—raw lacquer at the cabinetmaker's shop, chopped straw at the tatami-maker's, wood shavings at the box-maker's—but it is the aroma of food and cooking smoke that pervades, along with the unmistakable scent of the ocean.

We cross the tall, arched Nihombashi Bridge, the starting point for the five great roads and the point from which all distances are measured. It is the con-ceptual and spiritual center of the nation, yet it is basically just a crowded, noisy, ordinary wooden bridge, neither particularly grand nor elegant, and after crossing it we are disappointed to find that we don't feel particularly dif-ferent. To the left, the river is lined on both sides with massive whitewashed warehouses, and we can see the outer moat of the castle just two blocks away, tree-topped weathered gray stone walls guarding the opposite bank, white-washed battlements rising in the distance beyond. If we continued to the right along the central fish market we would soon find ourselves at the Sumida River. We will continue straight ahead, however, through the remaining four or five blocks of Nihombashi, across a small canal, and into Kanda.

If Nihombashi is the most densely populated part of Edo, Kanda is a close rival. Our friend Sadakichi the carpenter lives here—not surprisingly in a dis-trict called Kanda Daiku-cho ("Carpenter-town"). Though it was once very important to the lumber import business in Edo, all of the large operations have since been relocated across the river to an area less fire-prone and more convenient for transport and storage. Quite a few lumberyards remain clus-tered in the few square blocks of Daiku-cho, serving as distribution outlets to support the construction needs of both the surrounding commoners' city and also nearby government facilities and samurai homes. But most primary wood processing—turning the roughly squared timbers that arrive from the moun-tains in rafts into boards—takes place at Kiba ("wood place") across the river, and sawn wood makes its way to Daiku-cho by canal boat and handcart.

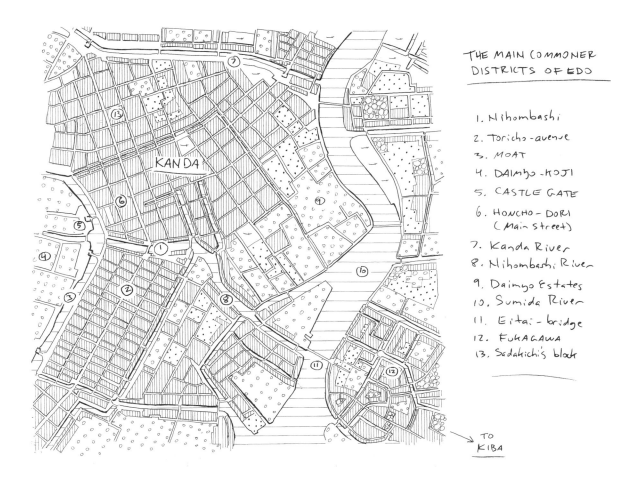

KANDA

THE MAIN COMMONER
DISTRICTS OF EDO

1. Nihombashi
2. Toricho-avenue
3. MOAT
4. DAIMyo-KOJI
5. CASTLE GATE
6. HONCHO-DORI
   (Main street)
7. Kanda River
8. Nihombashi River
9. Daimyo Estates
10. Sumida River
11. Eitai-bridge
12. FUKAGAWA
13. Sadakichi's block

TO
KIBA

| | |
|---|---|
| COMMONER |
| TEMPLE |
| DAIMyo |
| OTHER SAMURAI |
| FARMLAND |
| GOVERNMENT FACILITY |

## the fabric of edo: the block system

The urban layout of this district, based on a block system whose features are replicated with varying degrees in all of the districts in which commoners live, is marvelous in its rationality, efficiency, and flexibility. Though the terrain and natural watercourses make a true citywide grid impossible, most of Nihombashi and Kanda have been divided into urban blocks based on multiples of the standard structural grid used for houses, called the *shakkanho*.

Chinese in origin, the shakkanho has been in use with little modification for over a thousand years. One *shaku* is about 30 centimeters in length, almost exactly one Imperial foot; one *ken* is six shaku (1.8 m). Though the houses and businesses of the wealthiest and most prosperous merchants can be quite vast, most houses for commoners are either nine shaku (1.5 ken) or exactly two ken in width. The Edo city planners devised blocks whose dimensions are multiples

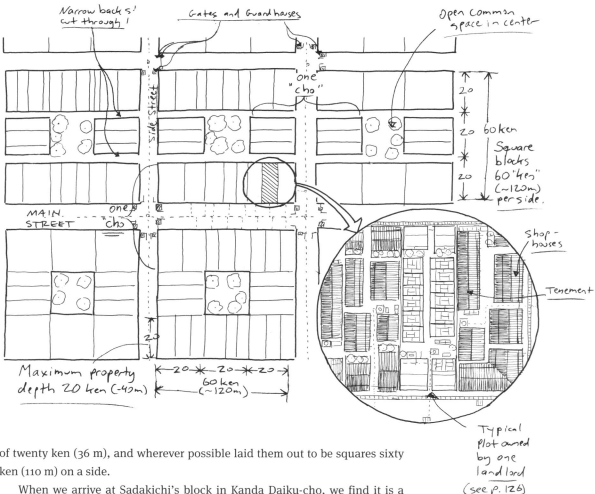

EDO URBAN BLOCK SYSTEM — KANDA DISTRICT —

Narrow backs! cut through!

Gates and Guardhouses

Open common space in center

one "cho"

Side Street

one cho

MAIN STREET

20

20 60 ken Square blocks 60 "ken" (~120m) per side.

20

Shop-houses

Tenement

Maximum property depth 20 ken (~40m)

20 * 20 * 20
60 ken
(~120m)

20

Typical plot owned by one landlord (see p. 126)

The Edo block system was made as rational as possible while still accomodating natural features. It is easily subdivided and administered.

of twenty ken (36 m), and wherever possible laid them out to be squares sixty ken (110 m) on a side.

When we arrive at Sadakichi's block in Kanda Daiku-cho, we find it is a typical one. This arrangement allows shops and houses to be built around the periphery of the block to a depth of 20 ken, leaving an empty 20-ken square in the center. Intended to be left as open fields to provide a safe gathering place in the event of fire or earthquake and to provide space for organizing activities like festivals, over the decades these spaces often become neighborhood vegetable gardens, wooded pockets, or grassy play areas for children. In one case, in a block adjacent to Kanda Daiku-cho, the authorities turned the central square into a major greenmarket, and the rest of the block soon followed, making it the city's prime greengrocer, even supplying the household of the shogun himself.

Though we see many varieties and degrees of sophistication and finish in the Edo merchant townhouses, the most common type found on the major streets is of two-story fireproof construction, with roofs of dark-gray tile. The exterior walls have been coated with thick plaster blackened with soot and then polished to a dull sheen, lending the streets a unity despite the great variety of detail from house to house. All adhere to the modular proportion system based on the ken. The most modest townhouses are only 1½ or 2 ken in width; larger ones are 3, 4, or more. Regardless of size, these houses are dignified, handsome, utilitarian, and efficient, and they are they are enlivened by colorful carved and painted signs, bright and attractive displays of goods, printed posters and advertisements, and numerous potted plants.

Street frontage is at a premium, so the houses are twice as deep as they are wide. Their ground floors are occupied by shops whose fronts are opened by means of sliding shutters. Most have generous street-side overhangs to protect pedestrians from the hot sun or downpours and to encourage them to linger, and even the largest shop-houses maintain an intimate scale on the street because of the low height of their overhangs. There is usually a dirt-floored space (doma) in front, which sometimes extends as a utility corridor all the way to the rear of the house, where the wood-floored workspace and kitchen are located.

Like their counterparts around Japan, these townhouses are models of natural climate control for high-density urban areas. Most have been designed with tiny gardens in back, and quite a few have gardens in the center. These shady and moist *tsubo niwa*—two-story green shade pockets, really—perform a critical environmental control function, providing a continuous supply of naturally cooled air that is drawn through the rest of the house with the slightest breeze. The tsubo niwa also links the living space on the second floor into the overall air circulation scheme, so that with the deft use of sliding doors and shutters it becomes a highly controllable bi-level cross-ventilation system. Street, shaded front, pocket garden, rear yard, unobstructed but adjustable flow-through ventilation: multiply these elements by the tens of thousands citywide and the genius of the system becomes apparent.

Each side of the block is a rectangular chunk with 60 ken of street frontage (room for thirty or more typical shops), and though the individual lots can extend 20 ken back from the street, most shop buildings require less than a quarter of that. The remaining space is filled with rows of small rental

NATURAL COOLING
Deep eaves, wide openings, and carefully placed shady gardens provide natural cooling.
"Tsubo niwa," center garden

airflow

street

Rear garden

airflow

Center gardens are more common in Osaka and Kyoto, while Edo folks get much the same effect from small rear gardens.

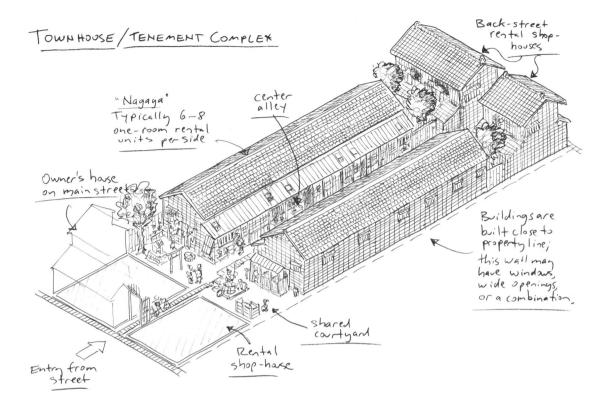

TOWNHOUSE / TENEMENT COMPLEX

"Nagaya"
Typically 6–8
one-room rental
units per side

center
alley

Back-street
rental shop-
houses

Owner's house
on main street

Buildings are
built close to
property line;
this wall may
have windows,
wide openings,
or a combination.

shared
courtyard

Entry from
street

Rental
shop-house

dwellings—single-story, one-room tenements for the most part. These are not slums, but home to people of all ages and from all walks of life: craftsmen, teachers, peddlers, doctors, as well as gardeners, porters, servants, day laborers, and others. There are families of every size and type: couples, unmarried adults, widows.

Though their homes represent truly minimal dwelling spaces and suffer wear and tear as they age, they are well planned, well organized and policed, and well provided with essential services. Beyond this, they are designed to encourage and enhance community interaction and communication. It is estimated that up to three-quarters of the commoner population of Edo, if not more, makes its home in such tenements, or *nagaya* ("long house"). Our friend Sadakichi, in other words, lives very much like his neighbors.

We enter the tenement zone of the block through a simple gateway that spans the space between a pair of two-story shop-houses. We immediately find ourselves standing in a small plaza, with the nagaya arranged on either side

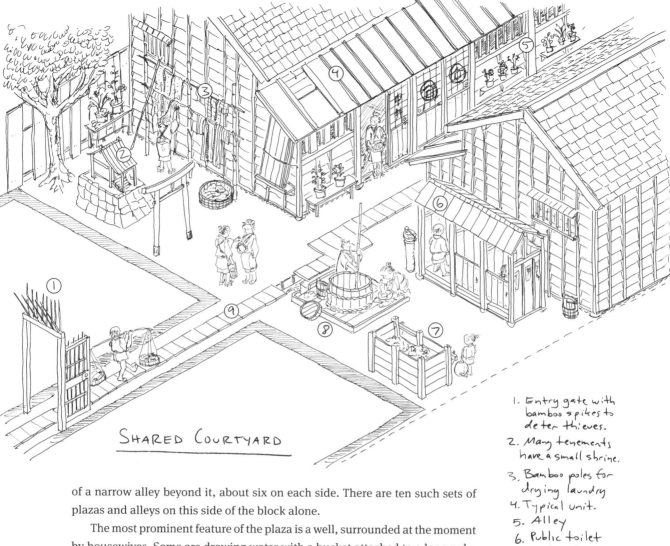

SHARED COURTYARD

1. Entry gate with bamboo spikes to deter thieves.
2. Many tenements have a small shrine.
3. Bamboo poles for drying laundry
4. Typical unit.
5. Alley
6. Public toilet
7. Rubbish bin
8. Well
9. Wastewater drain

of a narrow alley beyond it, about six on each side. There are ten such sets of plazas and alleys on this side of the block alone.

The most prominent feature of the plaza is a well, surrounded at the moment by housewives. Some are drawing water with a bucket attached to a long pole. Others are washing clothes in tubs set in the wide, shallow wooden basin at the foot of the well, or just passing the time of day with their neighbors. There is a rack with bamboo poles on which clothes are strung to dry, and some women have flattened their damp, disassembled kimono on tall freestanding wooden drying boards, which also removes creases from the fabric. There is a public latrine with two stalls used by both sexes and provided with a washbasin and clean water. There is a small red-painted Shinto shrine, this one for appeasing *kitsune*, the tricky fox spirit, and a board with notices and advertisements tacked to it. There is a large rubbish and recycling bin.

All of the residents pass through this plaza several times a day to use the well, latrine, and other facilities, or on their way to and from home, so it serves

as a natural communication center. The
tenement alley itself is technically a public space (even though privately owned
by the landlord) but, in a social sense,
it is clearly semiprivate. Strangers do not
feel comfortable entering the alley itself without
first identifying themselves at the plaza, and even
then they are likely to be initially regarded with suspicion.

The tenements are built on a scale and laid out in a way that
provides a strong local identity and sense of belonging, and this
shared identity extends outward to the main streets and includes the merchant landlords. As in a rural village, the residents of a block are considered
a political unit with interlocking and mutual responsibilities, and through the
tenement landlord, this responsibility devolves upon the residents as well. Just
as in the countryside, there are *go-nin-gumi* in the tenements, and everything is
reported. Shirkers are ostracized. The authorities usually leave the townspeople
alone and let them settle their own disputes, but when they intervene they usually come down hard.

The positive side of this is that things get done. Though the muddy alley
itself imposes a limit on how clean everything can be, all residents are expected
to pitch in to keep things neat. The landlord is expected to repair or replace broken latrine doors, clothes racks, basins, and other shared items promptly and
without undue complaint. In reality landlords come in many degrees of consci-
entiousness and frugality, but where public health and safety are at stake, even
the tenement dwellers have legal recourse.

### freshwater, and an ample supply

The public services—water, sanitation, and refuse—are all worthy of note,
though the people of Edo take them for granted. The water system is the
most complex of these and the most technologically advanced. The natural
lowland plain in which the city is located was selected partly because of its
rivers. Wells, however, presented difficulties from the beginning: because the
groundwater beneath the marshy coastland was usually too brackish for drinking purposes, adequate wells could only be dug further inland. As more ground
along the bay was reclaimed to house the rapidly increasing population, and
the rivers were diverted to form the basis for the castle moats, however, the
freshwater supply soon became inadequate to the demand, and ambitious,
large-scale water engineering projects were begun.

EDO BAY

N

0   10   20 km

## EDO WATER SYSTEM

SOURCES
Rivers
1. TAMAGAWA
2. ARAKAWA
3. FURUTONE

Ponds
4. INOKASHIRA
5. ZENPUKUJI
6. MYOSHOJI

MAJOR AQUEDUCTS

7. TAMAGAWA AQ. (longest!)
8. KANDA AQ. (oldest!)
9. SENKAWA AQ.
10. KAMEARI AQ. (incomplete)

DISTRICTS SERVED

11. EDO CASTLE + SURROUNDING SAMURAI DISTRICTS
12. KANDA, NIHOMBASHI
13. HONGO, ASAKUSA
14. AOYAMA, SHIBA
15. MITA, MEGURO
16. FUKAGAWA, HONJO (partial service)

Two independent aqueduct systems serve most the city, drawing from widely separate sources. The older Kanda River Aqueduct draws from the Inokashira spring pond in the hills to the west of the city and serves the northern half of Edo, including Kanda and Nihombashi. The more recent Tama River Aqueduct has the southwestern river as its source and serves the southern half of Edo. These aqueducts are low-gradient open canals passing through open farmland for most of their length; closer to the city the conduit is a large stone pipe. The Tama aqueduct starts 126 meters above sea level, decreasing in elevation to 34 meters by the time it reaches the Yotsuya sluice gate in the western part of the city 43 kilometers downstream. Here the flow is diverted into wooden underground pipes, with over thirty main branches and countless sub-branches.

The quality of the water in both systems is very high, equal to if not better than that of their European counterparts. The main reason is that the water at the source is particularly clean. Japanese mountains, as we have seen, are very steep, and consequently the rivers run fast and furious over stony beds for nearly their entire length. Centuries earlier, the government recognized the link between erosion and the health of rivers, and the policies implemented to protect the inland forests in earlier generations benefit Edo's current drinking supply as well. Relatively little organic matter enters the flow in the first place, and little is carried to the city. And though there are no filtration systems in place and no disinfection, the "wells" from which the populace draw their water are actually large, deep wooden settling tanks that allow sediment to collect at the bottom, well below the level at which water is drawn. The custom of boiling water for tea, thereby sterilizing it, also has clear health benefits. There are over five thousand wells in Edo connected to this system, and freshwater is available to all classes twenty-four hours a day—something no European city can boast at this time.

The buried wooden pipes and tanks that make up the urban delivery system would seem to be an inferior technology with technical problems that could diminish water quality, but the system is, in fact, well constructed and quite secure. The techniques used in the construction of the pipes and tanks is so similar to shipbuilding methods that it is likely that shipwrights—with their centuries of accumulated experience in watertight construction—were called upon

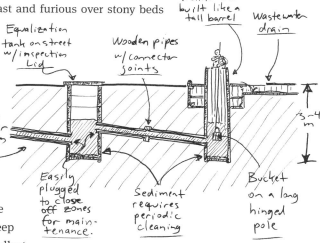

WELL DETAIL

wellhead is built like a tall barrel

Wastewater drain

Equalization tank on street w/ inspection Lid

Wooden pipes w/ connector joints

From feeder system

Easily plugged to close off zones for maintenance.

Sediment requires periodic cleaning

3~4 m

Bucket on a long hinged pole

to help develop the hydraulic technology. The major underground conduits are thick planks, fitted together with sturdy, lengthwise tongue-and-groove joints, caulked with fine cedar-bark shavings, and attached with giant recessed iron spikes. Round wooden pipes, bored their entire length, are sometimes used, but square pipes are far more common. Minor connections are made with narrow round pipes made from bamboo.

Burying the pipes has many advantages, from providing secure support to helping maintain a high moisture level in the planks; if they dried out, gaps and cracks would appear, possibly compromising the entire system and presenting the risk of contamination. The attachment methods are easily adapted to connect lengths of pipe and well tanks at odd angles, to provide for changes in elevation, and to allow easy maintenance. Lidded inspection points are provided at regular intervals (one every block at least), and a corps of trained waterworks inspectors makes frequent rounds.

This is an ideal example of a system that—despite a relatively high initial cost—uses inexpensive technology wherever possible and relies almost entirely on gravity to move the water from source to user. Water quality is easy to maintain because the cleanliness of the source is jealously guarded, requiring the cooperation of distant populations and otherwise disinterested sectors of society, such as farmers and woodsmen. Maintenance costs are low, and damage from earthquakes, for example, can be quickly located by examining the quality of the flow at each inspection point. Damaged pipes, which are only shallowly buried, can be easily exposed, repaired, or replaced. In addition, the system itself is a grid with built-in redundancy in most districts. If the flow is disrupted at one point—including the need to close off a section in order to make repairs—adequate flow can be redirected from another source.

The Edo water system has worked extremely well for almost two hundred years. The surveyors and engineers who designed this system demonstrated a profound understanding of watersheds and the interaction of water flow and terrain. Their system uses no energy but gravity, and it takes advantage of minor undulations and elevation changes within the city limits to effect efficient flow and distribution. The soundness of its initial planning will allow it to be used in future centuries with no change in layout, but with simple technical upgrades of pipes and sluices.

But there are still some parts of town that do not benefit, since the further one gets from Edo Castle, the less likely one is to be connected to the water grid. In the hillier parts of town, including some of the samurai districts north of the castle, there are no water mains. Luckily, good wells can be dug there, and

Parts of Fukagawa depend upon water-sellers for fresh water. Tanker barges are filled from aqueducts near Nihombashi and brought across the Sumida River, and from there water is distributed on foot this is how many samurai households obtain their water. Many of the outlying districts not yet connected to the grid are not heavily populated at this point, so they do not feel much of a freshwater pinch.

But the Fukagawa district just across the Sumida River from Kanda's piped-in water supply must go to great lengths to get its drinking water. The well water is brackish, the Sumida is just too wide to be bridged with an aqueduct extension using current technology, and a new aqueduct system lacks the political and economic wherewithal. Its drinking water must be trucked in, or more precisely, brought by tanker barge, and peddlers make the rounds selling their water by either the dipperful or the bucket.

At present the shortage of water rarely becomes more than a daily nuisance for most residents of Fukagawa. There are those, however, who cannot afford to pay even the nominal fee and who therefore are forced to take their drinking water from contaminated wells. Though the incidence of cholera and other water-borne diseases is still relatively low in Edo, when cholera breaks out significantly in future decades, this will be one cause.

Wastewater drains are covered with easily removable boards or blocks

## wastewater and hygiene

Because human waste is not emptied into the water supply, there has been no need to develop a large-scale sewage system. There is, however, a wastewater system that collects rain runoff, overflow and spillage from wells, and household wastewater from the kitchen and laundry use. For the most part this system consists of a grid of shallow, stone-lined covered channels—gutters, really—that crisscross the city and eventually empty into either the Kanda or the Nihombashi rivers. Here in the tenements, the channel is only about a 30 centimeters wide and deep, and it runs down the center of the alley; as we stand watching, a housewife who has been washing potatoes takes a single step outside her door, lifts a board covering the gutter in front of her house, and dumps the pail of dirty water directly into it. Wider channels line the main streets surrounding each block, these connecting at wide intervals to the outflow channels. In some parts of town, particularly in the great daimyo districts, the gutter is massive, one meter or more across and equally deep, requiring sturdy short bridges of wood or stone to allow them to be crossed.

Each neighborhood has an assigned "drain patrolman" responsible for keeping them clean

Great care is taken to prevent clogging that could result in backup and flooding, and each neighborhood has someone assigned to patrol its section of the system and unclog it where necessary. Anyone caught dumping trash or refuse into the wastewater system can be punished. Human nature being what

Large hot bath in enclosed space to conserve heat. Entered through decorated doorway.

Hot water for washing doled out by the bucketful from this window

Advertisements on wall

Lockers with wooden keys

Changing area

PUBLIC BATH ("Sento")

Owner or staff takes admission fee at entry, sells grooming supplies, snacks, and refreshments. Many "sento" have upstairs rooms for relaxation, amusement, and refreshment.

it is, continual vigilance is necessary, and in some areas—the Nihombashi fish-markets in particular, where fish guts and other noxious refuse are discarded in great quantities every day—the system can be overwhelmed.

In fact most households produce relatively little wastewater. The water that is used for cooking rice, noodles, and vegetables and that might be dumped as waste in the West, is commonly drunk as broth. Laundry is generally a communal activity performed at the well, and though waste is unavoidable, care is taken to minimize it. Individual homes rarely have baths either, since the *sento* public bath system is extensive, convenient, comfortable, inexpensive, and highly efficient. Even wealthy townspeople avail themselves of the public baths, as much for the social interaction and entertainment it provides as for the quality of the bath itself. With over five hundred public bathhouses in Edo, one rarely lives more than a couple of blocks away from one, and in neighborhoods like Kanda one can choose from several within easy walking distance.

# FIRE PROTECTION

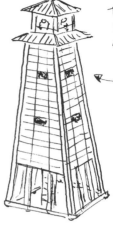

The city is dotted with tall lookout towers manned 24 hours a day, providing a round-the-clock fire watch.

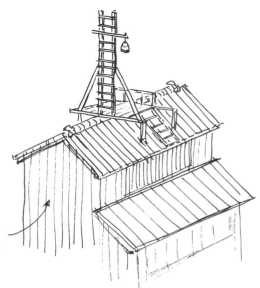

Each neighborhood has at least one rooftop watch platform and an alarm bell.

Each neighborhood is required to maintain filled barrels and fire-buckets in easily-accessible locations

In addition to semi-professional firefighting brigades, many measures are implemented to prevent fires from breaking out and to contain and quell them when they inevitably do.

Many homes and establishments keep rainwater barrels filled for the purpose

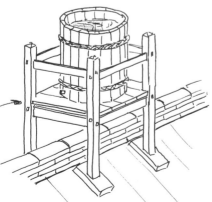

Almost every rooftop has a large water barrel mounted on top for firefighting.

The system conserves both water and fuel: a typical sento will use ten thousand liters of water per day and bathe three hundred customers. If each of these had bathed at home, water and fuel use would be thirty-fold and the wastewater system would be similarly taxed. Those who can afford it visit the sento daily, but these are the minority. Once every few days is more likely for most, who make do with daily cat baths taken at home. Still, rare is the person who is not seen in the sento at least once a week. Because of this excellent infrastructure and the social habit of making frequent use of it, the standard of hygiene in Edo is higher than in Western countries, where most people bathe only once or twice a year. In such a densely populated city as Edo, the public health benefits of this penchant for cleanliness are undeniable.

There are other systems that minimize the consumption of freshwater in the city, including the use of rainwater for firefighting. Many, if not most, of the two-story merchant houses around us have large open casks mounted on their roof ridges to collect rainwater. Firemen who climb roofs with buckets in hand to battle a fire find a ready supply of water close at hand. Rainwater barrels are also used to fill the ubiquitous fire buckets that stand in pyramidal stacks on every block. In the event of a truly large fire this supply will quickly run out, however, and the water system must be tapped. Edo firefighters—highly organized into enthusiastic corps—are equipped with a variety of hand-operated pumps that draw water from the wells and water system inspection points and can supply a steady stream.

## the high value of human waste

A farmer has arrived in the plaza to empty the neighborhood toilets. He left his home village with an oxcart laden with empty buckets several hours before sunup and arrived in Kanda as the city awoke. His village has a contract with several landlords in the area to empty their latrines, and so he makes this trip every couple of months, along with one or two other farmers from his village. He extends a long-handled scoop into the pit and skillfully skims off the liquid floating on the surface. This is kept separate from the rest, for it can be processed to extract ammonia and nitrates for various uses in both agriculture and industry. Then scooping out the night soil, he fills his buckets and carries them on shoulder poles to his oxcart that stands waiting on the street outside the tenement. It is almost noon and the day's collection is nearly complete.

At one time, the urban landlords paid to have this waste carted away, but there is now such demand that it has become a seller's market, and farmers must negotiate purchase of their supplies long in advance. At first it was mainly

## "Night Soil" Collection

Night soil is collected either by farmers directly or by brokers. It must be bought from the owner of the latrine, usually a landlord, and transported to farm villages.

The collector visits each latrine on his route, and empties them with a long-handled scoop into lidded buckets, which he hauls away

Pushcarts are the most common method of transporting large quantities out of town.

Some areas can be easily reached by special night soil barges.

an exchange of farm produce—usually a steady supply of fresh fruit and vegetables—but now most latrine owners demand cash as well.

The farmer doesn't have to pay the owner of the latrines today, because his village already paid the cash portion at the beginning of the year, and his partner has already delivered this month's allotment of radishes to this particular landlord. They should be home by sundown, and tomorrow they will add this fertilizer to the compost heap. After a month or so of the heat of decomposition, which will dry the material and kill most pathogens, the fertilizer will be ready to use.

The farmer and his fellow villagers are concerned, however, because the price of human waste has been steadily increasing. A nearby village lost its customary supplier and had to scramble to find other sources. Everyone knows that the price of night soil varies not only with quality but also with demand. For the landlords, as well as the samurai families and even the daimyo themselves, the sale of latrine waste represents a reliable source of income, and rents are often lowered for households with many members because of the value of their toilet contributions. Farmers expect to pay more for the feces of samurai than for commoners and must pay a lot more to empty daimyo toilets. They have a richer diet, after all. But the most valuable of all are the toilets of the actors and courtesans, because theirs is a life of nonstop feasting.

The night-soil collection system is highly organized, utilizing brokers and specialized transport systems. There are special wagons and even large barges designed specifically to carry the waste through the canals and upriver. Every afternoon, night-soil wagons on their way to farming villages north and west of the city crowd the gateway at Shinjuku, which has been nicknamed "Edo's anus."

Clearly a mutually beneficial symbiosis has been allowed to develop between Edo and the villages. The benefit for the farmers is obvious, in increased yields and therefore in income. For the townspeople, the steady income from the sale of human waste—which largely goes to the landholding classes alone—may be less significant than the health benefits that accrue to all from not having human waste accumulating for very long inside the city. Most European cities are dumping their night soil onto the street or into the water supply, both of which contribute to high disease rates and render entire cities noxious to occupy. Edo has escaped this fate by once again making a virtue of necessity.

As the night-soil collector hauls off his last bucketload, a young girl flings open the front door of her house, scurries to the communal trashbin, and after a furtive glance over her shoulder, removes a broken dish from under her kimono and tosses it onto the heap. Grabbing a nearby stick, she covers the telltale shards with some of the other rubbish and hurries back to her home. She is obviously afraid of being scolded, for while everyday pottery is not particularly precious, waste caused by carelessness is positively immoral. Curious, we cross the plaza to get a better look at the rubbish.

Considering the number of occupants of this particular tenement who use this rubbish bin, there's not much in it. What is there tends to defy description. It may be easier to list what is not found than to clearly identify what is. We find no paper, for instance, or cloth. No wood, bamboo, or anything else burnable, except for a few rotten fragments too soggy to burn. There's no ash, no metal, no broken umbrellas, cooking pots, candle stubs, barrels, sandals, or lengths of frayed rope. There's hardly any organic matter at all. We see some chunks of wall plaster, a few broken roof tiles, floor sweepings, dust, some odd, unsuccessfully burned chunks of something brown.

All of this will be carted off to become landfill, most likely across the river

Customer

Tobacco Pipe
repairman

Shoe repairman
(wooden clogs, sandals)

at Fukagawa. As we stand peering into the rubbish bin, a housewife rushes over, reaches in, and retrieves the broken dish. Walking briskly to the home of the young girl, she opens the sliding door a crack and calls in a conspiratorial whisper, "Mae-chan!" When the young girl appears, the housewife says to her, "Don't you know this can be repaired? I'll give it to the pottery repairman when he comes by this afternoon, and when he gets done with it it'll be good as new. Your mother need never know!"

"Oh, thank you auntie!" the girl says, bowing deeply and repeatedly, and wiping away a few tears. "She would have been so angry!"

"She'd have been more angry to know you'd thrown it away," the housewife replies. "Leave everything to me."

Itinerant Repairmen visit neighborhoods regularly, build up a steady clientele, and do top-notch work at a reasonable price. They carry their parts and tools in portable cases that are masterpieces of lightweight, compact design.

## the recycled city

In fact, in Edo, as in most Japanese cities, almost everything is made to be repairable and consequently to last a long time and provide years of useful service. And what isn't repairable is likely to be recyclable, with a well-established network for collection and processing. Most repairmen and recyclers are itinerant peddlers who make the rounds of the neighborhoods on a regular basis. In the case of dishes and other ceramics, the repairman reattaches the broken fragments with an adhesive made from rice starch, then fires the repaired item in a small portable kiln to set it. It may not really be as "good as new," but the repair definitely extends the useful life of the dish at a small fraction of the cost of purchasing a replacement.

Tinkers are a common sight as well, carrying a small portable forge and bellows on their backs that enable them to repair iron cooking pots, kettles, tools, and other metal items. Finding a repairman for copper items is also easy. Any metal items that cannot be repaired can be sold to the scrap metal dealers, who often involve neighborhood children in their work, singing out an offer to trade candies or trinkets for any iron nails or other metal scraps the children bring them. For the kids it's a great bargain, and fun as well.

On our way here today we've seen or heard at least half a dozen other types of repairmen on the streets, each with his own song, and at least as many recyclers, each specializing in a particular item or material. Among the more technically skilled are the locksmiths, who can repair almost any kind of iron or bronze lock as well as fabricate new keys to replace those broken or misplaced, and furniture repairmen, craftsmen with all the skills of a cabinetmaker but without the capital to open their own shop. They can deftly plane layers from old cabinets to reveal the fresh wood underneath, repair broken doors and drawers, or even make new ones on the spot. One can easily get chipped or cracked lacquerware touched up on the street, and knife sharpeners, grinding wheels on their backs, are equally plentiful. They will also refit new handles and regrind broken blades.

Everyone uses barrels to store liquids such as *shoyu*, sake, miso, vinegar, and a variety of dry and powdered goods, and cooperage is highly evolved. Not only are the well-crafted barrels and buckets tight when new, after extended use they can easily be retightened by adjusting hoops made of woven bamboo strips. The most common repair for barrels is to replace worn hoops, and itinerant barrel-hoop-makers are kept busy modifying and repairing the many barrels of various sizes in each household.

They can also find work as barrel recyclers. For some time Edo has had specialized tradesmen who collect, inspect, grade, refurbish, and send barrels out to be reused. Sake barrels must be handled differently than shoyu barrels, and the condition of each type is graded when it is returned. A brewer or liquor shop can specify what grade of barrel is needed—new, new-looking, slightly used, worn—depending on the intended use. The lower the grade, of course, the less expensive the barrel. It is a very refined system that prevents usable casks and barrels from being discarded too readily. Housekeepers can even pick up a bit of pocket cash by bringing their used barrels to the barrel recycler.

Footwear is often repaired several times before it is considered no longer

Crockery repairman.

Umbrella and lantern re-paperer

Used clothes seller

(Illustrations taken from an Edo-period guidebook)

wearable. In addition to *waraji*, the woven straw sandals whose straps must often be reattached or replaced, Edoites depend upon wooden clogs to keep their feet above the muddy streets. These clogs, or *geta*, suffer wear on the bottom and must be resurfaced from time to time. If the wood that contacts the sole of the wearer's foot splits or splinters, it might need to be smoothed. Clogs can be resized by fitting them with new thongs, and worn out or broken thongs can be replaced. Clogs must be fairly unwearable before they are relegated to the firewood pile, so the itinerant cobblers find a steady supply of work no matter where they go. Straw sandals, too, are never thrown away exactly, but become tinder and fuel.

Lanterns and umbrellas have a particularly involved repair ecology. Since both are made of paper mounted to thin frames—bamboo in the case of umbrellas, wood or bamboo in the case of lanterns—the methods used to repaper them are similar, and often the same craftsman will make a living performing both tasks. Umbrellas can be repaired and recovered many times before they are ready to be replaced, but the oil- and tannin-treated waterproof paper will eventually become too brittle to be rendered serviceable with just a few pasted-on patches, and the binding cords and bamboo slides and handles will break or become too worn to be reliable. At this point the umbrella can be sold to a used-umbrella buyer. They assess the umbrella's condition and assign it one of three grades, and the price they offer for it varies accordingly. These tradesmen are mainly interested in the frame, which can be disassembled, refurbished, rewound, recovered, and resold. Some of the work may be subcontracted out; umbrella- and lantern-making is a typical side job for low-ranking samurai. The old oiled paper—still waterproof—is favored by the few butchers in town for wrapping meat.

Paramount among the recycling specialists are the used-clothes dealers. Many are itinerant, but used clothes shops abound; some estimate there are as many as four thousand used clothes dealers in Edo. In fact, it is no exaggeration to say that the typical townsman rarely buys new clothes. It is more common to simply wash and spruce up an old garment and take it to a dealer to exchange at a small cost for a refurbished one. Because of their ingenious design, kimono can easily be taken apart, redyed, and reassembled, and though many people do this at home for their own use, it is one way that kimono are refurbished for resale.

Eventually, of course, a kimono becomes so worn and threadbare that even the used-clothes dealer won't want it, at which point it might be reworked into an apron or diapers, then perhaps a carrying pouch, then on down the line into wrapping material, cleaning cloths, and eventually fuel (and ultimately ash).

Some cloth pieces may end up as rags and shreds, but even these are not likely to find their way to the landfill, because ragpickers comb the neighborhoods for even these tiny scraps.

There is also a large and diverse market for used paper. The old notebooks, account books, and writing tablets that every merchant family accumulates are sold to dealers who sort and resell them to paper-makers. The old paper is pulped and blended into many kinds and qualities of recycled paper, which is considerably cheaper than new. Many frugal families make it a habit to use only recycled paper for daily communications and letter writing, saving the good stuff for when appearances are important, like New Year's greetings. Toilet paper is usually made from recycled stock. Like the people who specialize in scavenging rags, there are those who eke out a living by collecting discarded paper scraps from alleys and rubbish bins. These are sold to used paper merchants and find their way back into the product cycle. Used paper can always be used as fuel, too, and some is usually kept on hand in most households to help start the kitchen stove. Well-printed books, on the other hand, are expected to last for generations, and we have heard of one math textbook that has been in constant use at a local school for over a century.

The recycling extends to the most seemingly minor items. Abacus repairmen, for example, can reattach and reinforce frame corners, replace bamboo slides, and even come up with tiny counting beads to match any that have become lost. Tobacco pipe refurbishers make a living with similarly delicate work, cleaning out clogged wood or bamboo pipe stems, trimming and refitting joints, and cleaning and polishing the metal bowls and stem caps. They are also likely to have tobacco pouches, cords, and other fittings on hand to replace worn-out items.

Wax candles are relatively expensive, so their drippings are collected and sold to a candle-wax recycler. Used cooking oil is sold as well, whereupon it is filtered and reused as a lubricant and preservative. And there is a large market for ashes. Ash from straw and cotton cloth in particular is high in potassium and is valuable as an additive for fertilizer, as well as having many uses in ceramics, dyes, and the sake-making process. The ash from kitchen fires and heating braziers is never discarded but is kept in a special storage box at home and sold to the ashman. The same holds true for larger establishments like public baths, which generate a lot of ash in the course of business; storage containers of an appropriate size are always provided to hold the ash until it can be sold. Rope and all manner of straw refuse, such as sandals, hats, raincoats, and baskets, are better used as fuel and turned to heat and salable ash than consigned to landfill. Since the technology is heavily dependent upon plant products—wood, bamboo, straw, cotton—almost everything in daily use can eventually be either composted for agriculture or burned for usable ash.

## inside the carpenter's home

Informed by a neighbor of our arrival, our friend Sadakichi emerges from his house to greet us. He has just returned home from his boss's workshop nearby for the noon break, dressed in short, loose breeches that leave most of his legs bare, and a short cotton jacket printed in blue patterns, emblazoned with his employer's name in florid lettering. After exchanging pleasantries, he motions us toward his house. We decline his wife's offer to stay for lunch but accept the offer of tea. Because the family lives in a single room, we can see everything from where we sit. The house is only 9 shaku wide (3 meters), and half of the front opens by means of sliding doors made of thin wooden panels below and paper-covered shoji above. Sadakichi has painted his name directly on the shoji in bold brushstokes of black ink, like a logo.

A shallow overhang provides some protection from inclement weather and summer sun, and the alley itself is narrow enough to be shady except when the sun is directly overhead at noon. The thin, low wooden sill of the sliding doors separates the dirt surface of the alley from the narrow earthen doma of the house itself. This patch of ground and a wooden floor, like a wide step that extends the width of the house, together form the *genkan* entryway and provide kitchen space.

Raising several of the floorboards, Sadakichi's wife reveals a boxy storage area that is always cool and is ideal for keeping jars of shoyu, miso, or pickles. Woven straw raincoats and hats hang from pegs on the genkan walls, and an oiled paper umbrella stands in one corner. There is a large jar of water from the communal well, and a shallow wooden sink. A clay two-burner kamado cooking stove small enough to be portable sits on the wooden floor against the wall, and a sliding skylight hatch in the roof above can be easily opened with a long bamboo rod to let smoke out and additional light in. The kamado is used mostly for rice, soup, and stews. A small portable grill for fish sits to one side; because it generates so much smoke, this is used in the entryway or even taken outside. A simple set of shelves holds the family's dishes and a handful of wooden and bamboo kitchen utensils, and a couple of wooden pails lie close at hand.

The entryway/kitchen opens directly to the remainder of the house. It is a small room constructed in typical fashion with tatami floors (six mats in this case), and clay plaster walls, exposing the cleanly planed square wooden columns and beams. Being at the end of the row of houses, this particular unit has

# THE CARPENTER'S ONE-ROOM HOME

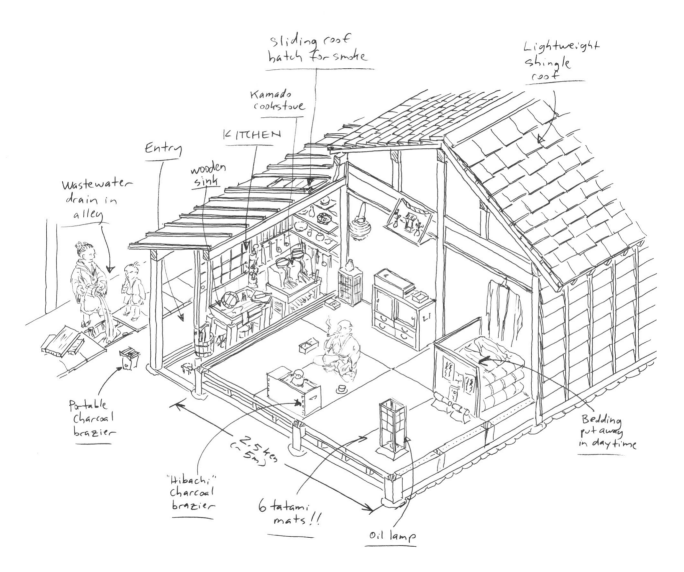

sliding roof hatch for smoke

Lightweight shingle roof

Kamado cookstove

KITCHEN

Entry

wooden sink

Wastewater drain in alley

Portable charcoal brazier

"Hibachi" charcoal brazier

2.5 ken (~5m)

6 tatami mats!!

Oil lamp

Bedding put away in daytime

Tenements ("nagaya") come in different sizes and varieties. This 6-mat version is considered adequate for a small family.

a small window that opens to the well plaza. It's a bit noisier than the others, perhaps, but the extra light and air circulation are welcome. The window has a lightweight wooden storm shutter outside and shoji inside. The rear of the house backs onto another tenement behind, so the windows there are small. Glancing up, we can see the entire roof structure: several sets of lightweight, cross-braced wooden beams supporting very thin rafters. We can also see the thin wooden boards of the roof underlayment above that; the roof itself is of cedar shingles.

This, basically, is all there is to the house. Like hundreds of thousands of other townspeople, Sadakichi and his wife live here in good health and reasonable comfort. Many tenement units are even smaller than this six-mat one, with only four-and-a-half mats of living space (or sometimes only three), but larger, more comfortable eight-mat rooms can also easily be found. Two-story apartments are also available but less common. What makes these minimal units livable is their convertibility and flexibility.

Aside from the architectural features described above, everything else used in daily life is in the form of a movable possession. This single room serves as bedroom, living room, workroom, and dining room. Bedding is stacked in the corner behind a low folding screen during the day and is laid out for use at night. The family doesn't own much in the way of clothing to begin with, and it all easily fits in a freestanding chest placed against the wall. There are shelves and racks for Sadakichi's tools, and a small sewing box sits against the wall. Meals are taken on little trays placed directly on the floor; the family has economized by not buying *zabuton* floor cushions, and they sit directly on the tatami, which is comfortable enough. Nighttime illumination is provided by a lightweight vertical oil lantern of paper pasted to a delicate wooden boxlike frame. Sardine oil is placed in a shallow dish inside with a wick of twisted paper or cotton. (In fact, lamp oil is a bit expensive, so the family tries to economize, only lighting it when really necessary. If they had more money they might use cleaner-smelling rapeseed oil instead.)

Like everyone, Sadakichi's family also economizes on fuel. In addition to the kitchen stove and fish grill, they have a *hibachi*—a portable brazier—for heating water for tea and for warmth when it gets cold. All are designed for use with charcoal fuel. The design of the small *kamado* is particularly ingenious in how the level of heat can be adjusted to save fuel. The hibachi is designed to warm people sitting close to it, but not the whole room. Though charcoal generates less heat than good firewood, it is lighter and more compact than wood, and it generates less smoke, so almost all Edoites depend on it. It is produced in the mountains, shipped downriver to Edo, and usually bought from peddlers who sell door-to-door. It is a significant household expense, but its use is reduced by the common practice of purchasing prepared foodstuffs.

Today, on his way home, Sadakichi picked up several skewers of *yakitori* chicken from a street vendor. Restaurants and food vendors use fuel more efficiently than the single household can because they prepare larger quantities of food. For the homemaker, prepared food costs only marginally more than raw foodstuffs, and when the cost of fuel is factored in, it is often cheaper overall. This approach to food preparation and fuel consumption has evolved in an unplanned way society-wide, being an excellent illustration of fundamental market economics.

Edo is a remarkable food city, not only because the highest quality and widest variety are available, but also because the food preparation and distribution infrastructure is so highly developed that one rarely needs to walk more than a few steps outdoors before encountering several vendors. It is estimated that there are over two thousand food vendors and restaurants in Edo. All take care of their fuel use, their water use, and their refuse, and they all sell their ash to the ashman for further use.

## the business of edo carpentry

Because Sadakichi is a house carpenter, he spends some of his time at the workshop preparing the beams and columns for the houses and storage buildings that comprise most of the company's business. The remainder of the time he is at the various worksites assembling the building frames and finishing the wood construction. Though they occasionally take work in distant parts of town, usually as a favor to a relative or an old friend of the master, it's usually a pretty short walk from home to a building site in Kanda or Nihombashi.

Sadakichi is a good carpenter, and he spent a long apprenticeship to become *ichi-nin-mae*, or "full-fledged," able to perform all the tasks he might be called upon to do. He is thirty years old, and while some of his colleagues have already become independent, Sadakichi doesn't yet have the capital or the backing from relatives to set up his own workshop. He is saving for that day, though, and his current humble lifestyle allows him to put away more money. He married at twenty-one, and although his son Yasukichi is only nine, he was apprenticed to a door-maker earlier this year. The door-maker and Sadakichi often work together on the same building projects, so Yasukichi is close by.

Sadakichi and his boss are members of a carpenters' guild, or *nakama*, one of dozens operating in Edo. The guild functions as a social and economic support system, coordinating the activities of the individual members so they don't

## PEDDLERS of PREPARED FOOD

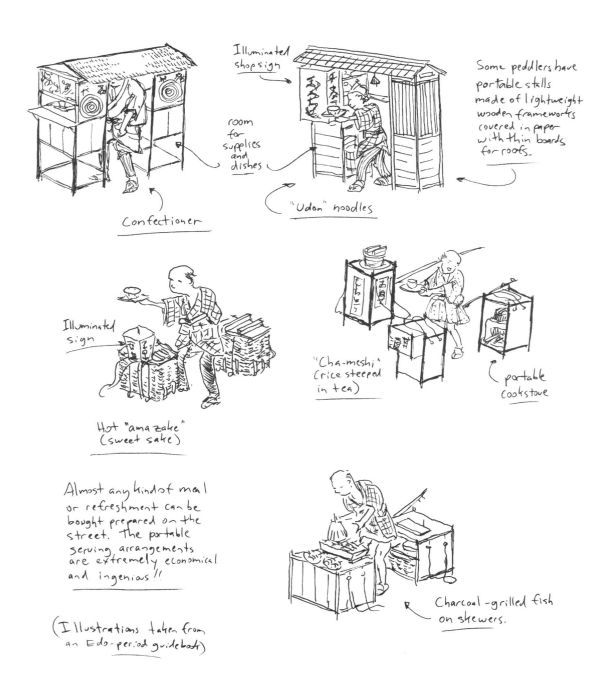

Illuminated shop sign

room for supplies and dishes

Confectioner

"Udon" noodles

Some peddlers have portable stalls made of lightweight wooden frameworks covered in paper with thin boards for roofs.

Illuminated sign

Hot "amazake" (sweet sake)

"Cha-meshi" (rice steeped in tea)

portable cookstove

Almost any kind of meal or refreshment can be bought prepared on the street. The portable serving arrangements are extremely economical and ingenious!!

(Illustrations taken from an Edo-period guidebook)

Charcoal-grilled fish on skewers.

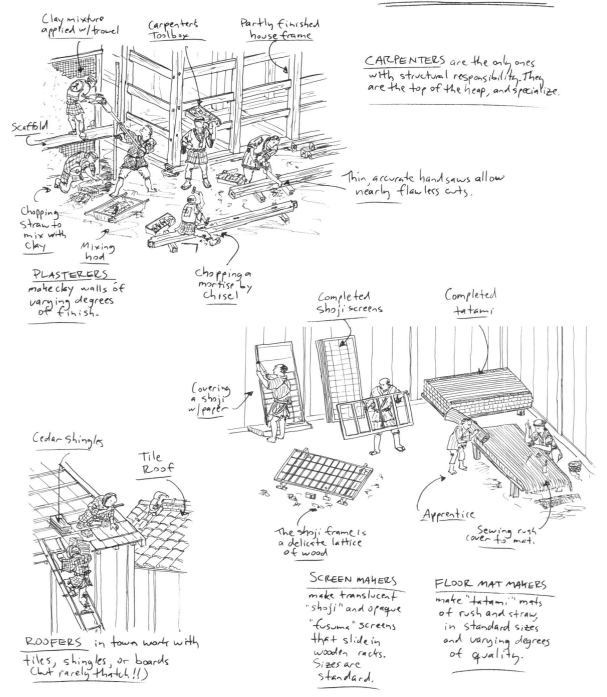

# HOUSEBUILDING TRADES

Clay mixture applied w/trowel

Carpenters Toolbox

Partly finished house frame

CARPENTERS are the only ones with structural responsibility. They are the top of the heap, and specialize.

Scaffold

Thin, accurate handsaws allow nearly flawless cuts.

Chopping straw to mix with clay

Mixing hod

**PLASTERERS** make clay walls of varying degrees of finish.

Chopping a mortise by chisel

Completed shoji screens

Completed tatami

Covering a shoji w/paper

Cedar shingles

Tile Roof

The shoji frame is a delicate lattice of wood

Apprentice

Sewing rush cover to mat.

**ROOFERS** in town work with tiles, shingles, or boards (but rarely thatch.!!)

**SCREEN MAKERS** make translucent "shoji" and opaque "fusuma" screens that slide in wooden racks. Sizes are standard.

**FLOOR MAT MAKERS** make "tatami" mats of rush and straw, in standard sizes and varying degrees of quality.

end up stepping on each other's toes. It lends its political and economic muscle to help settle disputes with suppliers or clients, and it has worked out solid arrangements with a couple of local lumberyards to make sure its members have not only an adequate supply of wood, but also first pick of prime material. (Sadakichi and his boss nevertheless sometimes make the trip across the river to Kiba to select from the best logs when the client wants something really special to grace his entryway.) The guild also has emergency funds that can be made available to help members in distress.

The wood they use comes from distant mountains, and like any carpenter worth his salt, Sadakichi can tell the difference between, for example, Yoshino sugi and superficially similar logs from Kai province, or between hinoki from a sunny northern hillside and some from a western valley. It's not only how the wood looks that tells them, but how it smells and how it feels under the hand plane. These carpenters know a lot about wood and how to make the most of it.

Carpentry is a highly stratified and specialized occupation. Sadakichi's boss doesn't get much government work, for instance, which means they don't build large villas, administrative buildings, barracks, jails, or schools. There are guilds of more elite carpenters in town who have hereditary ties to the various daimyo and to the shogun, and they're usually called on for this kind of building. But, in fact, the government hasn't been building much lately (purse strings are tight) so, despite the fact that master carpenters receive a yearly retainer, a lot of them have been moonlighting elsewhere. The temple and shrine carpenters are also elite, and they are quite busy. Many of them are also kept on retainer by a particular sect and are on call for whenever something needs to be built or repaired. Many Edo temples are already several hundred years old, and they need to be dismantled, refurbished, and reroofed every fifty to one hundred years. Temples also own a lot of property on which houses are built and rented to townspeople. Having connections with a temple is a pretty good deal for a carpentry concern, but Sadakichi's company has none.

Sadakichi's company does have the know-how to work for the more modest class of samurai, whose homes are neither very large nor very complicated compared to big merchants' houses. But not much of that work comes their way, either. Part of the reason is that a samurai is likely to hire someone connected with their boss when they need a house built. And since money is also tight for samurai these days, most are making do with what they have, even if their homes are beginning to fall apart.

While Sadakichi and his colleagues are not elite by any standard, business is booming for commoners all over town, so they have as much work as they can handle. A lot of it is technically ambitious and a lot of it is elegant, and this crew is up to the task. But they don't turn up their noses at building tenements. In fact, they built the one we're now standing in, and Sadakichi gets a break on the rent in exchange for occasional handyman work.

Most of what they build are merchants' rowhouses of the sort we see lining every downtown street. Though each owner takes pride in the unique design features of his shop, the overall design is fairly standardized. This makes it easy to estimate how much material is needed, minimizing waste and speeding up the process. There are lots of sumptuary laws and building codes that limit the amount of freedom a design can have: houses can't be taller than 20 shaku (7 meters) for instance, and second-story, street-side windows must have wide vertical bars in front to prevent commoners from looking down on any daimyo who might pass by. There are other laws that are clearly beneficial, mainly concerning fireproofing. But a few just seem like sour grapes. Commoners aren't allowed to build tearooms, for instance, and could get in trouble for interiors decorated in lacquer or gold leaf. Though tearooms and lacquer are supposed to be only for the samurai, most of them can't afford such luxuries these days, while many successful merchants can. Mum's the word, but Sadakichi and his fellow carpenters have built quite a few tearooms in the past few years, hidden deep inside the large townhouses of prosperous merchants.

Because everything is based on the shakkanho module system, even if a house is wider or deeper than its neighbor, they'll be very similar in how they're actually put together, and there's not too much variation in their structural layout. The shop and kitchen are downstairs, the living space upstairs. A small merchant's house might be 9 shaku wide by 4 ken deep (2.7 by 7.2 m), and have only a single shop room on the ground floor and two small ones upstairs. A typical large one might be 4 ken wide by 7 ken deep (7.2 by 12.5 m), with two or three good-sized rooms plus a nice kitchen downstairs and two or three rooms upstairs. This is about as grand as most merchants can hope to get, but there are plenty of even bigger shop-houses around, some taking up an entire block. About half of the shop owners also have *kura*, fireproof warehouses built at the rear of their lots, even if their shop is on the small side. It makes financial sense to protect your inventory and your important belongings before you think about making your house bigger.

No matter what kind of building it is, however, the actual layout and design are done by the master carpenter, and if he ever gets asked to build something unfamiliar, he's likely to tell the customer, "No problem, I build them all the time," before running off to the guild hall to look at design manuals. Over the years, carpentry manuals of all sorts have been published, and the guild keeps

## MODULAR LAYOUT SYSTEM FOR BUILDINGS

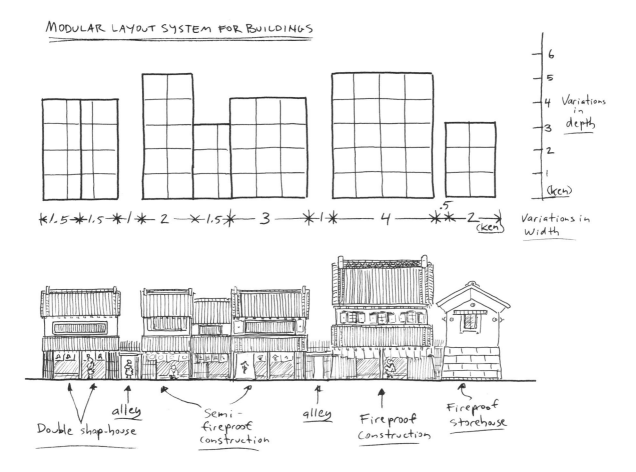

Variations in depth

Variations in Width

Double shop-house · alley · Semi-fireproof Construction · alley · Fireproof Construction · Fireproof Storehouse

a pretty good collection on hand for moments like these. Some of them are pretty well thumbed.

The other big difference in the type of house that gets built is the level of fireproofing. Storehouses are always fireproof, with a thick plaster called *shik-kui* covering the exterior walls of both stories—a gleaming white in most parts of the country, though Edoites add lamp black to make them a shiny black. These buildings have thick door and window shutters that can be sealed to make them almost airtight, and tile roofs—often with another fireproof plaster roof beneath that. Edo has gone up in smoke and flames—"The flowers of Edo," the fires are called—more times than anyone cares to be reminded, and eventually merchants started having their entire shops built like fireproof kura. It's the most expensive way to build, of course, and not everyone can afford it, but these chunky, massive-looking buildings line block after block of the merchants' districts, their gleaming black plaster adding to their mystique and dignity.

A lot of owners have to settle for "semi-fireproof," however, where only the second floor (considered more likely to catch sparks) is plastered and the first floor is covered with simpler board-and-batten siding. Like the fireproof houses, these almost invariably have tile roofs. Finally, the least expensive kind of building is left entirely unplastered, with thin wooden siding, and maybe even roofed with flammable wooden shakes. Nearly all the tenements are built this way, so if a fire breaks out it is likely to start in a tenement kitchen.

The carpenters are responsible for the primary wooden parts of the buildings: the frame, the wooden floors, the ceilings, the wooden roof underlayment, wood siding, if any, door and window frames, and maybe some of the simpler shelving. Other craftsmen, also organized into guilds, handle packing the earth and laying foundation stones; the roof covering (whether tile or shingle); interior and exterior plastering (though the wood and bamboo lath to which the plaster is affixed is part of the carpenter's job); the sliding doors, windows, and shutters themselves; the tatami floors; and interior details like fancy shelves and cabinets. The uniformity of the quality of workmanship applied to all construction is remarkable—for these craftsmen are well trained, conservative, and stubborn, and they demand to be allowed to do work in which they can take pride.

The inexpensive tenement is technically quite similar to both a rich merchant's house and a samurai mansion, and they share a distinct design sensibility in which centuries of trial and error have led to a convergence of framework design, spatial configuration, floor surfaces, wall coverings, roofs, and closures. What distinguishes a humble house from a mansion is primarily its size and the fact that larger rooms require a more robust structure and longer and thicker beams, with specific joinery details that, over time, have become stylistic flourishes. Next, an expensive house will be made of a higher grade of material. This means more desirable species of timber, more attractive grain, and greater length and girth where structure demands it. Finally, a lower quality house will show only a basic level of finish—which is, however, superb by any measure compared to what is available to the lowest strata of society in other countries.

Finish in some respects includes the presence or absence of interior design elements, like horizontal picture rails or built-in cabinetry. It may concern the presence or absence of decorative carving on exposed beam-ends on the exterior. And it may refer to staining, lacquering, or otherwise applying "fancy" finishes to wooden elements. A lot of what distinguishes a rich man's house from a poor man's is in the form of removable or replaceable fittings and their quality: the quality of the paper covering a sliding door, for example, or whether the door panels have lacquered surrounds, whether the cabinet doors are of strikingly grained zelkova or low-grade cedar, or the quality of the lamps, tables, cushions, and bedding. The quality of the poor workingman's house in Edo compares well with the rich man's because both are made by conscientious and skilled craftsmen who raise the level of construction and finish to an admirable norm—one that is basically humble to begin with.

## the life cycle of materials

The lumber used in building Edo, of course, must be supplied from a great distance and requires a sophisticated and well-coordinated infrastructure, particularly when great fires necessitate massive rebuilding. Government policy has sought to lessen both environmental damage from forestry practice and the overall consumption of timber through sumptuary laws limiting building size for most classes. Though ostentatious use of oversized beams for dramatic effect is sometimes seen, for the most part construction practice dictates efficient use of the material. Consequently, wherever possible, a multitude of thin, short wooden elements are carefully combined for strength, lending a delicate rhythm to most parts of the house, like in the roof rafters and wall bracing. Once again, technical skill and good design transform material shortages into aesthetic virtue.

The practice of concealing the primary roof structure behind lightweight drop ceilings allows wood of irregular form and appearance to be fully utilized there. Waste, wood shavings, and cut-off pieces are collected from the building site each day by low-ranking apprentices and carried back to the workshop, where they are used either in other aspects of the building effort or as fuel.

These wooden building structures can be easily dismantled to be repaired, reused, or moved, and the standardization of dimensions makes it a simple matter to reuse individual structural members elsewhere with a minimum of reshaping. In fact, the obvious reuse of old building material is an honored feature of the building aesthetic. Roof structures in particular are overengineered, however, because great mass is desired to act as damping during earthquakes. The house is built to last for generations, and the best-built ones can be used continually for centuries. Timber scavenged when houses are dismantled or destroyed is either recycled into other wood products or used as fuel, and ultimately ash.

Sourcing timber for Edo has a great impact on distant mountain environments as well as on the rivers used for transport, and it requires the mobilization of tremendous quantities of human labor. Nonetheless, excellent building

# WHAT HAPPENS to a Demolished Building?

Though most buildings are built durably enough to last generations, many eventually face demolition. Nearly every element finds a subsequent re-use.

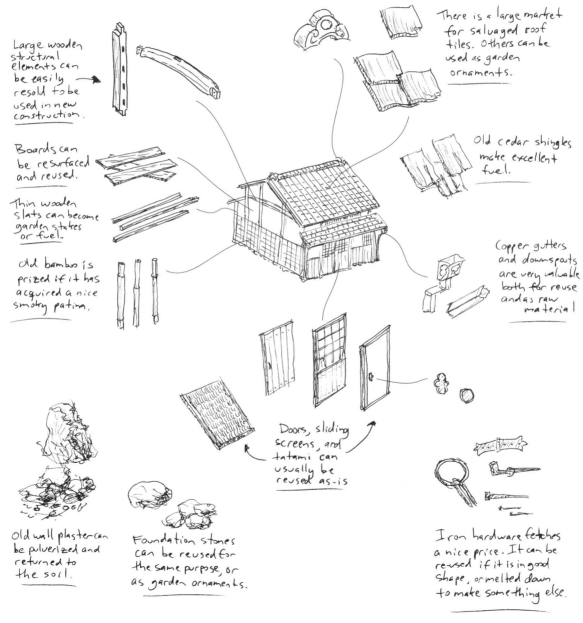

Large wooden structural elements can be easily resold to be used in new construction.

Boards can be resurfaced and reused.

Thin wooden slats can become garden stakes or fuel.

Old bamboo is prized if it has acquired a nice smoky patina.

There is a large market for salvaged roof tiles. Others can be used as garden ornaments.

Old cedar shingles make excellent fuel.

Copper gutters and downspouts are very valuable both for reuse and as raw material

Old wall plaster can be pulverized and returned to the soil.

Foundation stones can be reused for the same purpose, or as garden ornaments.

Doors, sliding screens, and tatami can usually be reused as-is

Iron hardware fetches a nice price. It can be re-used if it is in good shape, or melted down to make something else.

designs intended to minimize material use and to maximize recyclability and reuse are society-wide, and they significantly minimize the negative environmental impact of the building industry.

Walls are universally plastered with adobe-like clay on the interior, and though wooden siding is quite common for exteriors, clay- and lime-based shikkui plasters are more common in Edo. The clay must be mined within a reasonable transportation distance, and overexploited sources can soon become exhausted. It is a very gentle material, however. Various mixtures are in use, most including generous amounts of abundant rice straw as a binder and visual design element (sand and natural colorants are also used). Because Edo is situated in an alluvial plain, there are many sources of clay nearby, but higher grades of the material are brought from a great distance in order to satisfy demanding clients.

Shikkui wall plaster is made from slaked lime (hydrated calcium, usually obtained from oyster shells) mixed with sticky binders such as seaweed paste or red algae, and often colorants such as the lamp black preferred in Edo. Like clay wall plaster, it is applied in successively fine-grained layers, and the final layer is polished to a sheen. Clay wall material crumbles with age but is easily repaired, and at the end of its useful life it can be pulverized and returned to the soil. Shikkui can be repaired but is not as easily recycled, though the coating is usually thin enough to allow it to be pulverized along with the underlying wall clay. The inner wall structure to which either clay plaster or shikkui is applied is made of a lath of woven bamboo strips and hemp or straw rope; these can easily be used as fuel or composted and allowed to biodegrade.

Roofing presents a great technical challenge—one that has encouraged the development and extensive use of many materials and configurations. The earliest roofs in both rural and urban areas were of thatch, but these have been prohibited in Edo for over a century due to their flammability. Shingle roofs of thin cedar shakes are technically simple and aesthetically desirable, but their use puts stress on timber supplies, and because they are also flammable their use has also been discouraged. Nevertheless, they remain the most economical roofing material and so are commonly seen on inexpensive construction such as tenements. Neither thatch nor shingles are particularly durable, but old material can be reused on new roofs and eventually recycled as fuel.

Tile is the most durable and most expensive roofing material, but it is a multistep industrial process that requires ample supplies of high-quality clay and large quantities of fuel. It requires the skill of mold-makers and kiln-builders, and the finished product is heavy enough to discourage transportation over great distances. The kilns also produce enough smoke to be considered a source of pollution. In Edo, these disadvantages are all outweighed by tile's fire-resistance, beauty, and durability, and recent innovations in design have made roofing tiles both lighter and simpler to apply. Tile roofs are required by law for most uses.

Like most industrial activities, tile kilns are located on the outskirts of the city wherever possible, close to sources of clay and water transportation. The typical silvery gray roofing tile is essentially self-glazing and obtains its color from a reaction with woodsmoke inside the kiln, which leaves a thin but durable carbon film over the entire surface, rendering other glazing materials unnecessary. Though this surface reacts with rain and the atmosphere and slowly degrades over time, these tiles can last centuries; often they are the only salvageable item after a fire. There is an active market for salvaged tile, and even broken fragments are put to use as garden edging or embedded in earthen walls. Ultimately, many irredeemably broken roofing tiles find their way to landfill.

The floors of homes in Edo, like those in the rest of the country, come in three types, and most houses will usually feature all three. Merchant houses have a doma of packed earth, usually hardened with lime, in the ground floor of the shop. Tenements have a tiny doma inside the entryway as well. Shop houses are likely to have an ita-ma raised wooden floor in the kitchen as well as in the ground-floor shop space (depending upon the nature of the business), and tenements have a tiny bit of wooden floor for a kitchen. But the most characteristic flooring material is tatami, the thick, pliant, rectangular straw mats that have become ubiquitous in Japanese homes.

The doma is simply earth, of course, and this tough, rectangular patch of ground is often the only remaining relic after a house has been destroyed. If left undisturbed, it too will eventually erode and become a home to insects and weeds. Wooden flooring has the same virtues as other wooden building material: recyclability, easy reuse, potential as fuel. Tatami makes an excellent tinder when chopped into conveniently sized chunks, and it can also be pulled apart and used as mulch. It is thoroughly biodegradeable and makes very desirable ash.

Doors and windows are easily removed and come in standard sizes, so they can often be resold as is. Many are recovered in paper, refurbished, and put back to use. The same is true of cabinets, stoves, blinds, braziers, shelves, and screens. Nails, of which relatively few are used, are usually made from recycled iron hoes and spades. They can be pulled from the wood and reused if they are in good enough condition, or otherwise sold to the scrap metal dealer. Other metal hardware and fittings can be easily stripped and either reused or sold as scrap as well.

These abundant environmental virtues are easier to characterize than to quantify, particularly since adequate records are not being kept in most cases. But there is almost nothing used in building that does not have at least one good subsequent use, and even otherwise unusable clay wall plaster returns to the soil so cleanly and easily that it is as if it has simply been borrowed from nature for a few years. The energy used in the entire building material production system and in construction (and demolition) itself is overwhelmingly human muscle, followed perhaps by water currents and wind. Little food is diverted to livestock for production power or for transportation.

Of course not all is ideal. Extracting lime from shells for plaster requires as much fuel and is as locally polluting as tile making. Producing iron carpentry tools entails environmental degradation at the mine head as well as heavy fuel use in smelting and smithing, but metal products, particularly hand tools, represent a significant expense, and so they are treasured. The tools are so well made and so well cared for by their owners that they commonly last a lifetime, and most can be passed down to succeeding generations.

## dependent on the river and the sea

Taking our leave of Sadakichi and promising to meet up with him again in the evening, we return to the bustling street outside and continue our stroll. Following the salt air, we walk back toward Nihombashi, turn left, and continue several blocks to the Sumida River, where we stand facing the Eitai Bridge spanning the great river to the Fukagawa district on the opposite side. At the foot of this side of the bridge is an open plaza thronged with peddlers, hawkers, shoe repairmen, tinkers, temporary shop stalls, street performers, public notice boards, porters, palanquin bearers, mendicant monks, travelers, boatmen, teahouse girls, regular citizens, unsavory characters—a microcosm of Edo itself. Though not nearly as big as the entertainment area at the foot of the more important Ryogoku Bridge a couple of kilometers upriver, this plaza is just as crowded, mainly because of the commercial traffic heading to and from Nihombashi. These bridge-side plazas, left as open space primarily as firebreaks and to allow troops to mass for defensive reasons, lend themselves to commercial experimentation and easy reconfiguration. Anyone can set up a stall here, and everyone is welcome to people-watch and idle. Though policed and regulated, these *sakariba* are urban "free zones" whose importance to foot traffic makes them ideal communication nodes and essential parts of the urban pedestrian network.

Like most large bridges spanning the river, the Eitai Bridge is an arcing wooden structure supported by thick wooden piers that supports foot traffic

# COMMONLY SEEN WATERCRAFT

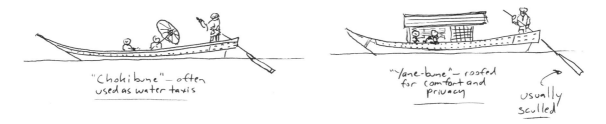

"Chokibune" – often used as water taxis

"Yane-bune" – roofed for comfort and privacy

usually sculled

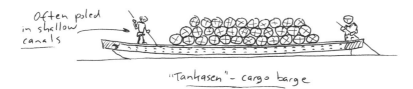

Often poled in shallow canals

"Tankasen" – cargo barge

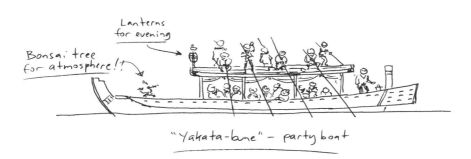

Lanterns for evening

Bonsai tree for atmosphere!!

"Yakata-bune" – party boat

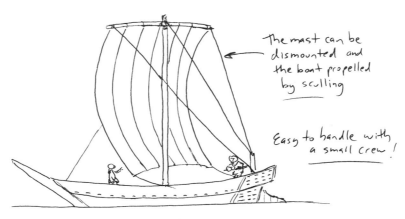

The mast can be dismounted and the boat propelled by sculling

Easy to handle with a small crew!

Small Fishing Boat

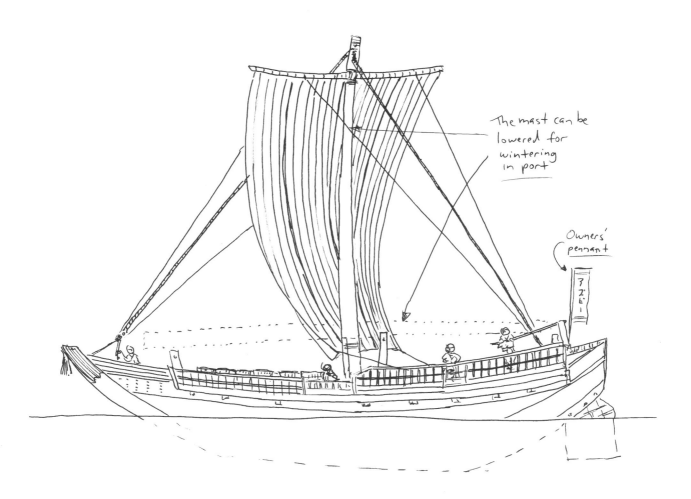

The mast can be lowered for wintering in port

Owners' pennant

"Bezai-sen" — Coastal cargo ship
(This one is a "taru-bune", built to carry barrels)

The boats seen in Edo's ports and rivers range from the very small to extremely large, and Edoites take to the water enthusiastically. Most small boats are sculled with a single oar, or poled along the inland waterways. Fishing boats are specialized for trawling, line fishing, or other techniques. The largest craft are coastal cargo vessels, which may boast multiple masts and sails, and require crews of 20 or more.

and the occasional draft cart, built high enough above the river to give ample room for river craft to pass underneath. As we pause at the highest point in the center of the bridge and look around, the immensity and variety of the river traffic is readily apparent—boats of all sizes and descriptions crowd the river and the innumerable canals opening onto it. Large passenger craft, packed ferries, tiny boats sculled by single occupants, and festive entertainment vehicles move back and forth from landings on one bank to others opposite, upriver, or out to the open bay.

Cargo craft are more numerous still, from small rafts and boats whose bulging straw tarps protect piles of goods, to barges stacked with heavy baskets and jars, nestling close to the larger coastal sailing ships that will carry the products to Nagoya or Osaka. There are also long, trim vessels bringing fresh farm produce to the markets in Nihombashi and Kanda. The degree of specialization is surprising, for we see wooden tankers filled with shoyu or vegetable oil riding low in the water, transporting these liquid goods from their canal-side producers to distant distributors, and rice boats equipped with wooden frames and palings designed to fit the standard rice bales precisely, allowing them to be lashed securely in place in gigantic towers. Cargo boats are custom fitted with tubs, racks, and compartments of many descriptions, indicating the highly evolved state of the waterborne transportation infrastructure.

Though Edo is both the largest and most evolved city in this respect, similar infrastructures—utilizing rivers, wharves, canal systems, and a variety of water craft—anchor the economies of every other major Japanese coastal city. It is small wonder that the major cities are all coastal ones. In nearly every case, with goods transferred from boat to handcart or carrying pole, the energy that propels the load is either wind, water current, or human muscle. There is no need to divert much of the limited grain stores to animal feed, or to contend with manure-filled streets. In fact, a mounted samurai is usually followed by an underling with a scoop and manure bucket to collect the precious droppings.

The activity along the riverbanks is both lively and complex. Boats can approach shops, storehouses, yards, restaurants, and inns directly from the innumerable landings, and there are quite a few houses, both ramshackle and handsome, built right on the river. Much of the construction is industrial in scale however, with a shipyard at the foot of the bridge and long rows of large, whitewashed warehouses on both banks. There are a few big lumberyards right on the river, as well as tile yards, stone yards, plaster yards, and businesses supporting every other aspect of the construction industry. At the same time, many people are obviously here just for diversion and relaxation, and for them a number of entertainment options are easily accessible. It is easy to get around

Gathering Mussels
in Fukagawa

Some people do it
for survival, some
as a diversion.
There is enough
for all!!

town by boat, and not much slower than walking. Nor, with the diversity of rivers, canals, and bridges, is it any less scenic.

The chaos and clamor of commerce that we see and hear as we look upriver from the bridge give way to something more fundamental and ancient as we turn our gaze to the bay itself. Most of Fukagawa, like the wide strip of coastal land where the older districts of Shiba, Ginza, Tsukiji, and Kyobashi lie, is land reclaimed from the existing tidal marsh. The waterfront of the older areas is fully developed, almost entirely devoted to commerce, traffic, and small settlements supported by fishing. But in Fukagawa, there are areas where the marsh and the sandy tidal flats remain, and the scene is both rural and bucolic.

In the tidal flats, we see small armies of commoners raking the sand for clams, some with a seriousness of purpose that would suggest that survival is at stake, others with a jocularity and good humor that suggests they're here for the entertainment. In fact, for some, what can be gathered here is an essential part of their diet, for there are always the poor who are barely making ends meet, and food free for the gathering can not only be eaten, but can be sold. Fukagawa clams are ideal in this sense, because even children and the elderly can gather them, and the source is just a stone's throw from home.

In addition to clams, there are a few varieties of edible seaweed to be gathered here as well, and the amusement of fishing. From where we stand we can see slender forests of bamboo palings in the shallows offshore that mark commercial beds of *nori* (laver seaweed). The tidal flats on the fringes of Edo and lining the surrounding areas of Chiba and Kanagawa support these same activities, as well as salt making. This essential and valuable nutrient is produced on a commercial scale here and requires large amounts of manpower, fuel, and time.

Edo, like most of Japan, has long been heavily dependent upon the sea. The earliest inhabitants found abundant shellfish, prawns, flounder, mackerel, and other fish in Edo Bay, as well as nori, *kombu*, and other varieties of edible seaweed. Whitefish, eels, and loaches make their homes in the Sumida and other rivers. Edo developed around the original fishing villages whose inhabitants possessed intimate knowledge of the bay environment and knew how to husband and utilize its many resources, and the city has been able to grow to great size without either overexploiting or despoiling its marine environment.

At present about a dozen fishing communities dot the bayshore, fully integrated into the city's transportation and service infrastructure. The fishing industry is well organized, with competing guilds and fixed distribution networks. It is also highly regulated, particularly regarding fishing rights to specific areas of the bay and rights to establish laver farms. An elaborate wholesale system centers on the main fish market in Nihombashi, with certain wholesalers maintaining close ties to their original marine communities. Though some seafood items can be preserved by drying, salting, or preserving in oil, by far the majority of Edo seafood must be eaten fresh—that is, on the day it was caught. It is a remarkable feat of logistical organization that brings the fish from the bay to the market and on to thousands of city kitchens in a matter of hours. Edo Bay is so productive and so well husbanded that the fishermen can supply the city while rarely venturing beyond sight of the shore, and their innumerable white sails dotting the horizon are considered a beautiful aesthetic complement to the sea itself.

Cuisine involves utilizing food resources, taking advantage of what is available and turning it into something to celebrate. Seafood has pride of place on the Edo dining tray, and the dozens of restaurant guidebooks published here every year list an incredible variety of delicious and innovative cuisines—like Edomae sushi, in which fish is served fresh and uncooked (and therefore prepared without consuming fuel) on little balls of rice, drawing travelers and epicures from afar. This cuisine, which one day will influence the way the rest of the world eats, attests to both the excellent use of ocean resources and ingenuity in their use and preparation.

## a representative of edo life

We've descended from the bridge on the Fukagawa side. Though somewhat irregular in layout, mainly due to the shape of the coastline and the bend of the river, Fukagawa nonetheless gives clear evidence of having been planned. Crisscrossing canals divide the district into islands, themselves cut

LUMBER ARRIVES IN KIBA

By raft or ship or a combination of the two, building lumber for Edo must pass through the labyrinthine canals that serve the KIBA lumberyards

by streets in such a way that rings of dense merchant blocks surround central green cores occupied by either the wooded grounds of shrines or temples or samurai houses and their gardens. There are even a couple of modest wooded daimyo estates in this part of Fukagawa.

Though the local clams are a big culinary attraction, the main occupation is lumber. Most of the traffic we see on the canals is either sawn wood products—columns, beams, and boards—on their way out from the yards, or roughly squared logs on their way in.

Fukagawa Kiba ("wood place") is low, swampy reclaimed land. It floods at high tides and during storms, and this makes it a less than ideal place to live but a perfect place for floating lumberyards. For one, the high water inundates termite nests and so Kiba lumber is largely termite-free. The low ground is also ideal for digging canals and basins, and an extensive network has turned the district into a web of waterways and pools linked by narrow strips of land. Since most timber products are moved by water, the arrangement is logistically ideal. The canals and basins also act as firebreaks, a very important consideration in such a fire-prone city.

There are over five hundred lumber brokers in all of Edo, and most of them are here. It is the home of several large wholesaler guilds that handle specific goods from specific regions, so there is specialization based on the source of the material, which is usually quite distant. In addition, each lumberyard or broker specializes in a type of finished product intended for a particular use. The lumber brokers maintain ties to the carpentry guilds, providing themselves with steady, reliable customers and the carpenters with guaranteed supplies

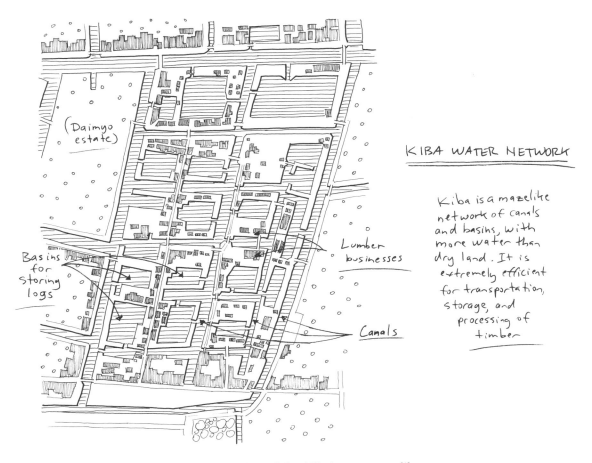

(Daimyo estate)

Basins for storing logs

Lumber businesses

Canals

KIBA WATER NETWORK

Kiba is a maze-like network of canals and basins, with more water than dry land. It is extremely efficient for transportation, storage, and processing of timber

and prices. Quite a few carpenters live nearby. While skilled carpenters, like Sadakichi, are more likely to live closer to the center of town, convenient to their worksites, Kiba is home to many less-skilled workers, who gather near the entrances of the lumberyards each morning in search of day jobs.

Fukagawa is an interesting representative of many facets of life in Edo. It is the point of entry for the crucial commodity of lumber. It is an industrial area filled with work yards and warehouses. It is an important nexus in the water transportation system. It has a prized natural food source. It is home to an important religious establishment, the Fukagawa Hachiman shrine. It is home to indigents and the poorest laborers, successful craftsmen, prosperous merchants, low-ranking samurai, and daimyo. And it is at the edge of the rapidly growing city. From where we stand, we can see suburban rice fields ripening in the sun. Fukagawa has an incredibly strong community identity and esprit, and the people who live here feel both fully a part of the city and also independent of it. It is a quintessential Edo neighborhood.

## a city of more with less

Late in the day, we find ourselves at a small, shady tea stall that overlooks the bay, enjoying a cup and a snack and resting our feet. Edo is an invigorating and overwhelming place to visit, and we are enjoying our time here. The people are entertaining and inviting, though we often feel like the targets of a fast-talking shopkeeper as much as we feel like his guests. What is most impressive here is the constant drive to maximize the utility of everything—to produce more with less, to make better buildings with less material, tastier food with less fuel, better colors with less dye, sharper blades with less steel, to turn necessity into virtue. And it is always done with a cosmopolitan flair for design and presentation.

The people of Edo rarely need to be convinced of the benefits of repairing, recycling, and reusing things, because they invariably save money by doing so. Edo works like a hive brain, which arrives at solutions like the public bath, which is both more fun than a bath at home and more economical. It is the power of the open market that leads to lightweight fired tile for roofs and the vast recycling market, and it is foresight and pragmatism, informed by environmental understanding, that drive the planning and construction of the water system. Edo is a remarkably well-functioning metropolis, and we have learned almost more than we can retain in our short time here. Still, we have seen only a fraction of the city. After a short rest, we rise to our feet and head back across the river.

*Fishing boats head out into Edo Bay under the watchful eye of Mount Fuji.*

# GROUND
# TRANSPORTATION

## IN TOWN

### COMMONERS

**On Foot**
Walking is by far the most common way to get from place to place in town. Edo is an ideal pedestrian city.

**Palanquin**
Commoners can hire an open-sided palanquin ("kago") and bearers, for a modest fee.

**Palanquin**
Wealthier commoners can afford to use a more dignified closed palanquin ("hosenji-kago").

### SAMURAI

**On Foot**
Most samurai walk to their destinations in town as well.

**Horse**
Samurai of middle rank and above are allowed to ride a horse. Attendants follow behind on foot.

**Palanquin**
High-ranking samurai, including "daimyo," are expected to use lavish "norimon" with several bearers.

### GOODS

**Carried**
Most items are carried on the back or shoulders.

**Pushcart**
Fairly large loads are transported around town on well-designed pushcarts. There are thousands of them in Edo.

**Oxcart**
The largest loads might require an oxcart. There are only about 600 oxen in all of Edo, however.

# LONG-DISTANCE

## COMMONERS

### On Foot
Even long cross-country journeys are usually made on foot. Most people find it entertaining and enjoyable!

### Palanquin
Many travelers hire "yama-kago" to help them over difficult mountain passes.

### Horse
A horse, led by a groom, can be hired for the day. Helpful for rough stretches.

## SAMURAI

### On Foot
Lower-ranking samurai usually walk long distances as well.

### Horse
Mounted samurai are often seen on the highways, usually on official business, retainers trotting along behind!

### Palanquin
"Daimyo" make their long journeys by "norimon" but may choose to ride their horse from time to time.

## GOODS

### Carried
Goods are hauled using shoulder-poles or backpacks, even for long distances!

### Packhorse
Because wheeled vehicles are prohibited on the highways, heavy loads must be carried overland by horse.

### Runner
Messages and other valuable information are carried by postal runners in relay.

### Posthorse
The most time-critical government information is carried by fast military riders.

# learning from
# the sustainable city

■ **city planning should be like gardening**

Something is deeply wrong with the way we
plan our cities. For the past century, at the least,
it has usually been a process of erasure, of
flattening and evening out the landscape, burying and redirecting waterways, and imposing
an abstract grid based on optimal automobile
access. Our cities are parts and fragments that
have been juxtaposed to each other and to the
landscape but not really connected.

Laying out a city should be more like gardening: husbanding the existing life and making
room for people but never allowing them to
lose sight of their dependence upon the natural world. Rather than wholesale clearing and
"improving," we need to relearn the process of
gentle shaping and incremental accommodation. Cities planned in this way, like Edo was,
can still support a large population and its
complex economic activity and transportation
systems.

While Edo was the only city on the planet
with more than one million people during the
mid-eighteenth century, and there were only a
handful a century ago, today there are over four
hundred. In addition, twenty urban conglomera-
tions boast populations of ten million or more.
The population density of cities requires collecting massive quantities of food, water, energy,
and materials, and taking care of the subsequent waste. Increasingly, the need to source
these things at a great distance—transconti-
nentally or even transoceanically—detaches
urban inhabitants from the natural ecosystems
in which they live, from the natural carrying
capacities of the places they inhabit, and from
a sense of connection to and responsibility for
their natural locales.

Cities that, like Edo, have been carefully
integrated into their local ecosystems enjoy
clear benefits for both the ecosystem and the
residents. Such cities are more easily heated
and cooled by nature, have more abundant and
diverse tree canopies, support food production

within the city limits, and have better and more reliable water supplies. The key lies in understanding how human habitation and natural systems form an interdependent, functioning whole, and in staying out of the way of nature wherever possible. The process is, in fact, a lot like gardening.

### ■ reinvent the urban waterway

Many cities were originally planned around waterways that played as large a role in daily transportation as they did in Edo. It was a mistake to allow these waterways to become obsolete as the automobile became more common. In their more advanced stages, still evident in Venice, Amsterdam, and Bangkok, but once quite prominent elsewhere as well, older urban water transportation systems were entirely separate from the road network but connected to it at discrete nodes, and physically the two were built on separate levels. This allowed heavy freight to be easily moved by boat without interfering with ground traffic, and the consequent decrease in heavy road traffic encouraged lively pedestrian networks.

Urban waterways are poetic and provide regular opportunities for a fundamental kind of enjoyment. Water transportation has historically depended primarily on wind power and currents, and it has remained the most energy-efficient bulk transportation method since the shift to fossil fuels. Recent technical developments that reexamine wind power for watercraft are extremely promising, so that in the near future water transportation may become both extremely clean and almost cost-free.

Reestablishing urban water transportation networks is only a part of the overall rethinking of urban transport that is necessary now. Ideally, use of the individual automobile should

## urban waterways

While Edo, Osaka, Nagoya, and other Japanese cities once resembled Venice or Amsterdam in the quality and extent of their urban waterways, these networks were allowed to languish over the course of the twentieth century, and most have disappeared under concrete and new roads, while those that remain are usually unattractive or inaccessible. During the boom years of the eighties, however, efforts began to reclaim and revive urban waterways as amenities that could increase property values, and many cities now think positively of the idea in general, if actual successes in this direction are few. One of the most regrettable lost urban waterways is the Nihombashi River, formerly the living heart of Edo, which held on until the early 1960s. For the 1964 Summer Olympics in Tokyo, an elevated expressway was built directly over it and the historic Nihombashi bridge itself, casting both into a dingy shadow that obscured their former beauty.

This is why it is extremely heartening to learn of serious plans to relocate the expressway into a tunnel under the river and to revive both river and bridge as part of the Nihombashi Restoration Project. While the project has not yet received the green light, and no completion date has been set, the many major stakeholders—the municipal government, local businesses, tourist concerns, and local residents—have all responded favorably to the plan—a welcome sign of recognition of the importance of having viable waterways and of acknowledging the cultural significance of historic urban elements like bridges and streetscapes.

be suppressed, and our cities should be made navigable by a combination of buses, light rail, bicycles, and pedestrians. European countries like Holland, Germany, and Denmark have made great progress in this direction, and their systems, which combine mobility, economy, and environmental and personal health, can serve as models for the rest of us.

### ■ allow a coordinated urban patchwork to emerge

No good argument exists for maintaining segregation in cities by rank, class, status, or race. The situation of Edo highlights the degree to which urban living conditions are the result of human decision making. Edo would have been dense even without class segregation, but the increase in the density in the commoners' districts provided impetus for ingenious problem solving in areas such as water supply, sanitation, transportation, and natural cooling. At the same time, it is doubtful if the samurai districts could have been as green as they were had the city's industrial, logistic, and mercantile activities not been so thoroughly segregated elsewhere.

However, though segregation was designed into this city from the start, much of the city was in fact a patchwork in which blocks of samurai housing and small estates were interspersed with commoners' blocks and religious institutions, and the environmental relationships between these disparate elements were carefully thought out. Ultimately, cities exhibit variable density as a result of natural topography, historical factors, economic disparity, and the configuration of the transportation systems.

The goal should not be to equalize density but to design a process that will lead to a deeply interconnected whole in which even the densest districts offer a high quality of life. Paradoxically, this may mean giving inhabitants more freedom in laying out their own neighborhoods, with less top-down planning on the community

scale in favor of a more incremental, self-organizing process that can more flexibly respond to and connect with developing urban and environmental conditions. Regardless, parks and public commons, which are both important urban connectors and form clear boundaries between neighborhoods, will always need to be established at the outset. The result will be a dynamic web of compact, pedestrian-scaled communities, each of which has a strong identity and strong connections to its neighbors.

### ■ pedestrian space solves problems

The gradual disappearance of pedestrian space in our cities has been lamented for decades, beginning at least in the early 1900s with criticism by Louis Mumford and Frank Lloyd Wright. That pedestrian space is a "good" seems to be easily accepted, and pedestrian zones are a prominent feature of many commercial and public developments. People communicate with others, even strangers, when on foot or on bicycles, but they avoid personal contact while in cars. Attractive and well-maintained public pedestrian space is probably essential to a smoothly functioning democratic society, because we are forced to develop and maintain a civic awareness there, our activities are visible, and we can meet as equals.

What is missing and has proven extremely difficult to replicate are the widespread pedestrian networks that linked every town and city in the West until the mid-twentieth century, and that were such an enduring feature of Edo. Our overall dependence on the car has not diminished in past decades; rather, the automobile-based lifestyle has recently taken root in many parts of the world that had preserved pedestrian life. What each city needs now is a "pattern" solution simultaneously addressing pedestrian space as a social issue as well as one of communication, transportation, urban planning, energy use, and the environment.

Better use of urban pedestrian space could

# local shopping streets

One reason Edo neighborhoods were so livable was their pedestrian scale, with lively and diverse commercial streets rarely more than a minute or so away. One might be surprised that it remains true in most parts of the city today. The *shotengai*, literally "shop street," is a direct descendent of its Edo-period forebears, and it often occupies the same real estate. The typical one is several blocks long and is lined with two-story shops whose owners live above or behind. It is a neighborhood gathering place, and business is conducted with a personal touch (the children of the shopowners attend the same schools as those of their customers, for example). There are always reasons to make the trek by car or train to a large-department store or big box appliance store, but despite the rapid inroads made by large-scale retail chains, the neighborhood-scale shopping street remains viable because most people prefer to shop there.

not only decrease our dependence on fossil fuel-based transportation and thereby save forests, improve our air quality, and help counter global warming, but it could improve our sense of community identity and our social responsibility and make it easier to care for our immediate environment and to make better decisions about the environment as a whole. An increased reliance on walking could help reverse the epidemic of obesity and bring many other health benefits. Besides, pedestrian cities are just more interesting, safer, and more fun.

### ■ maintain waste collection and scavenging as economic opportunities for marginalized populations

Priority must be given first to cutting down on waste, and then to recycling and reuse. Nevertheless, waste collection and recycling are legitimate employment, and where municipalities themselves have proven inadequate to the task, they are often done by otherwise marginalized populations—the homeless, the destitute, the disabled—who scavenge our cities and sell what they find to brokers in town. Participating in this business provides these groups with an acknowledged and valued role in their communities and the means of financial independence.

Efficient recycling and material reclamation of the sort practiced in Edo depended upon legions of recycling "specialists" who sorted refuse by hand; though large-scale technological fixes for the problem of sorting refuse are being implemented in many areas, this service business should always be maintained as an economic opportunity for those with few other choices.

### ■ make good use of the city block

The city block is a nearly ideal design unit for optimizing the use of shared water, wind, and energy resources, maintaining gardens, and monitoring joint waste output. It is also an extremely manageable scale for establishing and maintaining networks of people for communication and joint activity. A dense city block can operate in effect as a village, a vital subunit enmeshed within a greater whole. It can be self-organizing, speak with a unified voice, and work with other blocks on coordinated projects. All of this requires the sort of strong identity that comes from a high percentage of home ownership, the sense of permanent involvement that comes from having put down roots, and a vested interest in the future of the community.

There are many forces that hinder this kind

of neighborhood unity. Having a large transient population is one, as are poor design and real estate practices that efface uniqueness and idiosyncrasy in favor of an easily marketed uniformity. Segregation by age, with children attending schools far from where they live, and the elderly similarly institutionalized or effectively trapped in pedestrian-unfriendly homes, also weakens the community. Most of these are design problems, however, and so can be overcome. The urban block will be the site of many innovations in energy and resource use.

### ■ design the infrastructure for the long term

Infrastructure design can only be said to be successful if it is farsighted enough to provide the basis for adequate service several generations hence. In most cases this means that their operation should be based on inexhaustible natural energy sources like gravity, geothermal, tides, wind, and the sun, and that they should be designed to make use of terrain, natural watersheds, natural corridors, and collection points, in a way that enhances their natural functioning. Measured against this standard, very little of our infrastructure is truly successful. Most of it will cease to function when energy becomes too expensive.

### ■ remember: waste is food

As the designer and green design theorist William McDonough is fond of pointing out, "Waste is food." In the natural world all biological waste products, including dead plants and animals, provide nutrition for others. Removing human waste from the biological cycle by flushing it to the ocean or incinerating it represents a net loss of nutrients. Whether these nutrients are made available for use by humans, by other animals, or by plants is less important than that they be returned to the natural cycle. The Japanese night soil system provides an excellent example of a "pattern solution" that solves several prob-

lems at once: better urban sanitation and hence lower incidence of disease, increased crop yield, and mutual economic benefit.

Cities have a metabolism, and human waste is part of it. Water-based sewage removal and treatment can transform sewage into clean, drinkable water, but it is clear that it makes much more sense to separate our toilets from our water systems entirely, compost our own waste, and use it to help offset our alarming topsoil losses. Taking the toilet out of the water loop makes it much easier to purify and recycle household wastewater. As the Worldwatch Institute points out, "This switch would simultaneously help alleviate water scarcity, reduce the dissemination of disease agents in water systems, and help close the nutrient cycle—another win-win-win situation."

### ■ integrate self-policing recycling and reuse systems

Edo very closely approached the zero-waste ideal. This required a deeply ingrained set of ethical and aesthetic values and the establishment of habits of mind and behavior to guide daily life. It was a self-policing system, because nearly every waste product had economic value for someone and would quickly be scavenged for reuse. Manufacturing processes evolved to take advantage of refuse as material, and the logistics worked themselves out with simple mercantile self-gain as an impetus. Similar systems have evolved within unofficial urban economies in many parts of the developing world, but our society is capable of designing more thorough and widespread refuse utilization systems that would operate in a similar fashion.

### ■ makers should invest in the life cycle of their products

The craftsmen who made the homes, implements, and furnishings for Edo society took responsibility for maintaining them and keeping them in good repair throughout their useful life,

# the recycling community

Incredibly enough, given its past, Japan was a bit late out of the modern recycling starting gate compared to, say, Germany, but the country seems to have more than made up. Nearly every municipality has implemented recycling ordinances that mandate separate collection of recyclable materials, and citizens are increasingly willing to devote the attention and effort required to make them work as designed. Most municipalities require discards to be separated into five or six categories: glass, steel and aluminum cans, PET bottles, vinyl and styrofoam, paper, and other materials (including wet garbage). Drink manufacturers now make labels easy to remove from plastic and glass bottles, cardboard package design increasingly emphasizes easy flattening of used boxes so they will take up less space in the bin. And the systems are working: the recycling rate for PET bottles has topped 60 percent in recent years, and other materials show similarly increasing rates as well.

One reason the admittedly complicated systems work lies in close community relations. Garbage is not picked up from in front of individual homes, but each neighborhood has a designated collection point, where the collection schedule is usually posted. The use of clear garbage bags is the law in most areas, so violations are easily spotted. And not surprisingly, in the close communities everyone immediately knows from which household the offending discard has come. It is a living example of effective community self-regulation, reminiscent of the old *go-nin-gumi*, and one that clearly works for the good of all.

and often for ultimately recycling their materials. Product manufacturers today should recognize that a market exists for similar services and that they stand to benefit from accepting this responsibility.

## ■ base production on full use

When we throw away one kilogram of trash, either for disposal to landfill or incineration, or for recycling, there are over seventy kilograms of waste we don't see that were the result of extracting materials, transporting them, producing the goods, packaging them, marketing them, and transporting them again to stores and to our homes. Eighty percent of what we make is disposed of within six months of production, a one-way linear flow from raw material source to landfill. This is insanity.

The "disposable" economy itself is not the problem. Neither is mass production, obsolescence caused by steadily improving design, or

shifts in fashion. The problem lies in our inadequate notion of what it means to use something fully. Edoites didn't expect their straw sandals to last more than a few weeks; these were essentially disposable footwear that would be repaired a few times but were expected to wear out. But the discarded material reentered the production cycle as mulch or as fuel, to be converted into food or heat and ash. This illustrates "full use" downstream in the material cycle. Looking upstream, the same is true: the straw was essentially a byproduct of food production; instead of discarding the straw byproduct, it was fully utilized to make sandals and other items. Mass production can be based on full use, and replacement cycles can and should incorporate full use of materials both upstream and downstream. Most of the items we buy and use should be made to last to be easily repaired, and to have a clear downstream use path.

Until the market demands it, industry will

## packaging and reuse

Another aspect of recycling that has begun to catch on is the use of reusable containers and other items. One corporation, for instance, that sells *shoyu*, vinegar, *mirin*, and other liquid food products, took a hint from the reuse of barrels in the Edo period and decided several years ago to package their products in identical, returnable glass bottles, with different adhesive labels for the various products. A bottle that once held shoyu, for example, is washed, sterilized, and refilled with vinegar or whatever else needs bottling that day. It's a great system and deserves to be emulated.

Similarly, as laundries and dry cleaners in Japan transitioned from wire to plastic hangers over the past decade, environmental concerns were raised, as the latter were likely to be discarded after one use. In response, most cleaners began encouraging customers to return the used hangers, some offering a small cash incentive. Most households gladly comply.

turn to full-use and zero-waste methods and materials only slowly. Pollution and waste represent design failure. All of us must demand better designs.

### ■ design for both long use and removability

Ideally, our cities and buildings should be designed and built well enough that they can be used for centuries. The design and technical processes used should flexibly incorporate the possibility of incremental modification in order to smoothly accommodate unforeseen needs as the city and its buildings age. In reality, permanence often collides with easy reuse, and especially with the ability to easily dismantle and move buildings when that proves necessary. Our buildings today can only be dismantled through the application of destructive force—wrecking balls, jackhammers, cutting torches—and the debris represents a major source of waste. Add to that the fuel necessary to transport and process demolition waste and the environmental costs are very high. We need better designs.

Traditional Japanese wooden buildings were designed to be dismantled, and there was a highly developed market for reused materials, while permanent infrastructures were usually

built of stone or earth. Together these features enabled cities to be easily modified and reconfigured. Today many designers are experimenting with durable but easily dismantled buildings whose parts can be recycled or reused, and these ideas may soon reach the critical mass necessary for widespread adoption.

The Japanese system was extremely successful because standards for structural units, materials, and dimensional systems had developed over the course of several centuries until they reached a high level of perfection. Similarly, the trades evolved together with this system and were able to fully take advantage of it. We have nothing currently in place that approaches this system in sophistication and universality. Government, as a regulatory agency, undoubtedly has a role to play in hastening the adoption of these sorts of methods, but as in most cases, we can hope the market will recognize the long-term advantages of buildings capable of being dismantled and will begin to demand them soon.

### ■ utilize good building materials

Many people now accept that our buildings should be based wherever possible on renewable resources that have a low environmental impact and energy requirements for production and use—and can easily be returned to the environment. The Japanese made extensive use of bamboo, hemp, and other fast-growth plant species in their buildings, most of which are still available for us today. Similarly, earth was widely used then and remains a promising building material with many excellent applications. The design problem is to find ways to use materials like these that don't require complex and energy-intensive production processes or transportation over great distances.

Construction wood is rarely recovered in the West, except to be shredded for use as mulch or burned as fuel. Most becomes landfill. Similarly, though the recycling and reuse of glass bottles is highly developed, window glass is rarely recovered from demolition sites, and neither are tiles or plastics. These and other building materials need to be redesigned to enable easy recovery, but this kind of recycling will only solve part of the problem. We need to reduce the overall energy used in building material production and in building itself, including the transportation of materials. Better "green" building materials need to be produced locally, based on renewable sources that not only require little post-processing, but are inherently strong, flexible, attractive, and inexpensive. In

short, the ideal new building materials will need all of the virtues of bamboo.

### ■ moratorium, maybe?

Lumber for construction presents an excruciating problem. Sustainable forestry is possible and has gained acceptance in theory if not widely in practice. Wood should be a renewable resource, but deforestation nonetheless proceeds rapidly all around the globe. Should we impose limits on the allowable size of wooden homes? Prohibit the use of hardwoods and certain other species? Require that a high percentage of all new wood construction be from recycled material? Require the inhabitants of specific geographic regions to achieve self-sufficiency in timber? Call for a complete moratorium on the use of wood for construction?

To resort to any of these would be a hardship for us all, because wood is otherwise such an ideal building material. On the positive side, recent developments in wood structural design and engineering, as well as fabrication technology, are resulting in extremely material-efficient and low-waste wood-based building methods, but these admirable efforts may easily be undone by environmental catastrophe. The time has come to develop low-energy, wood-free

## room heating and cooling

Japan went from portable wood and coal *hibachi* braziers to portable kerosene, gas, and electric heaters, to wall mounted heating/cooling units, one per room. Heating or cooling the entire house at once was never on the table for most families, and one rarely encounters central heating in Japanese homes. This attitude has led to the development, marketing, and continuous refinement of a great diversity of localized systems, including heated carpets and lap rugs, oscillating electric infrared floor units, highly efficient freestanding gas heaters, and ideas like heating the toilet seat alone instead of the entire bathroom. It is undeniable that recent generations have come to expect more instantaneous comfort than their forebears, and this is reflected in unnecessarily high thermostat settings in many institutional buildings. But at home, where frugality rules, industry continues to help people keep the heat just where they need it.

construction methods, and to learn to build without using even plywood for concrete forms. We can hope we never have to resort to using them widely, but if sustainable forestry is not achieved in the next decade or two, wood construction will rapidly become an artifact of the past.

## ■ redesign kitchens to use less fuel

The kitchens of the developed world should be redesigned to require much less energy. Low-temperature food preparation is gaining in safety and viability, and means of preservation that do not consume energy for refrigeration, like dehydration, should be encouraged. Ironically, as the experience of Edo shows, making use of food that is prepared in large quantities or on a commercial scale is one way to use fuel efficiently. Few of us would preheat the oven for an hour just to bake a single cupcake; one can envision a closer technical coordination between home kitchens and food preparation services that would preserve the attractions of the former while maximizing the virtues of the latter.

We are saddled with kitchen systems, designs, and methods that were developed when oil was cheap and environmental concerns were not considered. Just as the shower and toilet account for the most profligate use of water in our homes, the kitchen, particularly the refrigerator, is the greatest consumer of power. True, recent designs are much more energy efficient than the ones our parents grew up with, but power use in the kitchen is still high. There is much room for decreasing our energy consumption at home, from replacing incandescent lights with compact fluorescent bulbs, to better insulation. But we can have the greatest impact by learning to use much less energy when we preserve and prepare food.

## energy-saving meals

Homemakers are sometimes criticized for serving their families dishes bought already prepared instead of cooking from scratch. The implication is that they are lazy or don't care enough. But in fact they are simply continuing a very old urban tradition. And just as in the Edo period, consuming food prepared (usually expertly, one might add) in large quantities is less wasteful in terms of fuel, refrigeration, transportation, and storage. As with everything in life, it must be approached wisely, from the standpoints of nutrition, packaging, and time. But people who organize meals for their families should feel reassured that buying several prepared dishes every week is not a sign of moral decline, but actually an excellent example of making use of what the market provides.

The ubiquitous, convenient, inexpensive, and highly evolved Japanese delivery services that thrive today are the direct descendents of those of the Edo period, and while their reach is now international, it's in what they can do locally that they really shine. No matter how narrow and labyrinthine the alleyway, how oddly shaped or unwieldy the parcel, how delicate or unusual the contents, deliverymen have learned from their ancestors: nurture personal relationships with the people on the route, become intimately familiar with the terrain, have the right kind of containers for every eventuality, and be physically fit. By eliminating the need to use personal vehicles in most cases, and integrating these functions into a specialized transportation system that can benefit from economies of scale and efficient use of time and fuel, Japanese delivery services point in a positive direction.

# greening the block

If older Tokyo neighborhoods today resemble their Edo-period counterparts despite the fact that the buildings themselves are quite different, it's because residents continue the practice of raising potted plants outdoors. Streets are still narrow, and homes and shops close together, and there's rarely room for real gardens or front yards that might provide a bit of green, but people adorn their streets, alleyways, balconies, and every possible nook and cranny with plants and flowers just like their ancestors did. Often the impression is somewhat ad-hoc and chaotic, with hints of competition among neighbors as well as evident loving care. Greening the block in this way is considered a public service, and in a sense efforts in this direction are expected. It's just one more way that the natural humanizing drive manifests itself in this vast metropolis.

## ■ create urban free zones

Urban free zones are essential for the health of communities, but as designer and theorist Christopher Alexander points out, we have forgotten how to make them. What we have instead are over-designed, dead plazas, scattered disconnectedly through our cities, most of which are not really public. Public free zones should serve many functions, have a place for all the members of the community to participate, and most importantly, enable the spontaneous chance encounters that form the basis of social interaction at all levels. A public space with real vitality can rarely be designed all at once but must be allowed to develop gradually by observing spontaneous social behavior and finding ways to support and encourage it. The *sakariba* of Edo were noisy and chaotic, and one probably had to be alert for pickpockets and hucksters, but in fact they provide an ideal model for the kind of self-organizing pedestrian plazas our cities need more of.

## ■ plan active waterfronts

Active waterfronts allow us to witness society, technology, commerce, and nature all at once. They are ideal for solitary meanderings and meditations, and for group work as well as for play. A large river or a bay is usually the primary feature of the landscape that surrounds it, and it was probably what made the site attractive for settlement in the first place. Being able to spend time on the waterfront helps keep us in touch with our locale, with the seasons, with birds and aquatic animals. Offering the possibility of travel and commerce, a waterfront provides a window onto the wider world outside. It also allows us to see an essential but otherwise hidden side of ourselves and other people. We should make sure all of our waterfronts are active ones.

## ■ gather food in the city

Food gathering also keeps us connected to our locale. Whereas being able to gather fruit or nuts, fish, or perhaps hunt near one's home was something our ancestors took for granted, it is now extremely uncommon. It is not merely that we should be able to find some food for free, but that we can be regularly reminded and reassured that our home locale can sustain us. Some towns and cities have begun planting fruit and nut trees in parks and other public areas, and encouraging citizens to do the same on their private land, partly as insurance against expected future food shortages. Having citizens who can help feed themselves will clearly be an advantage as the environment worsens.

# a life of restraint

## the samurai of edo

We are on our way to visit a friend in Ichigaya, one of Edo's samurai districts. Our route entails crossing bridges over crowded waterways and trudging up several of the slopes that connect the commoners' downtown neighborhoods with the more elevated avenues of the elite.

The city is literally divided into "high" and "low." The limited high ground of the low ridges and hills rises above the low and marshy plain, and it has been deemed most suitable for the military classes. The bridges are fortified and gated; they are defensive choke points augmenting the concentric moats of the castle. Samurai are warriors, and the layout of their residential areas surrounding the castle reflects the defensive considerations that dominated city planning when Edo was laid out in the sixteenth century. The geographic segregation of the city reflects the social hierarchy. Like is grouped with like, each in his place, with limited contact between levels. What contact occurs among people from different social strata is tightly governed by both law and custom.

Samurai dressed for work.

The daily functioning of society and the economy requires townsmen to have access to the samurai neighborhoods, however, and vice versa. Though we have no express right to cross the bridges, pass through the gates, and enter this neighborhood, as long as we observe proper protocol we will not be prevented from doing so, except in times of emergency or unrest. And so, having given satisfactory replies to the guards who inquired at several points about the nature of our business, we find ourselves standing at last on a narrow, leafy street in the Bancho neighborhood, home to hundreds of middle- and low-ranking samurai families, including one Hasegawa Yoshisada, who works in the quartermaster's office of the shogun at Edo Castle. An acquaintance of ours named Minoru, who lives in a nearby suburb, periodically tends the samurai's garden, and he has been given permission to show it to us this afternoon. But first we must get our bearings.

The castle stands a short walk to the southeast, and the high, pine tree-covered embankment of its inner moat dominates the skyline in that direction. Though we are on our way to a fairly modest home, there are over two hundred daimyo, or feudal lords, whose vast palace grounds are grouped in clusters around the castle. One such neighborhood, Daimyo Koji, lies to the south,

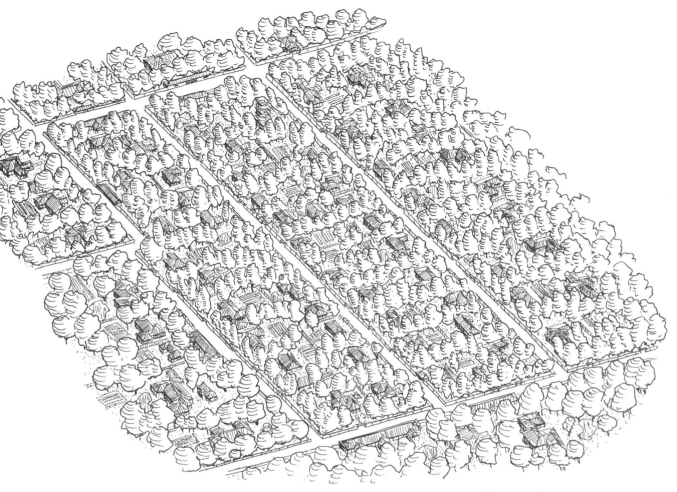

and its homes and gardens benefit from optimal placement on southern-facing slopes. To the north and to the west, beyond the outer moat, a patchwork of temples, samurai, and townsmen's homes gives way eventually to rice fields and the occasional garden estate beyond the city limits.

In addition to the two hundred and sixty daimyo-class households in Edo, there are over five thousand "bannermen" and over seventeen thousand "housemen." And the vast numbers of foot soldiers, porters, guards, and others at the lowest ranks bring the total number of samurai living in Edo to over six hundred and fifty thousand. Together with the daimyo they occupy 63 percent of the city's land.

By contrast, the six hundred thousand townspeople are crammed into only 18 percent of the city's land area (since more than 19 percent is devoted to temples and other uses). In fact, the area of the daimyo estates alone far exceeds the area allotted to the entire commoner population. The difference in

Residential districts for samurai are based on a grid of long rectangular blocks, but geographic irregularities often prevent an ideal layout. Nevertheless, all samurai above the lowest rank are provided with a lot big enough for a substantial garden, and over the course of centuries the tree canopy has grown and matured.

residential density between the samurai districts and those of the commoners is extreme to say the least.

As we stroll the wide streets, the difference between this area's infrastructure and that of the townsmen's district is immediately apparent. Many of the streets are paved, and all are flanked by wide stone gutters to carry rain runoff and wastewater, requiring the entries to many residences to be bridged handsomely with stone. The streets are cleaner and generally more neatly kept than those of the townsmen. While not deserted, they lack the bustle and noise of downtown, mainly because there are no shops. Because samurai women are generally not allowed to go out shopping, the merchants come to them, and we see quite a few peddlers singing their wares—food, household items, and other services. Almost every household need can be adequately met by a visit from one of these door-to-door deliverymen.

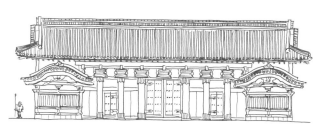

SAMURAI GATEWAYS

Samurai gateways run the gamut from immense and elaborate to quite simple and humble. The large gate at left marks the official residence of a Daimyo (Lord) of high rank (annual income of 325,000 "koku" of rice). The gate of a 100-koku rank samurai is shown for comparison.

The inhabitants here dress differently than the townspeople as well. While the actual cut of their clothes is nearly identical, particularly in their daily wear, because of the constraints of both frugality and propriety, the colors and patterns are much more sober: black, dark gray, dark brown, indigo. The fabric itself is nearly universally of simple weave, often expertly homespun by the women of the household, with cotton far outstripping silk in terms of frequency. Nonetheless, almost every samurai we see carries himself with a dignified, if not arrogant, air, and is as carefully groomed, from footwear to topknot, as his resources allow. All samurai carry two swords, at this point more as badges of status than as weapons, and their rank is displayed by subtly apparent differences in the quality and design of their clothes and accoutrements, as well as by the number and manner of their retinue. We see quite a few on horseback, most of them with grooms and porters trotting in front and behind, and we are frequently passed by samurai in palanquins, both open and closed.

# CLOTHING - MEN

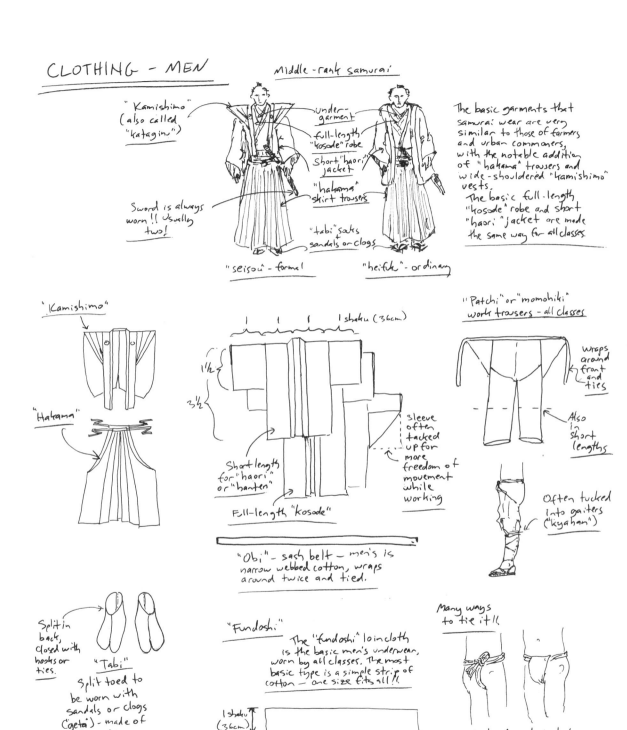

Middle-rank samurai

"Kamishimo" (also called "katagimu")

under-garment

full-length "kosode" robe

Short "haori" jacket

"hakama" skirt trousers

Sword is always worn !! Usually two!

"tabi" socks + sandals or clogs

"seisou" - formal

"heifuku" - ordinary

The basic garments that samurai wear are very similar to those of farmers and urban commoners, with the notable addition of "hakama" trousers and wide-shouldered "kamishimo" vests.
The basic full-length "kosode" robe and short "haori" jacket are made the same way for all classes.

"Kamishimo"

"Hakama"

1 shaku (36cm)

1½

3½

Short lengths for "haori" or "hanten"

Full-length "kosode"

sleeve often tacked up for more freedom of movement while working

"Obi" - sash belt - men's is narrow webbed cotton, wraps around twice and tied.

"Patchi" or "momohiki" work trousers - all classes

wraps around front and ties

Also in short lengths

Often tucked into gaiters ("kyahan")

Split in back, closed with hooks or ties.

"Tabi"
Split toed to be worn with sandals or clogs ("geta") - made of white cotton.

"Fundoshi"

The "fundoshi" loincloth is the basic men's underwear, worn by all classes. The most basic type is a simple strip of cotton - one size fits all !!

1 shaku (36cm)

← 6 shaku (2.2 m) →
"Roku shaku fundoshi"

Many ways to tie it !!

For hard work in hot weather, a man doesn't need to wear anything else !!

# CLOTHING - WOMEN

## Middle-rank samurai

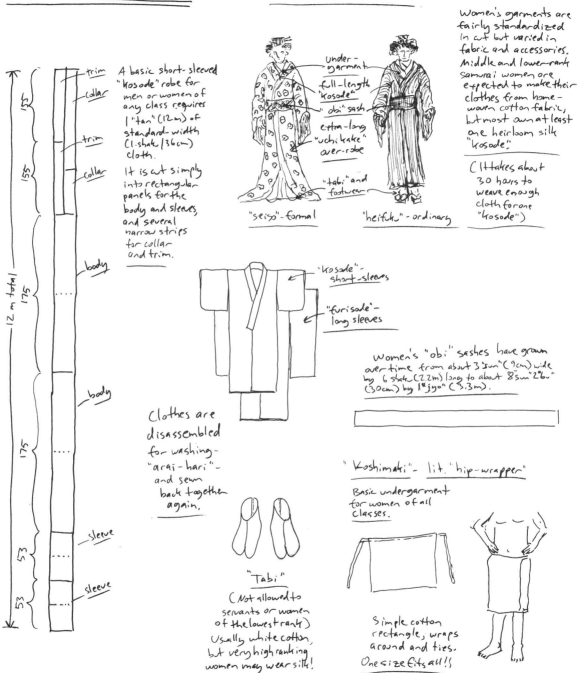

A basic short-sleeved "kosode" robe for men or women of any class requires 1 "tan" (12m) of standard-width (1 shaku / 36cm) cloth.

It is cut simply into rectangular panels for the body and sleeves, and several narrow strips for collar and trim.

Women's garments are fairly standardized in cut but varied in fabric and accessories. Middle and lower-rank samurai women are expected to make their clothes from home-woven cotton fabric, but most own at least one heirloom silk "kosode."

(It takes about 30 hours to weave enough cloth for one "kosode")

"seiso" - formal

"heifuku" - ordinary

under-garment

full-length "kosode"

"obi" sash

extra-long "uchikake" over-robe

"tabi" and footwear

"kosode" - short-sleeves

"furisode" - long sleeves

Clothes are disassembled for washing - "arai-hari" - and sewn back together again.

Women's "obi" sashes have grown over time from about 3 "sun" (9cm) wide by 6 shaku (2.2m) long to about 8 "sun" 2 "bu" (30cm) by 1 "jyo" (3.3m).

"Tabi"

(Not allowed to servants or women of the lowest rank) Usually white cotton, but very high ranking women may wear silk!

"Koshimaki" - lit. "hip-wrapper"

Basic undergarment for women of all classes.

Simple cotton rectangle, wraps around and ties. One size fits all!!

Whereas every block of the merchant districts is lined with two-story buildings whose first-floor shops open directly onto the street, we are now walking by long, high walls, punctuated at regular intervals by gates. The walls are of varied construction, some tiled and plastered, some made of wooden boards, and some topped by hedges. Over their tops we can see trees of every variety, quite a few with branches extending over the street, hinting at the gardens inside. All we can see of the actual houses are the roofs and gables, but from this we can tell that they are relatively modest, tile-roofed, one-story buildings, set back some distance from the street.

There is quite a bit of variety to the gates. Most of them are fairly simple roofed affairs of unpainted wood set slightly in from the wall. The roofs of some are tiled, but others are roofed with cedar shakes and still others with thin boards. A few of the homes have actual gatehouses, a small rectangular building that forms part of the surrounding wall, with a heavy wooden door at one end. These indicate that the occupant has enough status (if not necessarily the income) to warrant owning a horse, and the gatehouse is both stable and groom's quarters. A few blocks away we can see higher, grander, and more elaborate gateways; these mark the residences of higher-ranking samurai.

The size of gates, their configuration, and the decoration allowed or expected of each rank have long been standardized and legislated, and they are one of the more obvious and public displays of household status. The massive, sculpture-encrusted freestanding gateways legislated for daimyo were ruinously expensive to build, but the great fire in 1657 prompted a overall reconsideration of how newly scarce funds and building resources should be allocated. Daimyo gates built since then are still massive, but they are built into the wall as gatehouses and are not nearly as elaborately decorated.

The lifestyle of the daimyo, of course, with their large, luxurious estates and conspicuous consumption, is a far cry from how the middle-ranking samurai of this neighborhood live. Though nominally all these samurai are warriors, are trained as such, and adhere to a military rank system and chain of command, over a century of peace has seen the samurai mutate into a bureaucratic class of salaried workers. They are well educated, aware of history and precedent, but their daily life is entirely dependent upon the rice stipends their daimyo awarded their ancestors. For this, samurai owe intense loyalty to their lords. The actual income available to each family is dependent primarily on its rank and is measured in *koku*, measures of rice considered adequate to feed a person for one year (about five bushels). But many factors can influence the stipend—the local finances of their province being a major factor—and samurai of wealthy provinces live better than their counterparts from impoverished

Though most samurai dress modestly and unobtrusively, a few affect fashions that mark them as cultured connoisseurs of the arts, or "tsu." They are able to do this through subtle modifications of the pattern and fit of their otherwise standard garments.

(Illustration taken from an Edo-period guidebook)

ones. They are also often required to kick back a fraction of their stipend to their lords as forced loans, and excuses are often found to further reduce their rice payments. On the other hand, a samurai can increase his income through opportunities for special service, by finding good positions for his offspring, and by personal promotion.

The rank and position of a samurai are both hereditary and merit based. But the majority lack economic mobility.

The residents of this block could be considered lower-middle rank, and their incomes range from about 100 koku per year to about 300, though families with considerably larger stipends live nearby as well.

## a samurai retainer's house

We turn into a slightly narrower road and spot our friend Minoru, the gardener, squatting outside a modest, open gate, surrounded by baskets of leaves and cuttings and smoking a long pipe. We call out, and he waves to us. He taps out his pipe, rises with a grunt, and leads us through Hasegawa's gate.

The first thing to greet us is a simple, well-kept Japanese garden, nearly bisected by a straight, wide, stone walkway. Several trees grow just inside the wall: a fine *sakura* (cherry) that is a neighborhood landmark and that friends and neighbors drop by to view when it blooms in the spring; a pair of tall cryptomeria; and further back, a chestnut tree. There are ornamental shrubs, mostly camellias, of course, and several miniature azaleas. Some low flowerbeds have just started to bloom. The ground is covered partly with gravel, in the shadier spots with moss, and a well-trodden footpath has exposed the dirt elsewhere. To our right, a high bamboo wall punctuated by a simple hinged gate hides another part of the garden from view. It is the kitchen garden, and it has its own well for supplying water to the household. On our left is a tall boxwood hedge, beyond which we can glimpse a much larger garden.

The formal entry ("genkan") of the house as seen through the gateway ("mon"). The gardener has brought a full load of new plants from the nursery.

# SAMURAI HOUSE LAYOUT

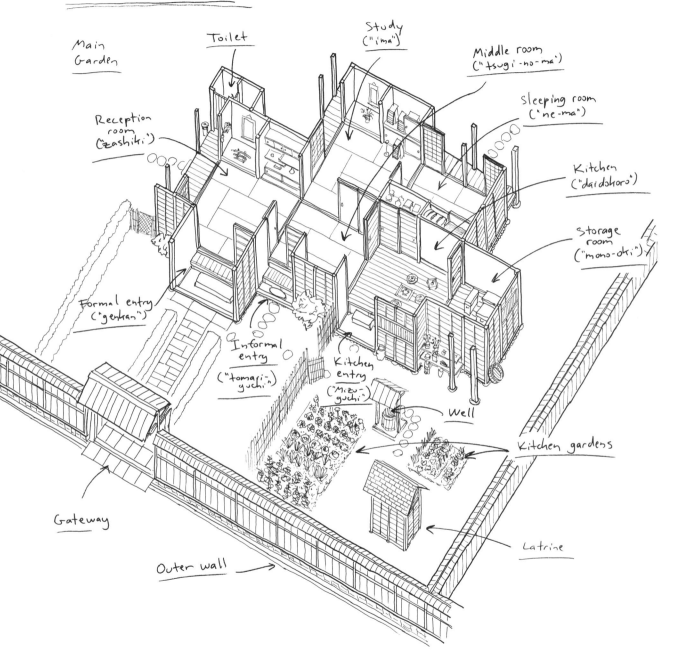

Main Garden

Toilet

Study ("ima")

Middle room ("tsugi-no-ma")

Sleeping room ("ne-ma")

Reception room ("zashiki")

Kitchen ("daidokoro")

Formal entry ("genkan")

Storage room ("mono-oki")

Informal entry ("tomari-n guchi")

Kitchen entry ("mizu-guchi")

Well

Kitchen gardens

Gateway

Latrine

Outer wall

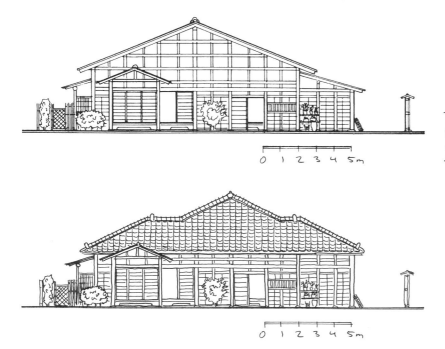

Though samurai of wealthy provinces like Kaga are accustomed to displaying their status by sober but noticeable decorative flourishes like half-timbered gables (above), the focus on economy in Edo itself means that samurai houses there are more likely to have subtle hipped roofs.

Hasegawa-san inherited this house from his father, and he lives here with his wife and two young sons, Yoshiharu and Yoshitaka. A maid lives with the family as well, and Kochi, a low-ranking samurai retainer, reports to the house every morning from his nearby barracks and accompanies his master everywhere. Many of Hasegawa's neighbors have enough space to house their retainers, and though he would like to add an extra room to his house for the purpose, the family can't afford it. Still, Koichi is trusted and considered part of the household.

Hasegawa's house is set back from the front gate by about 8 meters. Its gable end faces us, and the tiled roof is of shallow pitch. In the past, wooden shingles, boards, and even thatch were used for roofing samurai houses in the city, but as timber resources became scarce over the course of the past century, these materials became expensive enough to discourage their use. Coupled with the fire hazard, it led the government to require tile roofs for all new construction. The roof is low slung and hipped, its ridges topped by a line of decorative tile. In some parts of the country, samurai are encouraged to display their status by building houses with prominent gables in which exposed horizontal timbers are set off by gleaming white plasterwork. But in Edo, even this mild ostentation is frowned upon, and low roofs are considered more appropriate.

Though we know that Hasegawa-san is a member of the elite, however middling his status, his house strikes us from the exterior as boxy and utilitarian, and devoid of decoration. Though we've glimpsed handsome whitewashed exterior walls on some of the other houses nearby, and even rich ochre-colored earthen walls on a few, the walls of this house are of simple unpainted vertical boards and battens, now patinaed by time and verging on shabbiness. But the family has occupied this spot for four generations, and the slightly run-down atmosphere is accompanied by a sense of ease, grace, and permanence, as if the house and its gardens had emerged from the ground of their own accord. The formal entry to the house lies straight ahead. This is reserved for use by the master of the house when departing or returning from his post at the castle (the samurai of this neighborhood are all direct vassals of the shogun himself), and by guests for whom a show of respect is appropriate—mainly the boss, but also one's parents and in-laws, and individuals of equal rank but of no particular intimacy. There are two other entrances as well: one, the *tomari-guchi*, is the informal entry used by women and children and for daily puttering around; the other, the kitchen entrance, or *mizu-guchi*, is used for deliveries and by servants but exists mainly to make it easy to lug water from the well to the kitchen.

## a dignified ensemble

The main gate, the gable of the house, and the main entrance have been designed to work together as a dignified ensemble, and the *genkan*, the formal entry itself manages to be both inviting and sobering. It is recessed into the house, nestled under the wide overhanging eaves, and it has a small roof of its own. It is made of wood, simply treated and now handsomely aged. The stone entrance walkway ends at a low wooden sill marking the boundary of the entry; beyond this is a narrow paved surface, a low flat stone, and a wide wooden step, called the *shikidai*. All in all, the ensemble suggests both modesty and dignity.

The stone is actually a *kutsu-nugi-ishi*, or shoe-removing stone, and it is as poetic as it is practical. Formal entry into a house means stepping up from the ground level to that of the raised floor. In the case of farmhouses or townhouses, the main entry almost always leads to a doma, where one can remove one's shoes and step up to the raised, usually wooden floor. But shoe-removing stones are found in several contexts: they are provided as a means of access to the wooden veranda on the garden or courtyard side of a house, for entry into a teahouse, or, as here, as a means of stepping up from the ground to the shikidai of a samurai house. They are intentionally used in a nearly unfinished, natural state, implying a simple and direct interaction with nature, and are self-consciously archaic. In the ancient period, when most people occupied dirt-floored pit dwellings, a raised floor represented both a technological and social breakthrough, available initially only to the ruling class and so deserving of emphasis. The stone is as much an earthy totem of superior rank as it is a practical means of stepping up.

In every case, one steps onto it in one's shoes—straw sandals or wooden clogs—and slips them off while stepping up to the next level. This act of removing footwear marks the first stage of entry into the house. The wide entry platform of the shikidai is the setting for the next step, an exchange of greetings. Ostensibly intended to allow the master or an honored guest to alight from a palanquin without touching the ground, it is now a largely symbolic space. Like a small stage, it allows the visitor to sit on his haunches and compose himself, and it is usually wide enough to allow two or more people to occupy it at once, as protocol might demand. In cases where an extreme difference of status exists, a low-ranking visitor makes his greetings by placing just his hands on the shikidai while kneeling on the ground outside, as a sign of respect.

The shikidai is closed off from the house itself by a simple, sturdy wooden sliding door, made of dark wooden boards and thick horizontal battens, and beyond it is the first of a series of formal tatami-matted reception rooms. Depending upon the situation, Hasegawa-san or another member of his household will make formal greetings while seated on the tatami mats inside. They move aside to allow guests to enter the house, an action as simple as crawling

GENKAN DETAILS
Though their basic configuration is uniform, and the size and elaborateness are determined by the owners' rank, other variations are found.

"Shikidai"

wooden floor and walls

Ideally, the genkan should allow a high-ranking guest to alight from his palanquin with dignity!

Earthen floor and walls

The most modest samurai genkan have earthen floors, like a "doma."

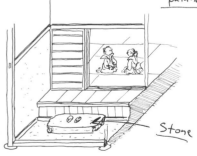

Stone

A shoe-removing stone ("kutsu-nugi-ishi") is less formal than a wooden floor, but it is a welcoming gesture.

forward the short distance from the shikidai to the tatami. There the greetings are concluded.

Though its lines and proportions are simple, the genkan of the samurai house can be seen as a carefully composed stage set where the ritual of greeting can be performed, allowing both parties to present themselves with dignity and to confirm the nature of their relationship with mutual respect. In more prominent households, the shikidai is deep, wide, and of high-quality material; the lowest samurai barely have room for even a simple one. Regardless of scale and status, the configuration of the samurai entryway is the same, because the ritual greeting is the same. This simple step, the shikidai, speaks volumes.

After a brief exchange with the maid, confirming that the master is away and his sons are at school, Minoru lets us into the main house. Passing through the genkan, we find ourselves in a well-appointed eight-mat room, the zashiki, which has the typical features of *shoin*-style architecture. Straight ahead is the *tokonoma*, a deep, slightly raised, decorative niche featuring a vertically hung calligraphic scroll. To the right of the tokonoma is another niche, topped by a fine, built-in cabinet, the *chigai-dana*. These are beautifully crafted and designed with simple forms, and lacquered in black. To the right, *fusuma* sliding doors covered in subtly patterned *washi* paper conceal the other rooms of the house. To the left, the entire wall opens by means of exterior shutters and sliding shoji screens to reveal the main garden, which serves as a backdrop for the activity within the room and is an essential feature of its layout and design.

There is a wide veranda running the full length of the room and a bit beyond, which serves as both a passageway and a place to sit. As seen from the room, the garden is designed to suggest endless depth and the possibility of privacy and contemplation. It gives clear evidence of the passage of time and the cycle of seasons, and it possibly serves as a reminder of the distant landscapes of an ancestral home.

In the quality of its craftsmanship, its proportions, the color and surface of every element, this room is perfectly articulated and extremely beautiful. More than this, it is reposeful. Quiet and uncluttered, it lends dignity to its occupants, and though it is intimately scaled, it enhances social interaction by allowing an ample measure of individual space while enabling physical proximity. The design elements, which incorporate many traditional features passed down through the centuries and are amplified by the many places in which heirlooms can be displayed, suggest great continuity with an aristocratic past. The space itself depicts a carefully maintained, timeless balance of individuals to others and of mankind to nature. This room, the formal heart of the house, feels like an independent garden pavilion, a scholar's retreat deep in the mountains. It is designed to age beautifully, to gain rather than lose impact with the passing of generations. That samurai of even modest means are granted a house and garden of such poetic richness and psychic fulfillment reveals much that penetrates to the core of Japanese longing and what it means to be fulfilled. It is the quintessential Japanese interior. We lower ourselves to sit for a moment, to better take it all in.

## appreciating the design

How does it work? What accounts for the uncanny quality of simultaneous soothing and invigoration? Faced with a design of such perfect integration, we should begin with the quality of sound. Though the street outside this house is relatively quiet, it is still the scene of many comings and goings, of peddlers' cries and shouts of greeting. The wall outside doesn't entirely block these sounds, but it does muffle them, as do the trees and vegetation. The house is set back some distance from the road, and the zashiki is oriented toward the garden instead of the entry, so that the street sounds are largely replaced by those of the garden: bird calls, the chirping and buzzing of insects, the sound of the wind in the trees, the croaking of frogs in the pond, the constant trickle of water. The room acts as a kind of auditory funnel that allows sound from the direction of the garden to be clearly heard by those inside, while shutting out sounds from other directions. With the sliding panels of the wall opened, the garden and zashiki form a fairly isolated island of garden sound, and this contributes a great deal to the overall sense of repose. Though now it is summer and opening the wall makes obvious sense due to the heat, in fact it is kept open year round, even in winter, except during the most inclement weather.

The room is also open to the breeze, and sitting inside here feels a lot like being outside, but shadier. Other sliding doors to the side and rear can be opened to provide more complete through ventilation when desired and to draw in breezes from other directions. The trees planted on nearly every side of the house provide a layer of shade and an envelope of cool air all around that can be easily drawn indoors through the wall openings. The wall facing the garden is a southern exposure, and the tree planting has been planned to maximize this shade zone during the summer while allowing the full strength of the available sunlight to warm the inside of the house during the winter. Breezes provide more than just sensations of warmth and coolness; they carry the perfumes and aromas of the garden as well, a scented banquet that persists throughout the flowering months; it is restful, if not therapeutic.

There are other aromas and physical sensations conveyed by the materials

used in the room's construction. Tatami mats have a characteristic grassy aroma, particularly when they are new, and this is especially noticeable when one is reclining on them. Tatami are rich in a tactile sense as well, their woven upper surface feeling slick if one brushes against it in the direction of the straw grain but giving quite a bit of friction when rubbed the other way. This is easily sensed by the hands, but also through the soles of the feet, even when clad with split-toed cotton *tabi* stockings. The mats are pleasantly yielding underfoot or under the body, and they are soft enough to sleep on without any extra padding.

Most new houses have strong characteristic smells that diminish as the materials are exposed to the air. In the case of this older one, the paper of both the shoji and fusuma have an aroma, partly leafy (from the paper itself), partly sweet (from the rice paste used as an adhesive). These aromas never really go away, perhaps maintained by the moisture in the humid air. Oddly, no matter how humid the air gets, the paper, the wood framing, the tatami, and the clay-plastered walls always feel dry. In the process of equalizing their internal

The well-appointed tatami-floored formal reception room, or "zashiki," and the garden with which it forms an ensemble, are a timeless expression of man's place in the world.

moisture levels with the ambient environment, they absorb quite a lot of water and release it back into the air on dry days as they equalize again. Of course this means that these elements are constantly swelling and contracting, which their design takes into account. It also makes the room more comfortable on both wet and dry days.

The clay walls are dry and sandy, slightly rough to the touch, and they smell like the earth itself. The exposed wood framing, almost universally left unfinished but smoothed as a final touch by expert hands wielding a razor-sharp plane that slices the individual cell walls cleanly open, is also dry to the touch, and—particularly in the case of hinoki or sugi—retains its aroma for years.

On the other hand, the lacquered surfaces, with their impeccably glossy black sheen, give the impression of perpetual wetness. When touched they adhere slightly to the fingertips like glass, because the air seal between the smooth lacquer and skin gives the sensation of stickiness or moisture. On close examination they seem dry enough, but in fact the lacquer is not dry but polymerized; it is technically as much liquid as solid and will continue to flow ever so imperceptibly for centuries under the influence of gravity. There are many ways to use lacquer without emphasizing its gloss, but often, as in this case, the surfaces are like tiny reflective pools tucked inside the room.

The room is truly brought alive by the changing sunlight, which at this time of day suffuses the environment with a unifying warm color almost devoid of glare. The light is filtered through the gently swaying leaves, dappling the ground and walls with pinpoints of dense color, enhanced by the vivid hues of

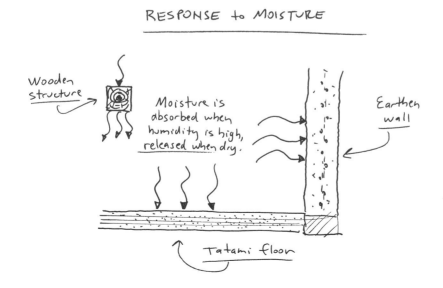

RESPONSE to MOISTURE

Wooden structure

Moisture is absorbed when humidity is high, released when dry.

Earthen wall

Tatami floor

the garden flowers. Light also reflects upward from the shimmering surface of the pond, from light-colored earth and gravel in the garden itself, and from the smoothly polished surface of the veranda boards. This upward-reflecting light casts an ambience that brightens even the ceiling. But despite this pageant of sunlight accenting the interior, there are pools of shadow as well, even on the brightest days. The deep recesses of the shelves, the inner corners of the wood-work, the darkened rooms beyond the sliding doors, all lend character to the space, transforming the play of sunlight into a tug of war between light and dark. And, of course, there are the innumerable filters that lend layers of depth and translucency to the walls: hanging reed blinds, partly closed shoji, trellises of climbing vines.

The light in this room is never simply on or off. Throughout the day and over the course of the seasons it mutates through countless gradations of bright-ness and color, focused by the occupants through clever use of shutters, blinds, and screens. And because the floor is an infinitely reconfigurable seating and reclining surface, one can easily move oneself to an ideally illuminated spot at any time.

Still half kneeling, half sitting, we shift our point of view a bit. The room is like a three-dimensional frame, less an object of observation than a foil to enhance the physical presence and character of the occupants and direct the gaze toward a handful of objects of contemplation: the garden, the hanging scroll, a decorative or votive object or two, some flowers, perhaps the book in which one is immersed. When meals or refreshments are taken here, attention and focus easily shift to the food and drink. The lifestyle, environment, and value system lend themselves more to the creative appreciation of well-crafted and culturally resonant items for daily use—vases, bowls, incense burners, stands, boxes, writing implements—than to works of art that have no practical purpose. The taste appropriate to a room of this style is understated, but bright and highly decorative items can be used, especially if they possess the virtue of age or bring with them an engaging story.

Works of art, like paintings or calligraphy, are usually expected to be instructive or inspirational. A desirable painting or line of calligraphy for the tokonoma is one that sets up poetic associations with the time of year or the occasion, that has a personal connection to the occupant, and that demon-strates a depth of cultural and historical knowledge. A painting is there to be "read" just like a line of calligraphy, its significance and the associations it brings appreciated and mulled over. The decorative objects and the fittings of the room itself—the door pulls, small pieces of hardware—are the only likely locations for surfaces of highly polished metal, tiny dancing glimmers of deeply

# MODULATING SUNLIGHT

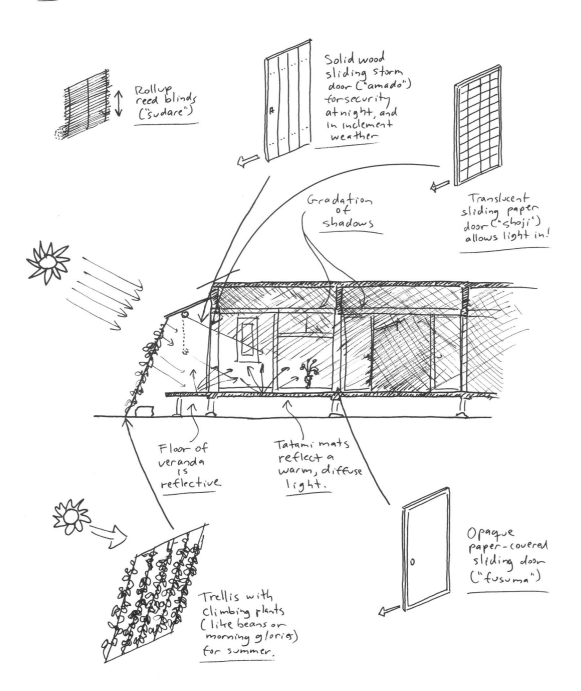

Rollup reed blinds ("sudare")

Solid wood sliding storm door ("amado") for security at night, and in inclement weather

Translucent sliding paper door ("shoji") allows light in!

Gradation of shadows

Floor of veranda is reflective

Tatami mats reflect a warm, diffuse light.

Opaque paper-covered sliding door ("fusuma")

Trellis with climbing plants (like beans or morning glories) for summer.

# SUNLIGHT MOVEMENT

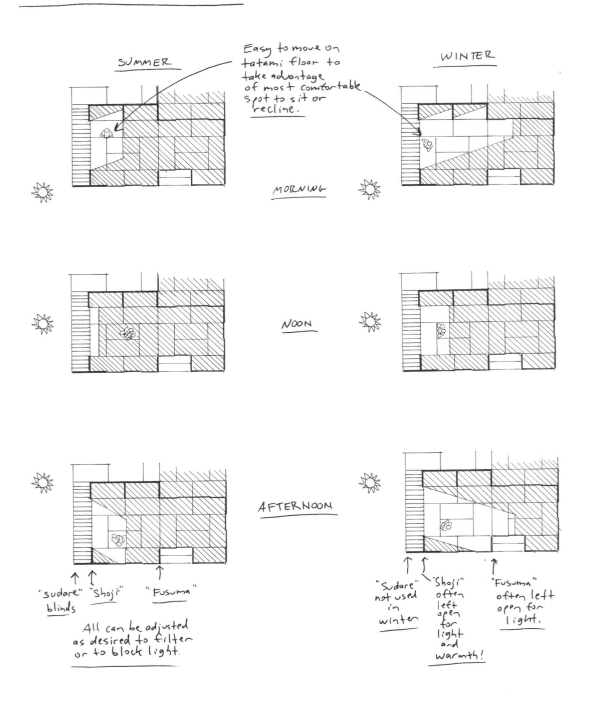

SUMMER

Easy to move on tatami floor to take advantage of most comfortable spot to sit or recline.

WINTER

MORNING

NOON

AFTERNOON

↑ ↑ "Shoji" ↑
"sudare" blinds "Fusuma"

All can be adjusted as desired to filter or to block light.

↑ ↑ ↑
"Sudare" not used in winter

"Shoji" often left open for light and warmth!

"Fusuma" often left open for light.

burnished silver and the incandescent glint of flecks of gold. The artworks, the hardware, the flowers are all conceived as places to rest the eyes, and whether they catch one's gaze momentarily or at length will depend upon their vividness. The more vivid, the more quickly one will feel compelled to turn away; the less vivid surfaces invite the gaze for an extended visit. A person of the best taste will place one vivid object in the room at most and use that as a kind of visual foil to direct the eye to a more reposeful view.

To the right, opposite the garden, sliding doors open to reveal another room. It is smaller than the zashiki and has a tokonoma but no built-in cabinets; it also has sliding doors on every side. This room, usually called the *tsugi-no-ma*, or "middle" room, is multipurpose. With the fusuma between the two rooms open when occasion calls for it, this room becomes a de facto extension of the other, though increasing perceptibly in dimness the farther one gets from the garden. This room also has the "family" entrance, the tomari-guchi, for the daily comings and goings of women and children.

One more formal room, the *ima*, or study, lies behind another set of sliding doors. It too has an entire wall opening onto the garden and both a *tokonoma* and built-in cabinets. This is the master's private domain, and it is decorated to feel both more masculine and more intimate. A certain idiosyncrasy expressing the occupant's personality is both excused and expected. A hanging scroll of monkeys reflects Hasegawa's personal taste and frame of mind, and a writing table and inkstand occupy the center of the floor most of the time. It is a garden room, and it shares in the conducive, pavilion-like ambience and sensibility of the zashiki, with the added benefit of relative privacy. It is easy to imagine Hasegawa-san spending long days here in his study, immersed in his reading and writing and in private discussion. He likely calls his children here, either for reprimand or praise, and his most familiar friends will be whisked through the zashiki to be received in this sanctuary.

These three rooms form the formal zone of the house, and though they are infrequently used, they take up more than half of its floor space. Better finished and more comfortable than the other rooms, they are kept immaculate and appropriately decorated in the event of unannounced visits from superiors. Poor design would be considered an insult to these guests, but design or finish that is ostentatious or inappropriately grand for one's rank would be not only be insulting, but possibly a prosecutable breach of sumptuary laws. For samurai, the reception of guests is a tense, protocol-ridden affair that requires a large outlay of money if for nothing else than to provide suitable space for it. But a large proportion of this inescapable and clearly codified protocol is intended to enhance the beauty of the occasion.

AESTHETIC DETAIL

A vase, incense burner, lacquer box, or other small decorative object may be quite striking in form and vivid in color, but only if it is the only thing in the room that has those characteristics.

If the eye is provided with a more restful refuge elsewhere as well — a subdued expanse of wall or floor, or natural greenery outdoors — then the result will be both soothing and stimulating.

# FLEXIBLE LAYOUT

## FORMAL OCCASION

The "zashiki" and "tsugi-no-ma" can be connected to receive a large group. The study ("ima") is closed, but can easily be used for private conversation. The kitchen and sleeping room ("ne-ma") are kept closed.

## VERY INFORMAL

The entire house is open "zashiki" to kitchen to allow breezes to cool the house during summer months. The study and sleeping room are opened to each other, but closed off from the rest of the house for privacy.

## DAILY USE

Typically the study and sleeping room will be connected during the day and used as a unit, while the kitchen and "tsugi-no-ma" will be connected for household work, etc. The "fusuma" separating the "zashiki" from the rest of the house may be opened for light and breeze, but the family will avoid using the room.

## the private zone

We hear the crunch of wooden clogs on the gravel path outside and the loud voices of the boys. They have returned from their afternoon classes at the neighborhood school, run as a business by an older, well-educated samurai who has more space in his house than income. A fusuma in the middle room slides open with a clatter, and the maid motions us quickly into the modest wooden-floored kitchen. Bringing our sandals, she directs us to sit on the edge of the floor. Minoru joins us, and the maid brings us cups of tea. We are now in the private zone of the house. The kitchen is considered appropriate for servants, workers, and tradesmen.

The boys loudly announce their presence as they cross the threshold of the family entrance. Kowtowing deeply with both hands on the floor as the boys enter the kitchen, the maid welcomes the young masters home with great formality. We follow Minoru's lead and bow as respectfully as we can, since the boys, though not yet twelve, are our social superiors. "They are with the gardener," the maid says by way of explanation rather than introduction, and we nod our heads without breaking into a smile. She pours them some tea and, ignoring us, they seat themselves at the sunken hearth and animatedly continue their discussion of the day's events.

We resume sipping our tea and look around at the kitchen. To the right is the doma's very small earthen-floored area and the *mizu-guchi* "water entrance" of the house (so-called because it provides the closest access to the well outside). The family's cooking stove and sink stand on the earthen floor. The sunken hearth around which the boys sit is in the center of the wooden floor. To our left is an entire wall of wooden-shuttered storage cabinets, filled with serving trays, dishes, kitchen implements, and other household items. Even this modest household must be able to serve a large number of people

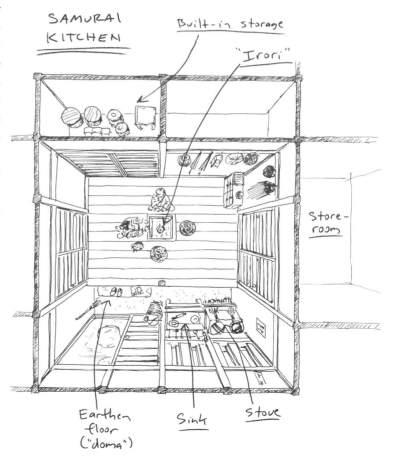

SAMURAI KITCHEN

Built-in storage

"Irori"

Store-room

Earthen floor ("doma")

Sink

Stove

on special occasions like weddings and funerals, and so space for twenty sets of dishes must be found.

Whereas the other rooms we have seen all had fine ceilings, this is open to the sooty rafters above. In several respects, the samurai kitchen is much like its farmhouse and merchant house counterparts. Like them, it is the main gathering place for the household, including menials and retainers. In particular it is the women's realm. In most formal situations, the presence of women in the reception rooms is neither required nor encouraged, and they are expected to perform their duties out of sight. Servicing a meeting between samurai is a job for males: sons, retainers, or menials. At the same time, while being entertained in style in the reception rooms is a sign of esteem, being invited to join the family around their hearth is a sign of acceptance, trust, and intimacy, and it is here that one is likely to enjoy the best hospitality the family has to offer.

Interestingly, if the character and quality of the formal rooms and gardens of the samurai house set them apart from what is enjoyed by the lower classes, the overall similarity of their kitchens and other functional areas is just as striking. The samurai kitchen is, if anything, smaller and more frugal than that of the typical merchant and certainly smaller than a farmhouse kitchen; but all are built with similar materials and technology, and reflect a similarly conservative attitude toward fuel use. One would have to visit the kitchen of a much higher-ranking warrior to witness the conspicuous consumption of fuel for cooking, lighting, and heating.

In addition to the kitchen, the private zone of this house includes a six-mat room for sleeping and a four-and-a-half mat storage and utility room. The sleeping room has its own veranda and opens onto the side garden. It is a very comfortable and well-lit place to spend the day. Though primarily for sleeping, when linked with the study it forms a snug but welcoming living room. Once the formal sequence of the zashiki and the study has been suitably taken into consideration, a samurai can lay out the rest of his home as freely as his financial resources allow. In fact, because of the placement of the sliding doors in this house, the middle room and the master's study can be easily reconfigured to form a larger private zone joined to the kitchen, thereby performing an economical double duty. Other samurai of similar rank might decide that another private room is necessary to adequately accommodate family life, particularly if they supplement their income, as so many do, with piecework and handcrafts. Depending upon the nature of the work, a wooden-floored space might be required, though tatami are suitable for others.

The Hasegawa house is a bit luxurious in that it has two toilets. The one

The samurai have a simple, wholesome diet. Most meals consist of a main dish like grilled fish, a small bowl of miso soup or broth, some pickled vegetables, and a bowl of white rice.

# SAMURAI COTTAGE INDUSTRIES

Umbrella-making and repair.

Basketry

Weaving cloth

Lantern-making

Letter-writing and calligraphy

As time has gone on, samurai increasingly find it necessary to supplement their incomes with other work. These are often crafts, intellectual work like teaching or writing, plant-breeding and bonsai, or other work in which education provides an advantage. Many samurai women are expert weavers.

designated for use by the family and household help is in an outhouse a few steps beyond the well, and access is through the "water entrance." This location is also fairly close to the front gate, so that the contents can be emptied by night soil merchants with a minimum of disruption. The samurai of this neighborhood get a higher price for their night soil than the average commoner, but not as high as a daimyo household or a house of entertainment. Another toilet is provided close to the main garden and zashiki; it is considered a "guest" facility. Though inconvenient from the kitchen and other private rooms, it is perfectly and attractively sited for guests, and though spare, it is considered the more presentable of the two.

This house has no separate fireproof storage building, and Hasegawa-san doesn't rate a horse and stable; besides the house there only a few garden sheds on the property. The house, therefore, is extremely compact. It is the

# FRUGALITY and ANTI-WASTE

## Paper

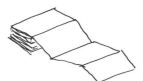

Most samurai use recycled paper for everyday purposes, saving new for important messages like New Year's greetings. Recycled paper is grey in color due to the presence of ink in the pulp!

"Andon" lantern

"Hibachi" brazier

## Fuel

Samurai often don't heat their homes at all during the winter, except for the coldest days, when health is at stake.
Many avoid burning lamps at night to save fuel.

## "Zabuton"

Most samurai consider cushions for tatami floors an unnecessary extravagance. (But used straw mats on the wooden kitchen floor)

## Clothing

Samurai families make most of their own clothes, from weaving the cloth to assembling the garment (though they usually send the thread out to be dyed).
The same cloth is often used for everyone in the family, to make it easier to patch the clothes. Children wear hand-me-downs, including split-toed "tabi" socks. Household help isn't allowed to wear socks, even in the cold months!

"Sembei" rice crackers

## SNACKS

While townspeople of the merchant classes wouldn't think of receiving guests without serving them a treat, samurai neither expect it from their hosts, nor provide it.

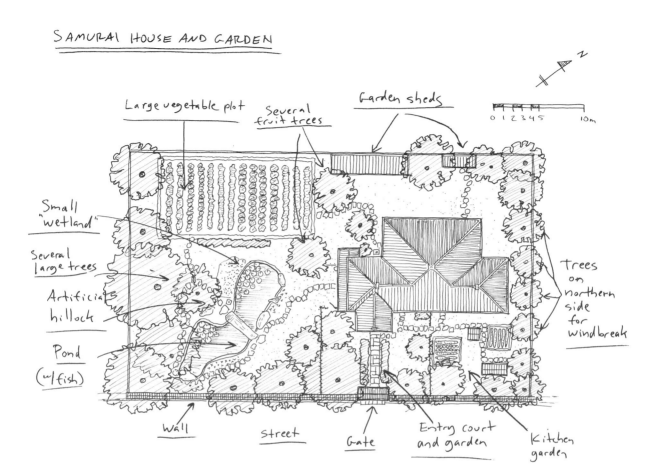

## SAMURAI HOUSE AND GARDEN

Large vegetable plot

Several fruit trees

Garden sheds

Small "wetland"

Several large trees

Artificial hillock

Pond (w/ fish)

Trees on northern side for windbreak

Wall

Street

Gate

Entry court and garden

Kitchen garden

0 1 2 3 4 5   10m

openness to the garden and its ease of reconfiguring, as well as the quality of the construction and detailing of the formal spaces, that make it so livable. If family fortunes improve, extra family and workrooms can easily be added; if they decline, a few simple one-room apartments could be built on the property and rented out to impecunious samurai grooms and porters.

Finishing his tea with a slightly overdone smack of his lips, Minoru calls, "Thank you for your hospitality!" to no one in particular, and as the maid approaches he stands and announces our departure. The boys glance in our direction and nod curtly, and we bow deeply before exiting through the water entrance.

Despite the compactness of the lot itself, the house is entirely surrounded by gardens. In fact, the house only occupies about one-eighth of the lot, and the rest is green. The "front" garden, the one we saw from the front gate, is the smallest

The house is 30 tsubo (99m²) in area, and stands on a lot of 300 tsubo (990m²) in size, about the largest size allowed samurai of the "100-koku" rank. The lot is large enough for both a vegetable plot and an ornamental garden, but it was not uncommon for nearly the entire garden of lower samurai to be farmed. (Based on Yamamoto House)

and simplest, but care has been taken to make it presentable and suitably ornamental; its wide paved stone entrance pathway lends it the air of a courtyard. The
main garden, the one visible from the reception rooms, is similarly decorative
and ornamental, and it is intended to make a good impression, though accommodation is made for idiosyncratic taste in the areas visible from the study.

## the self-sufficient samurai

Now, however, we are standing in the side garden, which, along with the
generously sized rear garden, is rarely seen by guests. It might be called a
"kitchen" garden because it lies outside the kitchen door, and in addition
to being where the well and family toilet are located, it has room for a small
vegetable plot. This is tended by household members, and Minoru's assistance
and advice are rarely required. As he leads us around the back of the house to
see the rear garden, we stop in our tracks. The rear garden looks very much like
a small farm.

Though not required to do so by law, samurai families like the Hasegawas
are encouraged to be as self-sufficient as possible. They have been granted fairly
generous plots, and with the increasing financial difficulties they face, this has
led to widespread urban farming. Like their neighbors, the Hasegawas are able
to grow a significant proportion of the vegetables they need for their own consumption, as well as herbs and medicinal plants, and they frequently exchange
their produce with relatives and neighbors (but never sell it). Rice farming is not
feasible because it would be impossible to provide the complex irrigation system that is necessary, but most families have a well on their property that taps
into the city water supply; this is more than adequate for raising vegetables.

Minoru points out that the trees surrounding the lot on most sides and filling the main garden have been selected for their food-bearing potential as well
as the provision of mulch and fertilizer. Many of the pines produce edible pine
nuts as well as needles for mulch, and a few of the larger broadleaf trees, like
chestnuts, provide food as well as considerable shade. Some, like plum trees,
are both highly ornamental and food-bearing, though varieties have been bred
to maximize either fruit or blossoms but rarely both. This is why the sakura
trees send the citizens into raptures when they bloom even though they don't
provide palatable cherries. Hasegawa's garden has enough fruit trees to qualify
as a small orchard, with an emphasis on seasonal variety. Many of the best
food-bearing specimens, such as persimmons, pears, loquat, and mikan, are
not really visually attractive enough to become an aesthetic focus but can easily be integrated into the ornamental *mise-en-scene* of the garden.

The vegetable garden has a compost heap, a pond, a shed for tools, trellises for climbing vines, and frames for shade, all on a scale that suggests a seriousness of purpose, and all of which Minoru helped set up. With his expert knowledge, the water cycle has been fully accounted for, and, being based on the same principles, this family garden replicates the functioning of its larger rural brethren in most respects. Hasegawa's pond is a miniature wetland, and taken in aggregate with the dozens of others in the neighborhood, it forms an important habitat for wetland species.

Though the bulk of the labor in the Hasegawa household falls to the servants and the women, everyone farms. Working the soil is not considered demeaning in any way, and the master's sons, barefoot and sweating in the late afternoon sun, are now weeding the radish patch. Samurai families can only provide for a portion of their needs by farming their home gardens in this way, but it is considered wholly worthwhile. In a sense, this lifestyle harkens back to centuries earlier, when the samurai were a class of rural landowners and farmers before their great relocation to the castle towns. Indeed, a few samurai-farmers still exist, though mostly in remote and difficult-to-govern provinces, where they live a life nearly indistinguishable from that of a typical village headman.

In cities like Edo, there is a strong aesthetic and philosophical component to the garden-based lifestyle. At the most cultured level, there is the tradition of the ascetic scholar, living in a mountain hut. Though neither Hasegawa-san nor his neighbors expects to actually replicate that life, it is constantly referred to in their art and poetry, and it is even depicted on the painted shutters of the built-in shelves in Hasegawa's study. For the many samurai who have accompanied their lords from distant provinces to take up periodic residence here in Edo, gardens can be a way of mimicking the natural environment of their

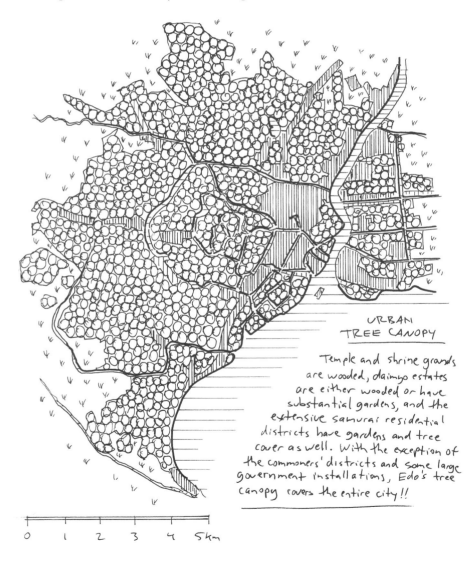

URBAN
TREE CANOPY

Temple and shrine grounds
are wooded, daimyo estates
are either wooded or have
substantial gardens, and the
extensive samurai residential
districts have gardens and tree
cover as well. With the exception of
the commoners' districts and some large
government installations, Edo's tree
canopy covers the entire city!!

0    1    2    3    4    5km

homelands, and by association, can serve as an expression of loyalty. It is very common for these displaced warriors to bring trees, shrubs, flowers, and vegetables from home to transplant into their gardens, surrounding themselves with familiar colors and aromas. The lords themselves, or others with the wherewithal, frequently have the landforms of home suggested in miniature by the rocks, hills, and ponds of their gardens. For persons of these upper classes, the only way to insure a supply of hometown garden specialties for the table is to have them farmed on their estate grounds.

Samurai are expected to be both blindingly obedient and ingeniously resourceful. Physical training and exertion are stressed, as are study and intellectual mastery. Growing one's own food demonstrates resourcefulness, lessens the financial burden one places upon one's lord, provides exercise, and entails mastering an essential body of environmental and botanical knowledge that is valuable and widely applicable. An expert urban farmer is better qualified to help monitor the agricultural production of the domain and to render technical advice to the peasantry.

Nevertheless, few samurai would have embraced urban farming with the zeal they currently display had they not been forced into it by necessity. The inadequacies of the food production and distribution system, and especially the inadequate stipends these middle and lower samurai are forced to live on due to inherent flaws in the economic system, have painted Hasegawa and his colleagues into a corner. They might not starve if they don't farm, but they can certainly eat better if they do. In time-honored fashion, they are making the best of an intolerable situation.

This pattern of land use, the urban farmstead, is replicated by thousands of households throughout the samurai districts of the Edo metropolis. Many townsmen also have gardens, including small kitchen ones, but land in their densely populated districts is so prohibitively expensive that they are most likely to satisfy themselves with small pocket gardens instead of expansive wooded plots. Still, with so much of the city given to samurai, thousands of whom devote about one-third to one-half of their property to farming, one can estimate that 50 percent of Edo's land area is used for growing food to feed its citizens. A large proportion of the remainder of the samurai homesteads is filled with densely wooded ornamental gardens, as are the temple grounds that make up another 13 percent of the city. Edo is an unprecedentedly green metropolis, both by design and by default. Water sources like ponds, rivers, and streams are all integrated into the overall natural green growth system, and the current peak of health and diversity of Edo's greenbelt is the result of generations of careful planning and nurturing.

Outside the gate of Hasegawa's house, we take our leave of Minoru and head back the way we came. The afternoon is turning to evening, and we enjoy the deeper shade and cooler breezes this time of day brings. Even this far inland, there is a whiff of sea air, and we are surrounded by the call of songbirds. Samurai are either returning to their homes or heading out for the evening, and we see the master of the house, Hasegawa-san, strolling back in an apparently good mood, a book tucked under his arm, followed a few steps later by his loyal retainer, Koichi. The aroma of supper cooking fills the air, wafting over the gardens walls from a thousand samurai kitchens.

We enter a wider avenue, cross a bridge, and from a large intersection can see the bay in one direction and Mount Fuji in another, and we feel both connected to the earth and protected by it. Just then, the earth shudders for a few moments, and everyone stops in their tracks. The tremor is a slight one, lasting just a few seconds, and when it passes, everyone—samurai and commoner alike—meets the eyes of whomever is nearest and laughs together in nervous relief. The people of Edo are constantly reminded that the earth both provides and takes away, and plan their lives accordingly.

Tomorrow we will make our way to the port and the ship that will take us home. The journey will only take a couple of days, heading south to a part of the country that is noticeably different in climate and vegetation, but where people live quite similarly to those we have been visiting.

What has struck us most is how closely all our lives are entwined, and how mutually dependent they are. In terms of resources, energy, water, food, shelter, and clothing, everyone's concerns are quite similar.

The farmers truly are the bedrock of society, custodians of the productive biosphere, and keepers of ancient wisdom necessary for sustainable habitation and cultivation. They are the most self-sufficient class of people in the country, making or producing almost everything locally, though their increasing integration with the market for cash crops, textiles, and industrial raw materials has given many of them both the income and exposure to goods with which to replace their homemade items.

The townspeople are undoubtedly the least self-sufficient, the most fully dependent upon the market for food and other necessities, and quite at the mercy of the government agencies that provide their water. And though a handful of commoners have acquired enough wealth to behave profligately, their behavior attracts as much censure as it does envy. Townspeople pinch their pennies, motivated in part by a drive towards upward mobility, and in this regard conservation is beneficial to the household economy. They've worked everything out in ways that are convenient, sociable, and entertaining.

The samurai lifestyle retains hints of their past as gentlemen farmers who have been transplanted to the city. While far more dependent upon the marketplace than the farmers, they are more self-sufficient than the townspeople, more likely to grow their own food, weave their own cloth, and to avoid commercial solutions to problems to which a homespun approach might be applied. Because his house opens onto a garden, the samurai's life is more reposeful than the commoner's, but at the same time, because he has no real economic mobility, his life is one of frugality and sameness.

If the lives of the many individuals we have met seems to be circumscribed in many ways, it is largely because this country is also circumscribed, set off from the rest of the world by beaches, rocky shores, and vast expanses of ocean. Japan in the Edo period is like a ship with no possibility of visiting port in order to reprovision. It all has to be grown and made on board, in a way that can be continued indefinitely.

We reach the top of a hill, and as we catch a view of Mount Fuji in the distance, silhouetted by the mauve and gold of the setting sun, we think the way of life on these islands is a good model for how to live on the vessel we call earth.

The Japanese garden is a selective model of nature, in which the primary elements of natural systems are integrated and allowed to interact with the surrounding environment.

# DAIMYO ESTATES ("YASHIKI")

Daimyo estates are not simply private homes, but function as military and administrative headquarters. Each daimyo is alloted three plots of land, an upper, a middle, and a lower estate, whose size and location indicate the family's status within the regime.

The daimyo residential ideal is a luxurious home open to nature in all its glory — a generous plot of wooded ground, robustly walled off so that the house itself can be made permeable and free-flowing.

It has woods, streams and waterfalls, hills and valleys, ponds, stones, flowers, fruits, and vegetables for picking, and is home to birds and small animals. As one descends the strata of samurai society and into the upper echelon of urban commoners, these features are all emulated on an increasingly intimate scale.

## UPPER ESTATE ("Kami Yashiki") —

functions as an official headquarters, and the buildings are of a scale and opulence appropriate for receiving the shogun himself. They are usually built as close to the shogun's castle as possible. Each has a uniquely-designed, intricate sequence of reception rooms, offices, guest rooms, and living quarters done in the free-flowing "shoin" style, as well as separate pavilions, interwoven with gardens and dotted with ponds. Service functions, such as large kitchens, baths, storage, offices, and housing for servants, are provided. The entire estate is walled off from the city by a layer of barracks for soldiers.

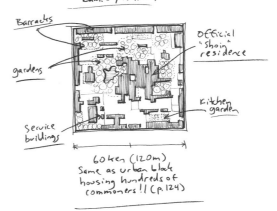

UPPER ESTATE
(Based on Matsudaira-Ikeda Kami-yashiki.)

Barracks
Official "shoin" residence
gardens
Kitchen garden
Service buildings

60 ken (120m)
Same as urban block housing hundreds of commoners!! (p.124)

## MIDDLE ESTATE ("Naka Yashiki") —

Is intended to serve as the home of the daimyo's family. Some are smaller in size than the upper estate, but they are often located away from the city center where more land is available, allowing larger gardens. Though it is a dwelling, it is clearly separated into public, private, and service zones, and the occupants live a very visible life with little privacy. Many servants are provided, drawn from the lower ranks of samurai, who serve, clean, act as porters and ladies maids, as well as valets. These estates are also walled off and often surrounded by barracks.

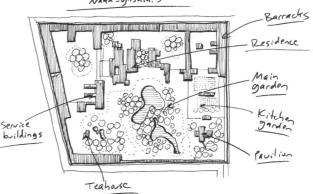

MIDDLE ESTATE
(Based on Matsudaira-Ikeda Naka-yashiki.)

Barracks
Residence
Main garden
Kitchen garden
Pavilion
Service buildings
Teahouse

## LOWER ESTATE ("Shimo Yashiki") —

Is designed as a retreat and a place of refuge, and is usually furthest from the city center — often outside the actual city limits, and close to a navigable waterway. Its location and size allow great freedom of design. The gardens are very large, often containing wilderness-like areas suitable for hunting, and the ponds may be more like small lakes. Due to the prevalence of fires, the lower estates are equipped to function as emergency headquarters, and feature many large fireproof storehouses and granaries.

Despite their leisure orientation, they also house a suitable military contingent.

## LOWER ESTATE
(Based on Mito shimo-yashiki)

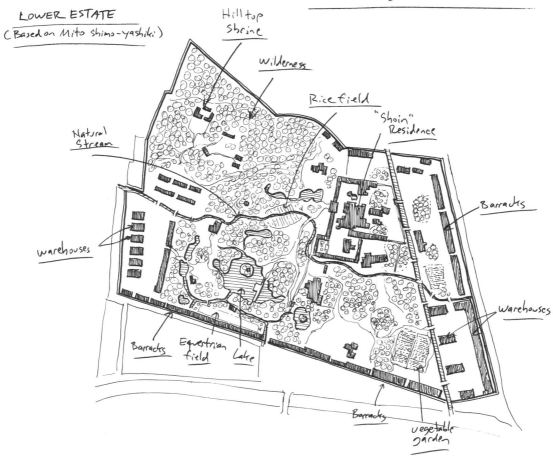

Hilltop Shrine

Wilderness

Rice field

"Shoin" Residence

Natural Stream

Barracks

warehouses

warehouses

Barracks

Equestrian field

Lake

Barracks

Vegetable garden

# learning from
# a life of
# restraint

### ■ promote new ethical standards

There have always been people who take advantage of status or economic power to consume far more food, energy, water, and building materials than they require, often purely in order to demonstrate that status or power. Though a grand lifestyle such as that enjoyed by the highest ranking samurai of the Edo period or a corporate baron of today may appear superficially beautiful, this beauty invariably conceals grotesque underpinnings. We can hope that our ethical values will soon change so that, instead of feeling proud of megalomanic overconsumption and waste, people will simply feel embarrassed.

### ■ aim for a locally sourced lifestyle

The root of the economy that supported the Edo ruling class was the long-distance transshipment of rice, which was both exploitative and wasteful, though it transformed this staple grain into a precious and therefore carefully husbanded commodity. Similarly, the expense and distance involved in supplying the capital with building lumber insured that it would not be wasted. Besides these two commodities, very few essentials were sourced at a great distance; vegetables, fish, and other foods were easily obtained from the immediate region, as were most daily items.

Ironically, though they were part of the ruling class, most samurai families could not afford luxuries, and in fact they were constantly exhorted to maintain a frugal and sober lifestyle, so that they only partly participated in the wider economy in which special goods such as foods, textiles, pottery, and furnishings were shipped from outlying regions. For the most part their lifestyle was locally sourced. This pattern of superimposed dual or multiple economies in the same region, one of which is local, "unofficial," and low impact, while the rest relies on a much greater expenditure of energy, is evident today in many places where great economic disparity exists. Achieving a higher degree of local sourcing and energy independence may mean emulating the underclass.

### ■ micro-economies result in better service

Samurai life depended on an extensive support economy that delivered goods and services to their doors. To put this in contemporary terms, these micro-economies relied upon close coordination and information sharing between supplier and customer, and frequent short-distance, "just-in-time" deliveries. For the suppliers, in this case peddlers, the benefits were close contact with end users, that is, market research, and the ability to build longstanding ties with customers. The system also provided opportunity for newcomers and the introduction of new products and services.

### ■ learn from legible housing

Though the language of the samurai house—the cultural clues provided by its entryway, its lay-out, and its garden—is now socially obsolete, it represents an unparalleled "legibility" of space. Virtually every detail is imbued with significance, with suggestion, and with information about the occupants, their history, their social standing. These homes express education and cultural background, unique tastes and idiosyncrasies. By its very layout, a house like this indicates expected roles and relationships, social norms, and the laws of loyalty and adherence. The design is based on longstanding, shared assumptions and is limited by regulations, but the design is nevertheless very free. The samurai house opens up to the first-time visitor like a valued book, all the more remarkably because it is so utilitarian. In our drive to preserve our privacy and security, we have perhaps allowed our homes to say less about us, on the one hand to conform to fashion and social norms and on the other to indicate nothing truly significant. Seeking freedom, we have perhaps achieved rootlessness.

## *sukiya* room design

Many new homeowners in Japan want to have at least one Japanese-style room, and by this they actually mean a traditional *zashiki* in *sukiya* style: tatami, the paper *shoji* and *fusuma* doors, a *tokonoma* alcove, and *tana* cabinets. In reality, these rooms are seldom used, and they often get converted into studies or guest rooms, or even storage. But the mere presence of the room satisfies a cultural longing.

Not many people these days can tell the difference between a well-designed zashiki and a cheap one, and the latter are numerous. But exquisite sukiya design is still being practiced. It is one of the most upscale ways of building, and affordable by only the wealthy, for it requires materials of a quality that is now hard to come by, and craftsmanship that demands high compensation. There are also some excellent new sukiya-style designs that are equal parts tradition and natural modernism, melding both sensibilities seamlessly and providing a high level of physical comfort. And true to tradition, though there are university-trained architects who are capable of very fine sukiya-style design, the true stars of the trade are master carpenters, *sukiya-daiku*, inheritors of the teahouse design tradition. We may lament the overall decline of taste and appreciation for good traditional architectural design, but it is reassuring to know that the core traditions have been passed on to the current generation of top-level craftsmen.

### ■ use the house as a natural theater

The life of a samurai was a life filled with ceremony and an acute awareness of how one appears to others. Homes should perhaps encourage a bit of self-consciousness, provide a sense of ritual, and allow us to present ourselves to strangers in a clear but carefully revealed fashion. This does not necessarily require separate formal spaces, but mainly concerns the experience of moving from our entryways into the family space, the inner sanctum, of the house. We could call this the "natural theater of the home."

### ■ utilize the enduring appeal of the garden pavilion

The garden pavilion, the cottage on the prairie, the intimate home set amidst greenery: why are these such enduring ideals for dwellings? While cultural resonance is undoubtedly a factor, there may be a genetic and physiological basis as well, linked to our evolution amidst green grasslands and forests. A house set within a garden lends repose, ease, and a sense of fertility and of being part of a supportive environment. The samurai use of garden space was ideal, made possible by favorable zoning and allotment of resources, but those of us in denser urban environments must provide ourselves with a sense of surrounding green in more spatially economical ways. Fortunately for us, the Japanese excelled in small-garden design as well, and they were masters at supplying the illusion of deep and wide green space where none actually existed. We can avail ourselves of many of their solutions.

### ■ find the poetic materials of the traditional house

No matter where they are found, the best traditional houses present a stimulating feast to the senses—of light and color, tactility and texture, air and aroma. The elements our houses are composed of, the actual walls, floors, doors, and fittings, should have a visual presence and identity, of course, but also characteristic scents, and they should respond to the fingertips in some telling and poetic way. We have become averse to aromas in the home and have become accustomed to living in spaces that are bound by characterless materials with neither sensual richness nor history. When judged by the standards and expectations of our forebears, ours are barely houses.

### ■ understand the meaning of "good" light

Light. Not enough can be said about it. Many of us would unhesitatingly agree that having good light in our homes is desirable. But few of us could actually describe what good light is like. We often make the mistake of equating good light with "bright light everywhere." In fact, good light means having an interesting continuum from light to dark, that lends the brighter spaces a special presence and beauty. It also means designing a house and siting living spaces—and even specific places to sit or rest—in a way that takes advantage of how natural light changes over the course of the day and from season to season. As light changes, so does the color of the home; this can be either dramatic or subtle, but the most beautiful solutions have both.

Light activates textures and patterns visually, making reliefs stand out more sharply and therefore allowing their character to emerge, and lends a suggestive shading and modeling to curved surfaces. It is light that gives spaces a three-dimensional character. In the contemporary home, as in the traditional Japanese one, we must assume that sunlight is an important energy source and direct it to where it can best be used to warm living spaces. At the same time, much as the samurai house made careful use of deep eaves for shading and careful planting of trees, we must take care to minimize unnecessary solar gain. From the outset this

## the openness of the *engawa*

In Edo days, the veranda, or *engawa*, was found in many contexts. In the farmhouse, it opened onto the workyard, in official buildings it overlooked formal courtyards. But it is the model provided by the aristocrat or warrior's house—the shoin- and sukiya-style house and garden unit—in which the engawa reached its poetic design potential, an intermediary space between the rooms of the house and the garden itself. It is this model that inspires most Japanese architects today and satisfies their clients when they include an engawa in their designs.

It is possible to make engawa of many sizes, to enclose them or leave them open, to detail them traditionally or make them out of glass and aluminum. An engawa allows a building or wing to work well with another as an ensemble, and it helps define and shape the exterior space as well as the interior. But it is essential that it lie between an important room and a garden, and that it is separated from the room itself by panels that allow most of the wall to open up.

Of the many traditional features from the Edo period that have continued in use in home designs until the present, the engawa has proven to be especially adaptable to new styles and materials, and to be stimulating for architects to think about. It allows homes to be both contemporary and traditional at the same time and to handsomely provide good natural air circulation and connection to the outdoors.

establishes a resonant continuum of light and shade.

### ■ build homes that are inspirational

Is it too much to ask that our homes be inspirational to us and to our visitors? To suggest that a home should be poetic does not mean that it must be "highly designed" or even "sophisticated." It doesn't even mean that it must be always clean and neat. It is our life that lends poetry to our homes, and if our lives are devoid of aesthetics then a house alone cannot provide it. Poetry, like spirit, often lies in the overlooked or overly familiar. Most of us surround ourselves with things that remind us who we are, where we've been, and how we've changed: photos, souvenirs, gifts, a child's drawing, a vase of flowers, some favorite music. A comfortable chair and a favorite view become a place we like to sit, become part of us. The samurai house was intended from the outset to highlight

prized aesthetic and personal objects, to have a place for writing, painting, and poetry, to have views, and to share all of these. The sharing this encourages is as important as the private contemplation.

### ■ appreciate the virtues of reconfigurable space

Farmhouses, commoners' houses, and samurai houses all used what we could call "soft" zoning to differentiate living spaces. The samurai house needed to accommodate the greatest extremes in formality and reflect the most detailed social hierarchy. Despite the limited space and modest technical means, it did this beautifully by assuming that all elements would serve more than one purpose and that by setting up slightly different combinations, approaches, and movement sequences within the same space, they would be perceived differently on different occasions.

## house and garden design traditions

While the image of the ideal home in Japan has changed significantly since the start of the modern era, and the reality of most people's dwellings is even more startlingly different from that of the Edo period, the ideal garden design hasn't changed much at all. Though new styles, like the English garden, and new features, like brick paving, have gained in popularity, the fully developed Edo-style garden is still considered the model to emulate. This is partly because the Japanese garden accommodates itself to so many different sizes and configurations: it can be made pocket-sized if necessary, or sloped or bent around a corner. And partly it is because of the kind of beauty and environment it provides. Part of the garden ideal, of course, is the house, or at least the rooms that open onto the garden, and this type of traditional connection is replicated wherever possible, through the use of sliding doors, shoji, tatami, and other features that make up the shoin-style zashiki ensemble. So, despite the tremendous differences in appearance, Edo tradition lives on quite vividly in millions of private gardens.

Our houses today rarely require the kind of formal reception areas that these houses did, but they can still benefit from a similarly flexible planning. The key is to envision dwelling spaces as reconfigurable, multipurpose areas, and to find or make furnishings, wall closures, and storage that accommodate this. As time goes on and the desire to live in homes with less of a negative impact on the environment becomes a guiding principle, we will see increasingly ingenious convertible and reconfigurable designs becoming more readily available, along with increasing standardization and interoperability. Many of these designs and products will bear the influence of their modular Japanese forebears.

### ■ design houses with multiple centers

Just as the brain is no less important than the heart, homes often have more than one "center." In the samurai house, the formal reception room is one, and the kitchen and its hearth are another. Each satisfies a different but equally essential need. The hearth is the most intimate and most private area, none the less so for being a working and communication center

and the place where sustenance is found. It is a social space but is concerned primarily with family. Significantly, in the samurai home, it is the women's realm, the control center of daily life and of nurturing and child rearing.

The reception room facing the garden is also a center, but one that is more intellectual and cultural, and more overtly social in that it is the preferred zone of interaction with people from outside the family circle. It is not purely a male center, but because this society dictated that most formal interaction was the responsibility of the men, it can be considered a masculine zone.

What is interesting is that both areas evolved into extremely comfortable and even physically and mentally healing spaces. The hearth offers a secure motherly embrace; the reception room offers nature and cultured reflection. Though in the West we have found many excellent reasons to abandon gender-based spatial zoning along with gender-based divisions of labor in most spheres, we still need to find ways to include similar dual centers in our homes. Just as we move through different moods and intellectual and emotional states over the course of the day, we should be able to move from center to center in our own homes, from an outward-gazing vantage point to an inwardly nurturing and reassuring embrace.

### ■ recognize the benefits of an urban tree canopy

The tree canopy of Edo was remarkable in its extensiveness and vigor, and it has had few parallels in dense metropolises, before or since. The benefits it provided were legion. Beauty is one, of course, but so is the shade it gives in summer (a mature urban tree canopy can reduce ambient air temperatures in a city by ten degrees Fahrenheit) and its use as a windbreak in winter. An extensive tree canopy provides connections to the surrounding ecosystem, both for botanical species and for birds and other animals that depend upon it for food and habitat. Trees and their roots aid the healthy functioning of the hydrological cycle, and their leaves provide natural compost and mulch. Many of them provide food for humans as well.

Edo reaped these benefits due to a combination of good planning, local direction, and simply staying out of the way of nature. And though it was the samurai who benefited most directly by having so many trees in their neighborhoods, the tree cover included innumerable temple and shrine precincts available for use by the lowest strata of society as well.

Trees, particularly in the form of tree-lined boulevards and in parks, have long been considered desirable additions to cities in the West, but it is only recently that they have begun to be recognized as essential for urban health and climate control and to reduce water runoff. Cities all over the world have begun planting trees to replace those cut in earlier years in the name of development, and the role trees can play in mitigating the urban heat island effect has led to a proliferation of rooftop gardens and other approaches considered extreme just a decade or so ago. These efforts are laudable and will likely have long-terms benefits. How much better it would have been if the original tree cover had simply been left in place.

### ■ consider an urban garden infrastructure

The samurai gardens of Edo have nearly all disappeared, and so it requires a strong imagination to picture what a large city filled with them

## cool green curtains

During summer months, Edo-period Japanese often used lightweight, removable trellises covered with climbing vines to help shade the interiors of their homes. Like "green curtains," they were often sources of food—beans and squash—or color—morning glories—as well as shade. Recently the "green curtain" idea has found renewed acceptance and has been adapted for use on institutional buildings. One large corporation has added them to five factories, using morning glories and edible bitter gourd plants to make living shade curtains over 140 meters in length. They found that the added shade greatly reduced the need for air-conditioning in the factories, particularly in the morning. Other groups have begun similar projects to add green curtains to schools and government buildings across the country, and they have established curriculum guidelines that use the creation and upkeep of the curtains to teach environmental science to elementary and junior high school students. The idea is excellent, inexpensive, easily approachable, and rooted in tradition, and we can expect to see it spread soon to other sectors of society as well.

was like. These were walled gardens, protected enclaves, each a microcosm designed to suit individual tastes, and so they displayed an incredible variety. If one could have seen this part of Edo from the air, one would have seen mostly trees. Existing woods were preserved wherever possible, and a vast number were transplanted, while the water flow of entire districts was planned to accommodate garden needs. Much of the soil of Edo was of a low quality, however, and so a large market for garden soil existed, with soil from the more fertile suburbs brought in by the cartload and boatload.

Over the course of a few centuries an entire layer of new topsoil had been laboriously introduced, and the overall ecological health of the metropolis improved correspondingly, aided by the continual addition of composted material. This urban soil renewal was an intensive and long-term infrastructure project that had government support but was also considered an appropriate use of financial resources by the residents themselves. The garden infrastructure of a city should be considered from the beginning in any urban planning scheme, not merely as a desired and optional "add-on."

The Edo samurai gardens had all of the most important features that successful urban gardens should have. Their trees were diverse, both naturally seeded and transplanted, and were selected according to their individual features—fruit, flowers, shade, medicinal properties—as well as for their interactions with other species—providing optimal understory conditions for flowers and shrubs or natural soil management for others. The trees in individual gardens connected with those in others to form the extended canopy. Samurai gardens had ponds and miniature wetlands that aided the hydrological cycle and provided habitat for birds, insects, frogs, and fish. When they didn't have space for larger water features, samurai used ponds of even one meter in diameter, sometimes in tubs or barrels, that were very

effective because similar ponds were in gardens nearby as well; the same is true of wetlands, which only need to be wet for part of the year in order to restore functions lost when land was developed. The Japanese made full use of scavengers such as snails and tadpoles to control algae growth, and their water features were extremely scenic as well.

A little forethought can insure that urban gardens can provide an attractive habitat for many species of birds, mammals, and beneficial insects. Gardens provide both horizontal and vertical areas, forming natural zones attractive to different wildlife species. Feeders, nesting boxes, and watering sites were provided for birds; but they also left hollow trees, fallen logs, and stumps, which are the preferred nesting sites for many birds (as well as for other wildlife).

Finally, Edo samurai improved their soil on a vast scale, each doing his part by improving his own garden. Though the original ground of Edo was so clayey and poor in nutrients that it made sense to cart in soil from outside, in most cases applying compost is the best method of increasing the nutrient content and general condition of garden soil. If carried out over the course of one or two generations by thousands of households throughout a city, as the samurai of Edo did, incremental soil improvement can have a remarkable effect whose benefits extend to the watershed and wider environment as well.

## ■ urban farming: difficulties lead to possibilities

Urban farming in Edo did not arise in a planned fashion. Rather, it was a spontaneous response to acute economic and agricultural conditions. Records show that, during the late Edo period, nearly every urban samurai family maintained a vegetable garden, and that over the years these gradually replaced large sections of their ornamental gardens. Consequently, to say that Edo was a vast urban farming area is no exaggeration.

It is ironic that it was the ruling class, underfunded, suffering from inflation, and deprived of real opportunity to improve its financial situation, that felt compelled to grow its own food. It was an "unofficial" economy, made possible by the fact that centuries of infrastructure work had already left every family with a large garden with good soil.

It is gradually becoming clearer that urban farming is necessary for us today as a means of reducing emissions from food transportation, as part of alternate water purification systems, to counteract the urban heat island effect, and also to help reconnect us to our locales. Many observers have witnessed a significant increase in urban farming in both developed and developing countries in recent years, and they expect to see it increase still more sharply as energy prices rise and affect food transportation.

Cities providing for a significant proportion of their food needs by farming done within the city limits or on the immediate outskirts include Hanoi and Shanghai. According to one report, 14 percent of the eight million London residents grow some of their own food, while nearly half of the households in Vancouver do. The United States in particular has vast untapped potential for urban farming in the form of vacant lots— seventy thousand in Chicago alone, hundreds of thousands nationwide. Farming can transform these blights into sources of bounty, with a regenerative effect that extends far beyond the garden wall. Farming provides a degree of self-sufficiency that is impossible to obtain in other ways, and it brings with it unquantifiable psychological and social benefits. In a way, if prohibitive fuel costs cause the widespread adoption of farming in our cities, then a threatening situation may have been transformed into something extremely positive.

## land for urban farming

Many neighborhoods are blighted by lots that became vacant during the real-estate bubble years, when existing homes and small businesses were demolished in preparation for new development that never happened. In most cases, these have been converted into unattended cash parking lots, and in others the lots have simply gone to seed and are overgrown. Some communities, like the town of Seki in Gifu Prefecture, have begun to convert vacant lots into urban farms, the labor being donated by volunteers. For the city governments involved, the vegetable gardens are considered part of the emergency food supply. In fact, some cities and towns, like Kanazawa, have always had a significant number of vegetable gardens and even rice paddies within the city limits, partly the result of slow development in which the rural nature of certain neighborhoods has persisted for centuries, and partly because they are a welcome feature of the townscape. Many urban places that are difficult to build on, such as riverbanks, ravines, or steep slopes, lend themselves to farming. The sustainability message has been trickling down, and it is becoming common to see vegetable plots in denser areas, were individuals and organizations have begun planting on rooftops and building vertical gardens that partly mitigate the lack of open space. Tokyo itself will probably never regain urban farming on the scale that was practiced in Edo, but it is rapidly becoming both socially more acceptable and easier for municipalities to accommodate through ordinances and regulations.

# acknowledgments

So many people assisted in making this book in ways both large and small that it is difficult to adequately acknowledge all of them. A number of people deserve special mention, however. I would like to thank Greg Starr, my editor at Kodansha International, for his enthusiasm for this project from start to finish, for steering it through the long production process, and for not being afraid to hurt my feelings when criticism was in order. Miyako Takeshita, curator and researcher at the KIT Future Design Institute, the think tank I founded in Tokyo in 2005, provided invaluable assistance with Japanese sources, tracked down individuals with expert knowledge in specific areas, and did an enormous amount of legwork. Nobuko Tadai also did crucial research for me, helping collate recent Japanese research in sustainability and tracking down historical images of the lumberyards of Kiba. The book designer, Kazuhiko Miki, demonstrated tremendous flexibility and imagination in accommodating my unconventional requests concerning the illustrations and captions.

Prof. Tatsuo Masuta, my colleague at the Kanazawa Institute of Technology, was extremely generous with his expertise on traditional architecture, particularly concerning merchant and samurai houses in the Kanazawa area. I am especially grateful for the insight he provided into the frugal reality of life for lower samurai and how that was reflected in the design of their homes. He also provided important introductions to specialists supervising the restoration of samurai homes at the Hyakumangoku Bunkaen Edo Mura (Edo Village), outside of Kanazawa, who allowed me unlimited access. Prof. Masao Takahashi, a grand old gentleman, entertained volley after volley of detailed inquiry concerning Edo period life, design, and technology, and directed me to a number of useful printed sources. I am incredibly indebted to his close analysis of the writings of Morisada Mankou, an Edo period traveler from Osaka who published an illustrated guidebook to the manners and customs of Edoites.

My work was made much easier by having access to a number of excellent museums. I'd like to thank Akihiko Toyama, curator at the Nihon Minka-en

(Japan Open-air Folk Museum), for arranging special access to the houses there, and for providing me with copies of restoration reports which clarified quite a few details concerning the history and construction of Japanese farmhouses. The collection and reading room of the Edo-Tokyo Museum were invaluable resources, as were those of the Fukagawa Edo Museum and the Tokyo Waterworks Museum. And the Edo-Tokyo Open Air Architecture Museum provided the opportunity to examine building types, such as a historical bathhouse, that are nearly impossible to find elsewhere. Many thanks also to the staff of the Japan Foundation Library, and of The National Diet Library, both in Tokyo. Their collections were invaluable.

There are also people I feel indebted to even though we've never met, particularly several writers and researchers whose approaches and findings informed my own. Conrad Totman has done groundbreaking work on Edo period forestry practices and the history of the period in general; Susan B. Hanley has illuminated daily life for people of the period by closely examining material culture; Anne Walthall's writings on the subject of "night soil" provided important insight into that issue. *The Cambridge History of Japan Volume 4, Early Modern Japan*, edited by John Whitney Hall, which deals with this period, is an essential resource and contains excellent contributions by leading specialists from Japan and abroad. There are quite a few other specialists who deserve mention, and I have tried to acknowledge as many of them as possible in the bibliography.

I'd like to thank John Poché and his family for allowing me to stay at their beautiful home in New Orleans for several weeks during the summer of 2008, which was very conducive to writing and enabled me to complete the text undisturbed.

And last but far from least, I want to thank my wife Mayumi and my son Max for their forbearance during my long absences and for not grumbling too much at the time I was devoting to this book instead of to them.

# bibliography

Akazawa, Takeru. "Regional Variation in Procurement Systems of Jomon Hunter-Gatherers," in *Bulletin No. 27, Prehistoric Hunter-Gatherers in Japan*, The University of Tokyo, (1986), http://www.um.u-tokyo.ac.jp/publish_db/Bulletin/no27/no27006.html (accessed August 18, 2007).

Alexander, Christopher, and Sara Ishikawa, Murray Silverstein. *A Pattern Language: Towns, Buildings, Construction*. Oxford: Oxford University Press, 1977.

Ando, Kunihiro. *Warabuki no minzokugaku* ("Ethnic Studies of Thatched Roofs"). Tokyo: Haru Shobo, 2005.
——and Naohiko Inui, Koichi Yamashita. *Sumai no dentogijutsu* ("The Art of Traditional Housing"). Tokyo: Kenchiku Shiryo kenkyusha, 1995.

Asano, Nobuko and Kiyoshi Hirai. "Scale and formation of samurai house in the castle town Ueda at the end of Edo period." *Journal of Architecture, Planning and Environmental Engineering* No. 537 (2000), 249-255.

Befu, Harumi. "Ecology, Residence and Authority: The Corporate Household in Central Japan." *Ethnology*, Vol. 7, No. 1 (January 1968), 25-42.

Berstein, Gail Lee. *Isami's House: Three Centuries of a Japanese Family*. Berkeley: University of California Press, 2005.

Bestor, Theodore. *Tsukiji: The Fish Market at the Center of the World*. Berkeley: University of California Press, 2004.

Brown, Lester R. *Plan B. 3.0: Mobilizing to Save Civilization*. New York: W. W. Norton & Co., 2008. Also available online at http://www.earth-policy.org/Books/PB3/index.htm.

Bushi Seikatsu Kenkyukai. *Bushi seikatsu shi nyumon* ("Introduction to the Life of Bushi"). Tokyo: Kashiwa Shobo, 1991.
——. *Bushi no seikatsu* ("The Life of Bushi"). Tokyo: Kashiwa Shobo, 2004.

Carson, Rachel. *Silent Spring*. New York: Houghton Mifflin, 1962.

Carver, Norman F. *Japanese Folkhouses*. Kalamazoo, MI: Documen Press, 1984.

Chamberlain, Basil Hall. *Japanese Things: Being Notes on Various Subjects Connected with Japan, for the Use of Travelers and Others*. Rutland, VT: Tuttle, 1971.

Coaldrake, William Howard. *Architecture and Authority in Japan*. London: Routledge, 1996.
——. *Way of the Carpenter Tools and Japanese Architecture*. New York: Weatherhill, 1990.

Cornell, Laurel L. "Infanticide in Early Modern Japan: Demography, Culture and Population Growth." *The Journal of Asian Studies*, Vol. 55, No. 1 (February 1996), 22-50.

Diamond, Jared M. *Guns, Germs, and Steel: the Fates of Human Societies*. New York: Norton, 1999.

Engel, Heino. *Measure and Construction of the Japanese House*. Rutland, VT: C.E. Tuttle Co., 1985.
——. *The Japanese House: A Tradition for Modern Architecture*. Tokyo: C. E. Tuttle, 1988.

Fujii, Yukiko and Koichi Amano. "The excursion in the amusement area of Edo. From the diary of Gesshin Saito." *Proceedings of Infrastructure Planning*, No. 22 (1999), 31-34.

Fujimori, Terunobu and Hiroshi Aramata, Yutaka Harui. *Tokyo rojo hakubutsushi* ("The Natural History of Tokyo's Roads"). Tokyo: Kashima Shuppan, 1987.

Fujio, Shin'ichiro. "The Beginning of Rice Cultivation and Paddy Field Cultivation with Irrigation in Japan," in *The 3rd Rekihaku International Symposium: The Formation of Agricultural societies and Civilization in East Asia*, (2000), http://www.rekihaku.ac.jp/kenkyuu/shinpo/fujio.html (accessed December 26, 2007).

Fukagawa Edo Museum. *Fukagawa Edo myujiamu katarogu* ("Fukagawa Edo Museum Catalog"). Tokyo: Fukagawa Edo Museum, 1987.

Furusawa, Koyo. *A Consideration on Sustainable Development and Civilization: Socio-cultural Ecological Perspective from Japanese Experience*. Tokyo: Kogakuin University, 2004. http://kuin.jp/fur/e-furusawa2.htm. (accessed December 26, 2007).

Fuse, T., and E. Shimizu. *Visualizing the Landscape of Old-Time Tokyo (Edo City)*. Tokyo: University of Tokyo (2005), www.photogrammetry.ethz.ch/pitsanulok_workshop/papers/21.pdf (accessed February 19, 2009).

Gensosha Editorial Dept. *Edo no daidokoro* ("Edo's Kitchen"). Tokyo: Jinbunsha, 2006.

Gerstle, C. Andrew. *18th Century Japan Culture and Society (Feh/Asaa East Asia Series)*. Detroit: Harry Ransom Humanities Research Center, 1991.

Goto, Kazuo, and Itsuya Matsumoto. *Yomigaeru bakumatsu* ("The Return of the End of the Edo Period"). Tokyo: Asahi Shuppan, 1987.

Haga, Toru and Masayuki Okabe. *Shashin de miru Edo Tokyo* ("Photos of Edo Tokyo"). Tokyo: Shinchosha, 1992.

Hall, John W. (ed.) *Cambridge History of Japan: Vol. 4*. Cambridge: Cambridge University Press, 1991.

Hall, Robert Burnett. "The Road in Old Japan," in *Studies in the History of Culture: The Disciplines of the Humanities, American Council of Learned Societies Conference of the Secretaries of Constituent Societies*, ed. Waldo Gifford Leland. Ayer Publishing, 1969.

Hanley, Susan B. *Everyday Things in Premodern Japan: The Hidden Legacy of Material Culture*. Berkeley: University of California Press, 1997.

Harada, Nobuo. *Edo no ryori to shokuseikatsu* ("Edo-period Cooking and Dietary Habits"). Tokyo: Shogakukan, n.d.

Hatate, Isao. *Irrigation Water Rights Disputes in Japan, as seen in the Azusa River system*. Tokyo: United Nations University, 1979.

Hayami, Akira. "Population Changes," in *Japan in Transition: from Tokugawa to Meiji*, ed. M.B. Jansen and G. Rozman. Princeton University (1986), 280-317.
——, and Satomi Kurosu. "Regional Diversity in Demographic and Family Patters in Preindustrial Japan." *Journal of Japanese Studies*, Vol. 27, No. 2 (Summer 2001), 295-321.
——and Matao Miyamoto. *Keizai shakai no seiritsu 17-18c* ("The Formation of the Economic Society of the 17th and 18th centuries"). Tokyo: Iwanami Shoten, 1988.

Hayashi, Hideo, and Michio Aoki. *Jiten shiraberu Edo-jidai* ("Encyclopedic Research of the Edo-period"). Tokyo: Kashiwa Shobo, 2001.

Heineken, Ty. *Tansu Traditional Japanese Cabinetry*. New York: Weatherhill, 2004.

Higuchi, Kiyoyuki. *Edo jijo, seikatsu hen* ("Life in Edo"). Tokyo: Yuzankaku Shuppan, 1991.

HIH Crown Prince Naruhito. "Edo and Water Transport," (address at 4th World Water Forum, December 2007). http://portal.worldwaterforum5.org/wwf5/en-us/ForumKnowledgeBase/4th%20World%20Water%20Forum/Programme%20of%20the%20Forum/Keynotes%20Speeches/Prince_Naruhito.pdf

Hirai, Kiyoshi. *Daimyo to hatamoto no kurashi* ("The Life of Daimyo and the Direct Retainers of the Shogun"). Tokyo: Gakken, 2000.

Hokusai, Katsushika. *Jitsubutsu manga*. Tokyo: Iwasaki Bijutsusha, 1969.

Ichikawa, Hiroaki, and Hidekazu Ishiyama. *Edo no Manabi* ("Learning from Edo"). Tokyo: Kawade Shobo Shinsha, 2006.

Ishiguro, Keisho and Yoshikichi Furui, Suehiro Tanemura, Koji Kata. *Natsukashii Tokyo* ("Nostalgic Tokyo"). Tokyo: Kodansha, 1992.

Ishikawa, Eisuke. *O-edo eneruji jijo* ("Energy Use in Edo"). Tokyo: Kodansha, 1993.
——. *O-edo tekunoroji jijo* ("Technology in Edo"). Tokyo: Kodansha, 1995.
——. *O-edo risaikuru jijo* ("Recycling in Edo"). Tokyo: Kodansha, 1997.
——. *O-edo seikatsu jijo* ("Life in Edo"). Tokyo: Kodansha, 1997.
——. *O-edo ekoroji jijo* ("Ecology in Edo"). Tokyo: Kodansha, 2000. Translation available online at http://www.japanfs.org/en_/column/ishikawa01.html.

Isoda, Michifumi. *Bushi no kakeibo* ("The House-hold Accounts of a Samurai"). Tokyo: Shinchosha, 2003.

Itonaga, Koji, and Kiyokazu Shidara, Moriyuki Konuki. "Permaculture In Japan: Suitable For The Natural And Cultural Conditions Of Japan," in *Proceedings of the Sixth International Permaculture Conference & Convergence* IPC-VI, (1996). http://permaculturewest.org.au/ipc6/ch07/itonaga/index.html. (Accessed December 26, 2007).

Ito, Teiji. *Traditional Domestic Architecture of Japan*. Tokyo: Heibonsha, 1972.

Iwai, Hiromi (ed.) and Kazuyoshi Kudo (ed.), Keiji Nakabayashi (illus.). *Mingu no jiten* ("The Encyclopedia of Folk Tools"). Tokyo: Kawade Shobo, 2008.

Jackson, David and Dane Owen. *Japanese Cabinetry the Art and Craft of Tansu*. Layton, UT: Gibbs Smith, 2002.

Jippensha, Ikku, and Sadakazu Shigeta. *Shank's Mare: Being a Translation of the Tokaido Vlumes of Hizakurige, Japan's Great Comic Novel of Travel and Ribaldry*. Tokyo: Tuttle Classics, 1960.

Kanazawa, the city of. *Kanazawa no rekishiteki kenchiku* ("Historical Architecture of Kanazawa"). Ishikawa: Kanazawa-shi, 1986.

Kanazawa shi Kyoiku Iinkai. *Kanazawa no rekishiteki kenchiku to machinami* ("Historical Architecture and the Cityscape of Kanazawa"). Ishikawa: Kanazawa shi kyoiku iinkai, 1992.

Kanko Shigen Hogo Zaidan. *Shokitsukuri no machinami to yonezawa kaido* ("The Unique Housing Structures and Cityscape of the Yonezawa Road"). Tokyo: Nippon National Trust, 1988.

Kanno, Shunsuke. *Edo no Ekoseikatsu* ("Eco Life in Edo"). Tokyo: Seishun Shuppansha, 2008.

Kawasaki shi. *Juyobunkazai Sasaki-ke ichikukoji hokokusho* ("Report on the Relocation of the Cultural property—the Sasaki House"). Kanagawa: Kawasaki-shi, 1969.

Kawashima, Chuji. *Minka: Traditional Houses of Rural Japan*. Tokyo: Kodansha International, 1986.

Kazuya, Inaba,, and Shigenobu Nakayama. *Japanese Homes and Lifestyles: An Illustrated Journey Through History*. Tokyo: Kodansha International (JPN), 2000.

Kerr, Alex. *Dogs and Demons:Tales from the Dark Side of Japan*. New York: Hill and Wang, 2001.

Kikuchi, Toshihiko. *Zufu Edo jidai no gijutsu* ("The Illustrated Guide to Edo-period Technology"). Tokyo: Kowa Shuppan, 1988.

King, F. H. *Farmers of Forty Centuries: Or Permanent Agriculture in China, Korea and Japan*. New York: Dover Publications, 2004.

Kinoshita, Futoshi. "Household Size, Household Structure, and Developmental Cycle of a Japanese Village: Eighteenth to Nineteenth Centuries." *Journal of Family History*, Vol. 20, No. 3. (1995), 239-260.

Kiple, Kenneth F. (ed.), and Kriemhild Conee Ornelas (ed.). *The Cambridge World History of Food*, Cambridge: Cambridge University Press, 2000.

Koizumi, Kazuko. *Traditional Japanese Furniture*. Tokyo: Kodansha International, 1986.

Kokichi, Katsu and Teruko Craig. *Musui's Story the Autobiography of a Tokugawa Samurai*. Tucson: University of Arizona Press, 1991.

Kurita, Akira. *Edo no gesuido* ("The Sewers of Edo"). Tokyo: Seiabo, 1997.

Maemura, Matsuo and Shunpei Matsuo, Takashi Akiyama, Toshio Kitami. *Nomin seikatsushi jiten* ("The Encyclopedia of Farmers' Life"). Tokyo: Kashiwa Shobo, 1991.

Masai, Yasuo. *Atlas Tokyo*. Tokyo: Heibonsha, 1986.

Maruyama, Masao and Mikiso Hane. *Studies in the Intellectual History of Tokugawa Japan (East Asian Studies)*. Princeton: Princeton Univ Pr, 1989.

Masuta, Tatsuo. *Kanazawa-shi no bushi jutaku*. ("Samurai housing in Kanazawa") Ishikawa: Kanazawa-shi, 1998.

Matsumoto, Zenjiro. *Edo Tokyo Kiba no konjaku* ("Edo, Tokyo, Kiba Now and Then"). Tokyo: Nihonringyo chosakai, 1986.

McClain, James L. "Castle Towns and Daimyo Authority: Kanazawa in the Years 1583-1630." *Journal of Japanese Studies*, Vol. 6, No. 2 (Summer, 1980), 267-299.

McDonough, William, and Michael Braungart. *Cradle to Cradle: Remaking the Way We Make Things*. New York: North Point P, 2002.
——. *The Hannover Principles*: *Design for Sustainability*. William McDonough and Partners, 1992. www.mcdonough.com/principles.pdf

Miyawaki, Akira, and Elgene Owen Box. *The Healing Power of Forests: The Philosophy Behind Restoring Earth's Balance With Native Trees*. Boston: Kosei Company, 2007.

Miyazawa, Satoshi. *Shirakawago gasshozukuri Q&A* ("Questions and Answers about the Thatched-roof Houses of Shirakawago"). Tokyo: Tomo Shobo, 2005.

——. *Nihon no minka* ("Japan's Folk Houses"). Tokyo: Gakushukenkyusha, 1980.

Mollison, Bill, and David Holmgren. *Permaculture One*. Bath: Eco-logic Books, 1990.

Morris-Suzuki, Tessa. "Concepts of Nature and Technology in Pre-Industrial Japan." *East Asian History*, 1 (June 1991), 81–97.
——. "Sericulture and the Origins of Japanese Industrialization." *Technology and Culture*, Vol. 33, No. 1 (January 1992), 101-121.

Murota, Takeshi. *Mawaru maware mizuguruma* ("The Turning Waterwheel"). Tokyo: Inax, 1986.

Nagata, Mary Louise. "Brotherhoods and Stock Societies: Guilds in Pre-modern Japan," in *International Review of Social History* (2008), 121-142, www.iisg.nl/hpw/papers/guilds-nagata.pdf (accessed August 20, 2007).

Naito, Akira, and Kazuo Hozumi (illus.). *Edo, the City that Became Tokyo: An Illustrated History*. Tokyo: Kodansha International, 2003.

Nakaya, Renjiro. *Kiba meishozukan* ("Illustrated Guide to Famous Kiba Places"), Tokyo: 1927.
——. *Kiba no omokage* ("Relics of Kiba"), Tokyo: 1938.

Nishi, Kazuo. *What is Japanese Architecture?* Tokyo: Kodansha International, 1985.
——, and Kazuo Hozumi. *Nihon kenchiku no katachi* ("The Style of Japanese Architecture"). Tokyo: Shokokusha, 1983.

Nishiyama, Matsunosuke. *Edo Culture Daily Life and Diversions in Urban Japan, 1600-1868*. Honolulu: University of Hawai'i Press, 1997.
——, Masakatsu Gunji, Hiroshi Minami, and others. *Edo gaku jiten* ("The Encyclopedia of Edo Studies"). Tokyo: Kobundo, 1984.

Nitschke, Gunter. *Japanese Gardens*. Los Angeles: Taschen, 2007.

Seidensticker, Edward. *Low City, High City: Tokyo from Edo to the Earthquake*. Boston: C.E. Tuttle, 1984.

Nitto, Kazuhiko. *Hokuriku no sumai* ("Housing in the Hokuriku Region"). Tokyo: Inax Shuppan, 1996.

Nosan gyoson bunka kyokai. *Nihon nogyo zensho* ("All About Japanese Agriculture"). Tokyo: Nosan gyoson bunka kyokai, 1983.

Ochiai, Ichiro. "Japan in The Edo Period: Global Impliations of a Model of Sustainability." In *Asia Pacific Journal: Japan Focus*. (2007). http://www.japan focus.org/-Ei-ichiro-OCHIAI/2346 (accessed August 13, 2007).

Oishi, Shinsaburo, and Chie Nakane, Saburo Okita, Conrad Totman. *Tokugawa Japan: The social and economic antecedents of modern Japan*. Tokyo: Columbia University Press, 1992.

Ooka, Ryozo. "Field Study on Sustainable Indoor Climate Design of a Japanese Traditional Folk House in Cold Climate Area." In *Building and Environment* 37-3 (March 2002): 319-329.

Rinoie, Masafumi. *Kawaya mandara* ("Outhouse Mandara"). Tokyo: Inaseito, 1984.

Roberts, Luke S. "A Case Study of the Restoration of a Samurai House in Shikoku," in *Abstracts of the 1999 AAS Annual Meeting*, (March 1999).

Saito, Osamu. "Land, labour and market forces in Tokugawa Japan," in *Discussion Paper Series* No.135; Hitotsubashi University Research Unit for Statistical Analysis in Social Sciences, Institute of Economic Research, Hitotsubashi University, (January 2006), http://hi-stat.ier.hit-u.ac.jp/ (accessed August 20, 2007).
———. "Population and the Peasant Family Economy in Proto-Industrial Japan," in *Journal of Family History*, (Spring 1983), 30-54.

Sasama, Yoshihiko. *O-edo fukugen zukan, shomin-hen* ("Edo Restoration Atlas, Townspeople Edition"). Tokyo. Yushikan, 2003.
———. *O-edo fukugen zukan, bushi-hen* ("Edo Restoration Atlas, Samurai Edition"). Tokyo: Yushikan, 2004.

Schumacher, E. F. *Small is Beautiful: a study of economics as if people mattered*. New York: Blond & Briggs, 1973.

Shimizu, E. and T. Fuse. "Rubber-sheeting of historical maps in GIS and its application to landscape visualization of old-time cities: focusing on Tokyo of the past," in *Proceedings of the 8th International Conference on Computers in Urban Planning and Urban Management*. (2003) CD-ROM.

Sloane, Eric. *Eric Sloane's America*. Chicago: Bbs Budget Book Svs, 1982.

Smith, Thomas C. *Agrarian Origins of Modern Japan*. Stanford, CA: Stanford University Press, 1984.

Smith, Robert J. "Aspects of Mobility in Pre-Industrial Japanese Cities." *Comparative Studies in Society and History*, Vol. 5, No. 4 (July 1963), 416-423.

Takai, Kiyoshi. *Nihon no minka* ("Japan's Folk Houses"). Tokyo: Heibonsha, 2006.
———and Teiji Ito, Hidetaro Sugimoto. *Nihon meikenchiku shashin senshu* ("A Photographic Guide to Famous Japanese Architecture"). Tokyo: Shinchosha, 1993.

Takahashi, Masao. *Morisada Manko zuhan shusei* ("Collection of Illustrations by Morisada Manko"). Tokyo: Yuzankaku, 2002.

Takayanagi, Kaneyoshi. *Edo no kakyu bushi* ("Edo's Lower-class Samurai"). Tokyo: Kashiwa Shobo, 1980.

Takeuchi, Makoto (ed.) and Kenichiro Yoshihara (ed.), Hiroaki Tachikawa (illus.). *Edo no machinami keikan fukugenzu* ("Illustrated Reconstruction of Edo Scenery"). Tokyo: Naigai Chizu, 2003.

Takishita, Yoshihiro. *Japanese Country Style: Putting New Life into Old Houses*. Tokyo: Kodansha International, 2002.

Tanahashi, Masahiro and Yuji Murata. *Edo no kurashi fuzoku daijiten* ("Encyclopedia of Daily Manners in Edo"). Tokyo: Kashiwa Shobo, 2004.

Tanaka, Yuko. "The Cyclical Sensibility of Edo-Period Japan," in *Japan Echo*, Vol. 25, No. 2, (April 1998) http://www.lian.com/TANAKA/englishpapers/cyclical.htm (accessed December 16, 2007).

Tani, Naoki and Atsuko Enshu. *Benjo no hanashi* ("All about Toilets"). Tokyo: Kashima Shuppankai, 1986.

Todd, Nancy J., and John Todd. *Bioshelters, Ocean Arks, City Farming*. New York: Random House, 1984.

Tokoro, Mitsuo. *Kinsei ringyoshi no kenkyu* ("Modern Forestry Industry Research"). Tokyo: Hirokawa Kobunkan, 1980.

Tokyo, the city of. *Edo fukugenzu* ("Illustrated Reconstruction of Edo"). Tokyo: Tokyo-to, 1989.

Totman, Conrad. *The Green Archipelago: Forestry in Preindustrial Japan*. Berkeley: University of California Press, 1989.
———. *Early Modern Japan*. Berkeley: University of California Press, 1995.
———. *The Lumber Industry In Early Modern Japan*. Honolulu: University of Hawaii, 1995.

Traganou, Jilly. *The Tokaido Road: Traveling and Representation in Edo and Meiji Japan*. Oxford: Taylor and Francis, 2004.

Tsukamoto, Manabu. *Edo jidai hito to dobutsu* ("People and Animals of the Edo Period"). Tokyo: Nihon Edita Sukuru Shuppanbu, 1995.
———. *Shorui o meguru seiji: Genroku no fokuroa* ("Folklore of the Genroku era"). Tokyo: Heibonsha, 1993.

Tsuya, N. O. and K. Hamano. "Mortality responses to rice price fluctuations and household factors in a farming village in central Tokugawa Japan." *The History of the Family*, Vol. 6, No. 1 (April 2001), 1-31.

Turnbull, Stephen R. *Samurai Armies, 1550-1615*. London: Osprey, 1979.

Uchida, Hoshimi. *Short History of the Japanese Technology*. Mitaka: The History of Technology Library, 1995. http://www.ied.co.jp/isan/sangyo-isan/JS7-history.htm (accessed August 20, 2007).

Vaporis, Constantine N. "Samurai and Merchant in Mid-Tokugawa Japan: Tani Tannai's Record of Daily Necessities (1748-54)." *Harvard Journal of Asiatic Studies*, Vol. 60, No. 1 (June 2000), 205-227.
———. "Caveat Viator. Advice to Travelers in the Edo Period," in *Monumenta Nipponica*, Vol. 44, No. 4 (Winter, 1989), 461-483.

Waley, Paul. *Tokyo: City of Stories*. New York: Weatherhill, 1991.
———. *Japanese Capitals in Historical Perspective: Place, Power and Memory in Kyoto, Edo and Tokyo*. Oxford: RoutledgeCurzon, 2003.
Walthall, Anne. *Peasant Uprisings in Japan: A Critical Anthology of Peasant Histories*. Chicago: The University of Chicago Press, 1991.

Watanabe, Kazuji. *Ikiteiru suiro* ("Living Waterways"). Tokyo: Tokyo University Press.

World Commission on Environment and Development. *Our Common Future*. Oxford: Oxford University Press, 1987.

Yamakawa, Kikue. *Women of the Mito Domain: Recollections of Samurai Family Life*. Stanford University Press, 2001.

Yamamura, Kozo. "Toward a Reexamination of the Economic History of Tokugawa Japan, 16000-1867." *The Journal of Economic History*, Vol. 33, No. 3 (September 1973), 509-546.

Yonemoto, Marcia. *Mapping Early Modern Japan: Space, Place, and Culture in the Tokugawa Period, 16030-1868*. London: University of California Press, 2003.

# index

*Bold type denotes illustration.*

（英文版）地球を救う江戸先進のエコロジー
Just Enough

2009年10月26日　第1刷発行

著　者　　アズビー・ブラウン
発行者　　廣田浩二
発行所　　講談社インターナショナル株式会社
　　　　　〒112-8652　東京都文京区音羽 1-17-14
　　　　　電話　03-3944-6493（編集部）
　　　　　　　　03-3944-6492（営業部・業務部）
　　　　　ホームページ　www.kodansha-intl.com
印刷・製本所　　大日本印刷株式会社